Designing a European Fiscal Union

Does the European Union need closer fiscal integration, and in particular a stronger fiscal centre, to become more resilient to economic shocks? This book examines the experience of 13 federal states to help inform the heated debate on this issue. It analyses in detail their practices in devolving responsibilities from the subnational to the central level, compares them to those of the European Union, and draws lessons for a possible future fiscal union in Europe.

More specifically, this book tries to answer three sets of questions: What is the role of centralized fiscal policies in federations, and hence the size, features, and functions of the central budget? What institutional arrangements are used to coordinate fiscal policy between the federal and subnational levels? What are the links between federal and subnational debt, and how have subnational financing crises been handled, when they occurred? These policy questions are critical in many federations and central to the current discussions about future paths for the European Union.

This book brings to the table new, practical insights through a systematic and comprehensive comparison of the EU fiscal framework with that of federal states. It also departs from the decentralization perspective that has been prominent in the literature by focusing on the role of the centre (which responsibilities are centralized at the federal level and how they are handled, rather than which functions belong to the local level). Such an approach is particularly relevant for the European Union, where a fiscal union would imply granting new powers to the centre.

Carlo Cottarelli is a Special Commissioner for Public Spending in Italy. Previously, he was Director of the Fiscal Affairs Department of the International Monetary Fund (IMF).

Martine Guerguil is a Deputy Director of the Fiscal Affairs Department of the IMF, where she oversees the preparation of the IMF flagship *Fiscal Monitor*.

Routledge Studies in the European Economy

Designing a European Fiscal Union

Lessons from the experience of fiscal federations

Edited by Carlo Cottarelli and Martine Guerguil

LONDON AND NEW YORK

First published 2015 by Routledge

2 Park Square, Milton Park, Abingdon, Oxfordshire OX14 4RN
52 Vanderbilt Avenue, New York, NY 10017

Routledge is an imprint of the Taylor & Francis Group, an informa business

First issued in paperback 2020

British Library Cataloguing in Publication Data
A catalogue record for this book is available from the British Library

Library of Congress Cataloging-in-Publication Data
Designing a European fiscal union : lessons from the experience of fiscal
    federations / edited by Carlo Cottarelli, Martine Guerguil.
        pages cm — (Routledge studies in the european economy)
    1. Fiscal policy—European Union countries.   2. European Union
countries—Economic policy.   I. Cottarelli, Carlo.   II. Guerguil,
Martine.
    HJ1000.D47 2014
    332.4'566094—dc23
    2014019981

ISBN: 978-1-138-78322-5 (hbk)
ISBN: 978-0-367-66911-9 (pbk)

Typeset in Times New Roman
by Apex CoVantage, LLC

Contents

Introduction and overview

Carlo Cottarelli and Martine Guerguil

This book examines fiscal arrangements between the central and subnational governments in federations from the perspective of the center. In that sense, it differs from most of the literature on fiscal federalism, which largely focuses on the devolution of fiscal responsibilities to the subnational level. But the Great Recession, by reigniting the debate on the counter-cyclical role of fiscal policy, has brought to the fore the question of the role of central governments in countries with a decentralized fiscal framework – and of the instruments they could use to safeguard macroeconomic stability and the sustainability of public finances.

More specifically, this book tries to answer three sets of questions:

- What is the role of centralized fiscal policies in a federation and, hence, the size and features of the central budget? To what extent are fiscal policies harmonized at the central and subnational level – and how? In particular, what is the typical size and function of transfers from the federal to the subnational governments?
- What are the institutional arrangements between budget authorities at the federal and subnational level? How common are rules or constraints on subnational governments at the operational or procedural level?
- What are the links between federal and subnational debt, and how have subnational financing crises been handled when they occurred?

These are critical policy questions in many federations. And they play a key role in the current debate about the future of a fiscal union in Europe. The European Union (EU), although not a federation, faces many issues that closely relate to those arising between the central and local levels in federations. When relevant, the book explores this parallelism and compares the situation in federations with that in the EU. Drawing from these experiences, and looking back at the genesis and unfolding of the euro area crisis, the last chapter sketches out possible steps that could be taken to strengthen fiscal integration and governance.

The comparison should, however, be taken with a few grains of salt. For example, labor mobility in the EU typically remains much lower than in federal states, and approaches that work well in a political union may not work at all in the absence of a political union. Moreover, this book describes prevailing practices but does not assess performance under those practices, so its findings should not be interpreted as normative statements. Yet, looking at what is common (or uncommon) practice elsewhere is a useful starting point for a reflection on the design of arrangements and institutions in a new fiscal union.

To answer our set of questions, we look at the experiences of 13 federations (Argentina, Australia, Austria, Belgium, Brazil, Canada, Germany, India, Mexico, Spain, South Africa, Switzerland, and the United States). These are the largest federations monitored by the Forum of Federations, the global network of federations established in Canada.[1] Some of them may not be federations at the constitutional level (e.g., Spain), but all have a regional level of government that is intermediate between the central and the local level and is endowed with wide fiscal autonomy. This intermediate level of government fulfills important budgetary and fiscal tasks of its own – as distinct from a regional delegation from the central government or an association of neighboring local governments. The relations of the central authorities with this intermediate level of government are thus qualitatively different from those observed in unitary countries.

Our sample covers all regions of the world and is quite diverse: national GDPs range from $400 billion to $15 trillion, per capita income from $300 to close to $28,000, the land area from 30,000 to 9 million square kilometers, and the population from 8 million to 1.2 billion people (Table I.1). The degree of decentralization, measured through the share of subnational governments in total public spending or through their taxing capacity, also varies across the sample – from highly decentralized federations, such as Switzerland and the United States, to relatively more centralized ones, such as Germany and India. Nonetheless, regularities and common patterns do emerge, which the book tries to evince.

Given the diversity of the sample, a terminological clarification is in order: unless otherwise indicated, the term "central" or "federal" government is used in this book to refer to the highest national government level; the term "local", "state" or "subnational" government is used to refer to the highest level of subnational government, regardless of the actual designation applied to this level in its federation. The term "general government" refers to the consolidation of central and subnational governments. In some cases, when relevant for the analysis, data referring to all subnational government entities (that is, all levels of government below the central government, including state or regional government and local or municipal governments) is also discussed.

To centralize or not to centralize: The distribution of tax and spending responsibilities in federations

The benefits of decentralized spending and revenue decisions have long been acknowledged in public finance: allocating fiscal decisions to a level of government that is closer to the taxpayers allows a closer tailoring of fiscal policy to local preferences. But efficiency still calls for the centralization of some fiscal responsibilities. The first chapter of this book discusses how, typically, three key functions are allocated to the center. First, fiscal federations invariably confer the

Table I.1 Basic information on the countries in the sample (2011, unless otherwise indicated)

	Land area (sq. km)	Population (millions)	GDP (USD bn)	Nominal GDP per capita (USD)	Subnational government revenue (percent of total general government revenue)	Subnational government revenue (percent of total general government revenue, excluding shared taxes)[1]	Subnational government spending (percent of total general government spending)[2]	Transfer dependency[2]
Argentina	2,736,690	40.8	446	10,941	...	14.6	...	...
Australia	7,682,300	22.6	1,372	60,642	50.7	19.8	49.9	44.1
Austria	82,430	8.4	418	49,707	31.6	5.0	31.3	45.0
Belgium	30,280	11.0	512	46,469	38.4	10.0	36.9	64.1
Brazil	8,459,420	196.7	2,477	12,594	32.1	27.3	28.9	25.2
Canada	9,093,510	34.5	1,736	50,345	67.0	49.1	66.6	16.5
Germany	348,610	81.7	3,571	43,689	39.0	7.0	37.9	54.2
India	2,973,190	1,241.5	1,848	1,489	61.7	...	53.9	31.3
Mexico	1,943,950	114.8	1,155	10,064	48.8	4.0	46.7	88.6
South Africa	1,214,470	50.6	408	8,070	57.7	...	19.6	70.4
Spain	498,800	46.2	1,491	32,244	51.0	18.0	49.6	49.7
Switzerland	40,000	7.9	636	80,391	56.9	40.2	57.4	14.9
United States	9,147,420	311.6	15,094	48,442	59.6	37.2	46.2	18.3

Sources: IMF, *Fiscal Monitor*; OECD; World Bank, *World Development Indicators*; and IMF staff estimates.

[1] Data for 2010. Argentina, Australia, Brazil, and Mexico refer to 2009.
[2] Transfer dependency is defined as (grants + revenues sharing)/total subnational government revenue. Data for 2005.

responsibility for defense, foreign relations, and other traditional public goods (such as countrywide justice and law enforcement, communications, and key transportation systems) to the federal government. Second, since the introduction of a national social insurance system in Germany in the 1880s, and more broadly in the aftermath of the Great Depression, the center has also increasingly assumed social welfare and redistributive functions. Third, and more recently, the central government has been responsible for carrying out macroeconomic countercyclical policies, offsetting the risks of economic or other shocks affecting all or some regions.[2]

These core functions imply that the federal government needs a minimum size to operate. Even in the most decentralized federations in our sample (Canada, Switzerland, and the United States), the federal government's own revenue and expenditure represent about half of general government final spending (or 15–20 percent of GDP). This is in sharp contrast with the minimal size of the EU budget – it barely accounts for 2 percent of general government spending (1 percent of EU GDP). In contrast to established federations, the central taxation basis in the EU is very narrow (largely limited to custom duties), and most spending policies remain the responsibility of member countries. This difference reflects, first, the fact that the EU is not a political union, thus precluding the existence of a common defense and common external policy. But it is also a byproduct of the initial design of the union, which by construction did not include the common provision of public services nor a common macroeconomic stabilization or risk-sharing function, even within the bounds of the euro area.

To fulfill its core tasks, the center requires resources. In principle, these could be transferred from member states – and this is largely the case in the EU. In practice, central governments in established federations always finance themselves through their own taxes, with some regularities across the sample:[3]

- *Corporate and personal income taxes are usually centralized, but often supplemented by regional taxes.* The centralization of income taxes matches the stabilization function given to the federal government: when revenue from such highly cyclical taxes accrue to the central budget, the automatic stabilizers are also centralized. Centralization makes them usually more effective, as they might not operate as well at the state level if states face more binding financing constraints than does the federal government (as is generally the case). But the benefits from centralization go well beyond macroeconomic stabilization goals. The centralization of corporate taxes supports market integration, providing a level field for competition and minimizing distortions, while the centralization of personal income taxes enables the federal government to have a redistributive and inter-regional equalization role. At the same time, regional income taxes (often in the form of surcharges or piggybacking) are also frequent, reflecting dissimilar preferences or revenue needs across regions.

- *Consumption taxes are also mostly centralized, although largely for efficiency reasons.* In principle, consumption taxation meets most criteria to be levied at the local level (e.g., its basis is relatively less mobile). However, the VAT – the most common and efficient form of consumption taxation – is not easy to decentralize operationally. In practice, it is challenging to preserve the integrity of the VAT credit-debit chain (and the administrative advantages associated with the VAT) without imposing internal border controls of a kind federations inherently seek to avoid. Because of these difficulties, only a few federations (Brazil, Canada, India, and the United States) have decentralized consumption taxes; in almost all U.S. States and some Canadian provinces, the decentralized consumption tax is a retail sale tax, with some efficiency loss compared to a VAT. In some federations (Germany, Mexico, and Spain), the tax proceeds from the centralized VAT are shared between the central and subnational governments based on a formula.

In most cases, revenue ends up being more centralized than spending, leading to the emergence of the so-called vertical imbalances – the need for transfers from the center to the subnational level. The extent of these transfers, however, differs widely across federations. They are as high as 60 percent of state revenues in Belgium but play a relatively small role in the most decentralized countries (e.g., in Canada, Switzerland, and the United States, they account on average for 16 percent of state revenues). Vertical transfers can be expected to be larger in countries with a strong social preference for inter-regional equalization (to compensate regions with a low tax mobilization capacity) and for harmonized spending policies (to ensure minimum national standards). In those countries, transfers are usually calculated on the basis of distribution formulas based on population and demographics and, at times, on economic variables (such as unemployment or infrastructure gaps). In our sample, the United States is the only federation with no explicit equalization transfer. As mentioned, transfers in the EU have the unusual feature of flowing upwards (from country members to the central budget); about 80 percent of the EU budget is financed through such transfers.

Beyond redistribution, central transfers can also help offset the impact of macroeconomic shocks – either common shocks or region-specific shocks. Chapter 2 presents the results of an econometric study based on the experience of Australia, Canada, and the United States over the past two decades which yield interesting insights on the response of transfers to such shocks:[4]

- Changes in vertical transfers in response to cyclical shocks are neither large nor common, although there are exceptions (such as the transfers from the U.S. federal budget to the states as part of the 2009–10 fiscal stimulus package).
- In contrast, *net* transfers are relatively sensitive to shocks, and particularly common shocks. Net transfers encompass all financial transactions between the central government and all residents of a given state – in addition to unrequited payments from the central to the local budget, they include transfers made by the central government to residents of the state, net of the taxes paid by these same residents of the state to the central government. The sensitivity of net transfers to shocks primarily comes from the centralization

of output-sensitive spending (e.g., unemployment benefits) and, especially, taxes (e.g., corporate and personal income taxes) – the main automatic stabilizers. Net transfers are found to offset approximately 15–20 percent of common shocks for the three federations under study – a number roughly in line with the share of federal taxes in GDP.

In sum, in federations net transfers from the center play a non-trivial role in offsetting shocks and to some degree distributing risk across regions, although this occurs primarily as a by-product of the centralization of revenues and spending, rather than from specific, dedicated mechanisms.[5] In contrast, transfers play a very marginal role in the euro area at present. Yet, in principle, lower labor mobility and the lesser synchronization of economic cycles would call for higher risk-sharing in the euro area. A central budget would be one possible risk-sharing mechanism – but other, less ambitious options could achieve the same goal. These include, for example, a stabilization or "rainy day" fund that pools together resources from member states and distributes them to states when they are hit by a shock. However, a larger central budget (and the attendant establishment of common policies, such as a common self-financed unemployment insurance scheme or, even, a common pension scheme) would bring additional advantages. In particular, common policies would foster macroeconomic convergence over the medium run, thus strengthening the basis of the union.[6]

As for the policies that are decentralized, Chapter 1 discusses steps taken in federations to harmonize policies across subnational entities:

- *On the spending side,* minimum provision levels have often been established to limit regional disparities while allowing subnational governments wide discretion to allocate spending. For example, the provision of education services and their financing is generally highly decentralized, but national education standards are frequently defined, either by the central government or by a coordinating body of subnational authorities. In many cases, central transfers are used to induce subnational governments to follow harmonized standards. For infrastructure, central transfers reduce regional disparities or encourage local contributions to contribute to national priority projects, while retaining central control over projects with important externalities or of national scope.
- *On the revenue side,* some degree of tax harmonization is common in federations. The intent usually is to limit spillovers from decentralized tax policy decisions and reap the benefits of economies of scale through information sharing and other collaborative arrangements. Frequently, the tax base is harmonized and member states can set the tax rate either freely or within a centrally defined range, and in some cases can still provide a small number of simple tax allowances or tax credits.

Here again, the situation in the EU differs significantly. Spending policies are generally not harmonized, and on the revenue side, degrees of harmonization and mandatory minimum taxation apply only to the VAT and some excise taxes.

To constrain or not to constrain: Institutional arrangements across levels of government

Because the vertical structure of government in a fiscal federation can raise moral hazard and bailout expectations, explicit institutional arrangements are often in place to ensure that fiscal policies at the different levels of government are mutually consistent. Constraints can be placed on fiscal targets such as revenue, spending or financing, to shape the design of subnational fiscal policy (Chapter 3); they can also affect the procedures governing the budget process, in order to steer policy implementation (Chapter 4).

Constraints on subnational fiscal targets can take four main forms, generally non-exclusive of each other. These include, first, direct (administrative) controls set by the central government; for instance, the central government may set and revise regularly limits on subnational borrowing. Second come fiscal rules. They constrain fiscal discretion in a less binding manner than do direct controls, because they preclude the central government from micromanaging subnational fiscal policy, and because subnational governments have generally some margins to comply with them. A third option is comprised of cooperative approaches which, unlike fiscal rules, allow subnational governments to negotiate their fiscal targets on a regular basis. And finally, federations can just rely on market discipline.

In practice, fiscal rules – often in the form of balanced budget rules – are by far the most common form of constraint found in federations. In about half of the cases these rules are self-imposed, as for example, in Australia, Canada, Switzerland, and the United States. However, it is possible that, in the absence of self-imposed rules, rules would have been imposed by the center.

In contrast, cooperative arrangements are found mainly in European economies. For example, in Austria, annual fiscal targets are negotiated by federal, regional, and local governments via the Austrian Stability Program. A similar negotiation process occurs in Belgium through cooperation between the federal and regional levels and the High Finance Council.

Direct controls from the central government are relatively rare (this is an important difference between federations and unitary states) and mostly appear following an extended breach of fiscal targets or a severe subnational fiscal crisis that requires sizable financial support from the center. Finally, purely market-based discipline remains atypical, although market signals would also keep subnational behavior in check, as a complement, rather than a substitute, to institutional arrangements.

In most federations, well-designed constraints seem to have been effective in shaping the behavior of subnational fiscal authorities, although they cannot compensate for flaws in the decentralization framework – such as, for example, structural mismatches between revenue and spending responsibilities. Constraints on subnational fiscal policy are, of course, particularly effective when the central government is strongly committed to enforcing them and able to resist pressures to fill in subnational funding gaps in case of breach. This in turn enhances the effectiveness of market mechanisms and reduces both the level and volatility of subnational borrowing costs. Cooperative approaches, although appealing, have had a mixed record and require strong enforcement and coordination mechanisms to be effective.

The monitoring of institutional constraints is greatly facilitated by the adoption of *common public financial management tools.* However, few federations in our sample have standard, homogenous guidelines for the formulation, execution, reporting, and audit of subnational budgets. Harmonization is somewhat more common downstream (through the use of accounting and reporting standards), in some cases because past crises have showed the importance of timely monitoring, but also in response to public demands for increased transparency. However, important gaps remain. Annual financial statements are often available only after a significant delay – anywhere up to a year – and consolidated accounts are produced with an even longer time lag, and more for statistical purposes than for analysis.

The harmonization of upstream procedures (fiscal projections and budget formulation) is even more limited, perhaps because it is seen as more intrusive of state autonomy. More extensive oversight by the central government is often associated with a lack of capacity at the subnational level and, in some cases, a history of past subnational debt crises.

Notwithstanding all these differences, the overall trend is of increasing harmonization in most federations. In many cases, an instrumental factor has been the establishment of legal frameworks that are common to all levels of government, such as fiscal responsibility laws, a common public finance act, or the enactment of common principles of public financial management. However, harmonization has also gained ground in cases where there is no such legal obligation, such as the United States.

How does this compare with the current situation in Europe?

- Like most federations, the EU relies on fiscal rules, rather than on direct controls and cooperative arrangements – with the 3 percent deficit rule, the 60 percent debt rule, an expenditure benchmark, and medium-term budgetary objectives defined in structural terms. The fiscal compact also requires countries to enshrine a structural balance rule in national legislation.
- There is also a yearly cycle of economic policy coordination (the European Semester), but this exercise cannot be described as a full-fledged cooperative approach, as fiscal plans are examined rather than negotiated between Brussels and Member States.
- The EU framework does not resort to direct controls from the center, although there have been proposals in that direction for countries in breach of the rules.
- Harmonization of budget processes across EU members is relatively limited, although efforts are underway to increase the comparability and coverage of fiscal data.

There are three important differences, however, with the practices in federations. First, the EU rules apply to the general government, with countries being responsible to distribute the target internally among government units. By contrast, in federations, central constraints generally apply separately to different government levels, and states are not responsible for the achievement of lower–level targets. Second, most federations tend to impose a smaller set of constraints.[7] Third, sanctions for breaching the rules are relatively mild in the EU: they usually consist of opportunity costs from financial deposits. The conditions to convert these deposits into outright fines are strict and, so far, never have been applied. In addition, the EU framework does not provide for administrative sanctions, which exist in several federations (for example in the province of British Columbia in Canada, ministerial salaries can be withheld, and in Brazil, officials who violate the rules may be subject to criminal penalties and fines).

Below the line: Subnational debt and subnational debt crises

Financing arrangements between central and subnational levels of government have attracted enormous attention in the euro area during the last two years. A central issue – also the subject of a heated debate – has been whether shared financial instruments (such as euro bonds or euro bills) should be developed to facilitate the funding of member states.

Chapter 5 shows that in federations, the largest share of debt is held at the central level, with the share declining with the degree of centralization. While highly centralized governments rarely borrow on behalf of or directly lend to sub-national governments, there are exceptions, primarily related to special programs and development purposes. For example, central governments in Australia, Canada, Germany, and the United States provide small specific-purpose loans to state governments for housing and infrastructure or, in the United States, for unemployment compensation. In India, over the last decade, the central government has been phasing out its large direct loans to states. Austria is a notable exception. The Austrian federal government's debt management agency is tasked to raise debt and on-lend to states through direct loans. While these loans are not large (about 2.5 percent of GDP in 2011), they cover a significant part of states' financing needs (in 2011 the federal government held about 32 percent of states' debt).

In some federations, central governments finance subnational governments indirectly, by channeling loans through centrally owned financial entities. In emerging market economies, central governments also provide guarantees to sub-national governments. This is not common in federations in advanced economies, although in Germany, the federal government provides guarantees on a very lim-ited scale to Länder for specific projects.

In the end, the bulk of subnational borrowing comes from markets, through securities and loans. But interestingly, borrowing costs often reflect the underly-ing financing arrangements between the central and the subnational governments: the more decentralized the federation (or, the lower the transfer dependency of subnational governments, and thus the lower the expectation of bailout), the closer the borrowing costs are aligned with the observed fiscal performance at the local level.

So in practice, common borrowing of the kind that has been the topic of a heated debate in the euro area is unusual in federations. This does not mean that

Eurobond proposals have no merit. Historically, in the early stages of a fiscal union, the center has sometimes taken over sub-entities' debt on a one-off basis. In the United States, for example, the federal government took over states' debts in 1790. But operations of this kind were a bridge toward the creation of common debt backed by common revenues, as in the case of federal debt in existing federations, not a permanent feature of federation arrangements.

Chapter 6 reviews experiences in the management and resolution of subnational financial difficulties in the context of a federation – a topical issue, given persistent sovereign debt pressures in the euro area.[8] Over the past decades, when faced with a financing crisis, subnational governments have been rarely allowed to default on their private creditors. In fact, subnational debt restructurings have been limited to smaller political entities or to situations where the federal government debt itself was restructured. With only a few exceptions, pre-set crisis resolution frameworks such as bankruptcy procedures are absent for subnational governments. Instead, the federal government may provide financial support through a range of ad hoc mechanisms such as guarantees, loans, and extraordinary transfers, rather than standing support facilities. In a few cases, the central government simply increased (although by a substantial amount) the financing it was providing to the subnational government through its regular arrangements. But in most cases, the central government created a new, separate vehicle to channel its financial support. Loans and extraordinary transfers have been most frequently used. In the most severe crises, the form of support evolved from guarantees to loans to transfers as the amount of financing (and its cost to the central government) increased.

Loans and transfers have commonly been associated with conditionality, typically aimed at controlling deficits, and including in a few cases structural reforms, such as privatization. Conditionality was limited in time and often could not prevent the resurfacing of subnational fiscal stress later on. Nonetheless, about half of the countries that experienced open subnational fiscal crises did subsequently strengthen their subnational fiscal frameworks, including through legal changes and stepped-up transparency and reporting requirements.

The response to the euro area crisis shares many similarities with those experiences – most notably, the provision of financial support from the center and ambitious subsequent institutional reforms, both somewhat more formalized than has been observed in federations.

Lessons from the crisis in Europe

Chapter 7 looks back at the genesis and unfolding of the euro area crisis and sketches out possible steps that could be taken to strengthen fiscal integration and governance. The euro area crisis is found to have exposed a few critical gaps. Country-specific shocks have remained more prevalent than expected, while increased trade and financial integration created the potential for substantial spillovers. Weak fiscal governance and the absence of an effective market disciplining mechanism compounded these problems. Sovereign and bank stresses have moved together, setting off a vicious dynamic once markets started to price in default.

Although the scope and shape of fiscal integration remains a matter of social and political preferences, four sets of measures would help limit immediate crisis risks. First, better oversight of national fiscal policies would help build buffers and limit fiscal policy indiscipline. Second, some system of temporary transfers or joint provision of common public goods or services would increase fiscal risk-sharing − although it would have to be subject to strong oversight to limit moral hazard. Third, a credible pan-euro area fiscal backstop for the banking sector would prevent the buildup of financial imbalances. And fourth, some common borrowing could be considered to finance the above-mentioned risk-sharing mechanisms and provide a common safe asset.

Conclusions

This simple comparison − without normative implications − between a sample of federations and the EU highlights that, as could be expected, the mechanisms of fiscal coordination in place in Europe are much weaker than those prevailing in federations. A few other conclusions emerge:

- The role of the center in existing federations has often been shaped by a combination of historical circumstances and social and political preferences. For example, the most decentralized federations are often those where states were independent entities before the establishment of the federation − cases that may be in that dimension more relevant for the EU. On the other hand, a succession of severe and protracted subnational financial crises led to the introduction of substantial constraints on local budgets in a previously relatively decentralized federation like Brazil. The current crisis in the euro area could thus influence the future shape of the union beyond the resolution of the financing crisis itself.
- Even in highly decentralized federations, the central budget plays a significant role that involves both redistribution and stabilization. This role stems from the central government's own economic weight, due to its own taxing capacity. In contrast, institutional constraints on member states in Europe are arguably more overbearing than those in existing federations due, to some extent, to the absence of an economically-meaningful center.
- Harmonization of budget processes is advisable on efficiency grounds but carries little weight in existing federations, suggesting that it is an area for improvement in all types of federations or semi-federative arrangements, independently of their degree of centralization.
- Some of the proposals recently put forward in the euro area (such as common debt issuance and self-standing lending facilities for crisis support) are not a permanent feature of federal institutions, although they have played a role in the early life of federations. Conversely, it remains to be seen whether the "reverse transfer dependency" that is now at the core of the EU budget can

survive as a permanent feature or if new sources of trans-European revenue would need to be developed.

Notes

1 Our sample includes all federations with a nominal GDP above $400 billion in 2011, with the only exception of Russia, due to the lack of comparable information. Incomplete information also prevented the inclusion of all countries of the sample in some of the analyses and discussions in this book.
2 Stabilization and social protection were crucial factors in the growth of central governments in fiscal federations through the 20th Century. For example, in 1929 the U.S. federal government budget was about 2.5 percent of GDP, about one-third of the states' budgets; in 1939 the shares were 10 percent for the federal and 9 percent of GDP for the state budgets, respectively. In most federations, social protection and redistributive policy programs such as public pensions and unemployment insurance now account for the lion's share of federal spending, while public order and safety, waste and water management, and education – all allocative functions – are highly decentralized.
3 Transfers from the subnational to the federal level have been more common early in the life of federations, for example in Germany during the 1870s and 1880s, and in the United States before the reforms introduced by Alexander Hamilton.
4 The study focuses on how net transfers respond to output shocks (both common and idiosyncratic) rather than on their level (which could be high because of large vertical imbalances that are unresponsive to cyclical fluctuations).
5 The centralization of automatic stabilizers reduces of course the size of the stabilizers under the control of local governments, but the total impact on local economies will in the end be higher if borrowing at the decentralized level is subject to tighter borrowing constraints, or in the presence of fiscal rules that would not allow the operation of automatic stabilizers at the local level. Note also that, even though the econometric evidence shows that transfers do not respond much to idiosyncratic shocks, the existence of central transfers still imply a degree of risk-sharing following a common shock, because not all states may be able to access financial markets at sustainable rates when hit by a common shock.
6 See Cottarelli, 2013.
7 Spain, however, adopted an extensive fiscal rule framework during the crisis.
8 A subnational fiscal crisis is defined as a situation in which the subnational government faces payment difficulties that required exceptional financial support, either from its creditors (debt restructuring) or from the central government. This excludes situations in which subnational financial difficulties are resolved solely through subnational fiscal consolidation.

Reference

Carlo Cottarelli, 2013, "European Fiscal Union: A Vision for the Long Run," *Swiss Journal of Economics and Statistics* 149 (2): 167–174, available at http://www.sjes.ch/papers/2013-II-5.pdf.

1 Distribution of fiscal responsibilities in federations

Julio Escolano, Dora Benedek, Hui Jin,
Carlos Mulas Granados, Masahiro Nozaki,
Joana Pereira, Gregoire Rota Graziosi,
Laura Sinn, and Jose Torres

I. Introduction

This chapter discusses the distribution of the main budgetary functions (revenue, expenditure and inter-government transfers) across levels of government in a sample of fiscal federations.[1] It takes a primarily descriptive perspective, although drawing as appropriate from the vast body of theoretical and empirical studies on fiscal federalism. The theory and practice of fiscal federalism has evolved substantially in recent years. The current literature typically distinguishes between two approaches to fiscal federalism. First generation fiscal federalism theory, rooted in the normative approach developed during the 1950s–60s, studies the performance of decentralized systems under the assumption of benevolent social planners. The second generation fiscal federalism theory builds on those models, but also incorporates the fiscal and political incentives facing subnational officials.[2] This chapter draws on both approaches to assess and put in perspective the practices of federations in our sample.

Since we focus on fiscal federations, not surprisingly, these countries are characterized by the allocation of a large proportion of the total revenue and expenditure to subnational governments (SNGs). While fiscal decentralization is seldom undertaken in pursuit of fiscal efficiency, there are well-established efficiency reasons to allocate budgetary decisions to lower levels of government whenever possible – the "subsidiarity principle." Essentially, allocating fiscal decisions to a level of government that is closer to the taxpayers and beneficiaries of the government services allows a closer tailoring of fiscal policy to regional social preferences and a tighter accountability (Oates, 1972). This may potentially lead to efficiencies in spending and to a tax-expenditure package with better balanced costs and benefits. Indeed, empirical evidence indicates that the fiscal performance of the government sector as a whole tends to improve with decentralization (Baskaran, 2010; Escolano et al., 2012; European Commission, 2012).

Potential gains from decentralization notwithstanding, a minimum size of the central government is necessary for the effective dispatch of its core functions. From inception, fiscal federations have invariably conferred on the central government national defense and foreign relations, as well as other traditional public goods such as countrywide justice and law enforcement, communications (e.g., postal service), and key transportation systems. Since the 1880s introduction by

Bismarck of a national social insurance system in Germany, the center has also increasingly assumed social insurance and redistributive functions and expanded the provision of public goods and services with large positive network externalities, such as national transportation, energy, and communication grids. In addition, the central government is invariably responsible for carrying out macroeconomic counter-cyclical policies, providing risk-sharing against regional idiosyncratic and asymmetric shocks (such as natural disasters), and responding to other aggregate shocks. Stabilization and social protection were crucial factors in the growth of central governments through the 20th Century. For example, in 1929 the size of the U.S. federal government budget was about 2.5 percent of GDP, about 33 percent of the states' budgets, while in 1939 after the New Deal, the figures were 10 percent for the federal and 9 percent of GDP for the state budgets (Vanistendael, 2011). In all, the evidence from fiscal federations shows that, today, the central government often accounts for more than half of total government spending.

The distribution of functions is somewhat different in the European Union. Regional equalization and cross-country transportation networks consume an important share of the joint budget. While social protection policies remain in the hands of member countries, stabilization policies are increasingly coordinated and overseen at the central level, including through a single monetary policy for euro member countries, a strengthened framework for fiscal policies, and Union-wide central firewalls to help maintain financial stability.

The rest of this chapter is divided in four sections. The following two sections discuss in detail the assignment of responsibilities in fiscal federations across levels of government in the areas of taxes and spending. The next section covers the design of inter-governmental transfers, followed by a section which discusses the European Union's budget. The final section draws some conclusions.

II. Distribution of revenue responsibilities

A. *Inter-governmental tax assignment criteria*

The underlying criteria for the distribution of taxing powers between the central and subnational governments are similar to those that apply to fiscal decentralization in other areas: delegation to a lower level of government allows for a better matching of the tax system to the preferences of the community, closer accountability, and more participatory and transparent decision-making. On the other hand, economies of scale, risk-sharing, and externalities argue for the centralization of taxes where these features are dominant. These considerations apply both to the tax policy decision-making powers and to the administration of the different tax instruments – an aspect that has often been overlooked by the theoretical literature (Box 1.1). Finally, decentralization of tax powers often aims at minimizing transfer dependency, allocating as an integral package the decision-making on public services' provision and their funding.

Taking into account the interplay among intrinsic features of different tax instruments, their administration requirements, and the allocation of government

Box 1.1   Fiscal federalism and tax administration

The assignment of tax administration and collection responsibilities between the federal and SNGs reflects a trade-off between minimization of administration and compliance costs and SNGs' sovereignty. Solutions take several forms including decentralization to SNGs of most central taxes (Germany, Switzerland), coordinated but separate administration of their respective taxes, and central administration of some SNG taxes (Australia, Canada, Spain).

Germany combines a decentralized tax administration and a highly harmonized tax system: PIT, CIT, and VAT are regulated by federal law but administered by the SNGs' fiscal authorities. However, the Constitution provides the federal government with power to secure a homogeneous enforcement of tax compliance. For instance, the Federal Ministry of Finance is entitled to issue instructions, supervise, and contribute to federal audits in SNG operations to safeguard the interests of the federation and the uniform application of tax law. Other federations (Australia, Canada, Brazil, India, and the United States) have independent separate tax administrations for each level of government.

The administration of two-level (federal and local) consumption taxes can be particularly challenging. Brazil has state VATs levied by SNGs at multiple rates and with a hybrid model combining the destination and origin principles – the introduction of the latter was motivated by low SNG administrative capacity and the absence of borders controls – with national tax rules applying to interstate trade. In the United States, SNGs (states and municipalities) have and administer separate sale taxes, with voluntary partial harmonization and coordination taking place among some SNGs. Most Canadian provinces with VATs delegate their administration to the central Canadian Revenue Authority, so that both VATs (central and provincial) are administered centrally, except for Quebec where the federal and the provincial VATs, which share the same base, are administered by the provincial tax administration. In Australia, Mexico, and Spain, a single VAT is administered centrally.

Income taxes (CIT and PIT) are often administered centrally to minimize costs – occasionally with formal or informal agreements between the center and SNGs. In Canada, almost all SNGs (except Quebec for PIT and Quebec and Alberta for CIT) have voluntarily delegated the administration of income taxes to the central tax administration.

functions, the literature on fiscal federalism points to the following principles for assigning taxing powers across levels of government (Musgrave, 1983; Dahlby, 2001; Bird, 2010a):

*   *Central taxation of bases that are highly mobile across regions minimizes distortions; reciprocally, less mobile bases are well suited for SNG taxation.*

This is a particular case of the Ramsey's optimal taxation principle that postulates that taxation should be inversely related to the elasticity of the base. When tax avoidance leads to a shift of the tax base across regions, it gives rise to economic inefficiency as a result of suboptimal location.

- *Inter-regional equalization argues for central taxation of tax bases unequally distributed across regions.* While this policy objective is present to some extent in all countries, it is often balanced, particularly in fiscal federations, by the desire to protect the economic policy autonomy of regions and allow the more dynamic regions to reap the benefits of their economic success. Also, most countries allow natural resource-rich regions to benefit from a portion of the tax potential associated with these resources that goes well beyond the local costs and negative externalities generated by the resource exploitation.
- *Centralization of progressive taxation instruments (e.g., progressive personal income taxation) facilitates cross-regional income redistribution.* As with inter-regional equalization, the concentration of progressive taxation at the center is a function of the social demand for redistribution. Central taxes typically contain a certain level of progressivity, which regional authorities can complement with an additional tier of regional tax progressivity to achieve intra-regional redistribution according to regional preferences.
- *Risk-sharing and counter-cyclical policies are enhanced by centralizing volatile and pro-cyclical taxes – as the central government is better able to absorb revenue shocks over the cycle or across SNGs.* Part of the risk-sharing function of the central government – that is, insurance against idiosyncratic regional shocks – can be achieved by allocating centrally the most volatile revenue sources, such as the corporate income tax. The central government is also better placed to absorb revenue shortfalls stemming from business cycles, as central governments have better access to financing than do SNGs, while SNGs are sometimes constrained by thin debt markets or management capacity.

In light of the principles above, some tax assignment features appear desirable. The corporate income tax (CIT), with the most volatile and pro-cyclical revenue, is well suited to be a central tax. Moreover, its centralization promotes market integration by removing tax-induced barriers to firms' cross-regional activity. Footloose bases also argue for the centralization of financial transaction taxes (FTTs) and other financial taxes. The VAT is also a good candidate for centralization since its reliance on an unbroken credit-debit chain creates difficulties in the treatment of cross-regional trade, and VAT fragmentation hinders cross-regional market integration and effective administration. If these taxes are allocated to SNGs, or SNGs have a second tax layer on these bases, harmonization provides significant benefits. On the other extreme, property taxes come closest to an ideal SNG tax, followed by personal income taxes (PIT). However, country-wide income redistribution objectives argue for allocating the PIT (or a tier of it) to the central government.

An important choice regarding the system of tax allocations is whether a tax base should be assigned to only one level of government or there may be co-occupancy of tax bases (Bird and Smart, 2010). In the case of *India*, for example, the Constitution prescribes full tax separation (Bird, 2012), whereas in Canada different levels of government share the same or similar tax bases for the consumption, corporate, and personal income taxes. If tax base overlapping is allowed, the case for harmonization and tax policy coordination is strong:[3] to minimize inefficiencies – as the tax policy of the central government or of an individual SNG has important spillovers beyond its jurisdiction – and administrative costs (including to the taxpayers).[4] Harmonization implies that SNGs have some tax design power, but they are subject to well-defined limitations (Box 1.2).

Box 1.2 Tax powers, harmonization, and base sharing

Most federal-type countries provide substantial discretion to SNGs over the base, rates, and other rules regarding their own tax revenue. However, the manner on which this power is exercised differs. In highly decentralized federations, such as the United States, Canada, and Switzerland, states have, individually and unilaterally, full discretion over the tax base and tax rate of their own taxes, which represent a large proportion of total general government taxes. On the other extreme, in most European fiscal federations, each SNG must often exercise its tax power in a joint manner – either jointly with the central government, or with other SNGs, or with both – rather than individually and unilaterally. States in Germany receive a large share of total tax revenues, but on almost 90 percent of these revenues states have no unilateral individual decision power. Under this type of arrangement, tax and revenue-sharing decision power is exercised jointly by SNGs, by SNGs and the central government, or in some cases only by the central government – the revenues are then distributed as transfers. In Spain almost 40 percent of regional revenue is subject to some form of shared tax policy authority and in Austria tax policy decision power over 45 percent of states' revenue is exercised by the central government.

A common form of harmonization is when the tax base is harmonized and SNGs can set the tax rate either freely or within a centrally defined range, typically piggybacking on a central tax. In some cases, the tax base is largely unified but SNGs can provide a small number of simple tax allowances or tax credits. Tax harmonization might allow for administration efficiencies: harmonization allows regional tax administrations to benefit from central taxpayer audits (since the tax base is the same) and, in the case of piggybacking, the central tax authority may fully administer the tax.

An alternative to piggybacking is granting the central government autonomy in administering the tax – but sharing the tax revenue among the different government levels. The design of the base, rates, and revenue split formula can either be decided at the central level or with the participation of the SNGs (Blöchliger and Rabesona, 2009).

B. *Structure of tax revenue in fiscal federations*

Reflecting the federal-type fiscal frameworks in the country sample, the tax revenue of the central government (excluding social security funds) represents a relatively low proportion of the total general government tax revenue: on average, slightly over 55 percent versus 62 percent in the whole The Organisation for Economic Co-operation and Development (OECD). This is particularly the case for Switzerland and the United States, followed by Canada, Spain, Brazil, and Germany – all of them below the sample average. Central government tax revenue (again excluding social security funds) is also lower than average as a proportion of GDP, particularly in the highly decentralized federations (Figure 1.1 and Appendix Table A.1.1),[5] where it represents approximately 10 percent of GDP – versus an average of 21 percent in the whole OECD.[6]

The structure of the central government tax revenue is diverse in our sample of countries, mainly reflecting whether there is a central consumption tax. Most central governments derive substantial revenue from the VAT, except in Canada and the United States, where most consumption taxes are subnational (Figure 1.2). The other main sources of general government revenue are taxes on income. Most fiscal federations have central corporate and personal (except India) income taxes – sometimes complemented by parallel regional taxes on similar income bases. SNGs receive most of their revenue from taxes on consumption (including from shared taxes of the central VAT); the regional tier of the corporate and personal income taxes (often also shared taxes), and property taxes.

Corporate Income Tax (CIT)

All fiscal federations in the sample have a central CIT. The CIT is well suited for allocation at the central government level: it favors the development of an integrated market, its tax base is strongly pro-cyclical and easy to shift across regions, and its distribution can be highly uneven across SNGs. While many countries share CIT revenues with SNGs, the CIT is usually imposed solely by the central government (Appendix A.1.2).[7] The exceptions are Canada, Switzerland, and the United States, where some states have their own CIT in addition to a federal CIT.

In countries with regional CITs (or a regional tier of the CIT), an important issue (even when the CIT is harmonized across regional jurisdictions) is the apportionment of the tax base amongst SNGs for firms that operate in more than one region – that is, the proportion of corporate income that can potentially be subject to tax in each region. In the United States, this problem has not been fully solved, since different states use different apportioning rules. The apportionment is often based on a formula containing a firm's sales, property, and payroll within each state (either with equal weights or with sales having higher weight). Another formula, applied by 11 states, uses only sales as a basis of apportionment (Gichiru et al., 2009). States also differ in their rules applied to subsidiaries: some only tax companies within their borders and disregard subsidiaries in other states, while some states tax income aggregated with subsidiaries.

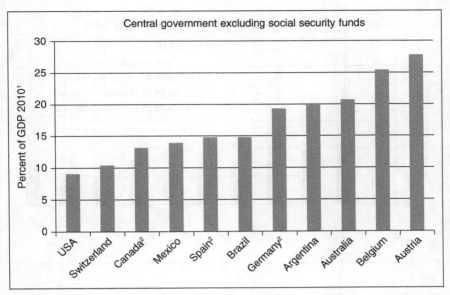

(a)

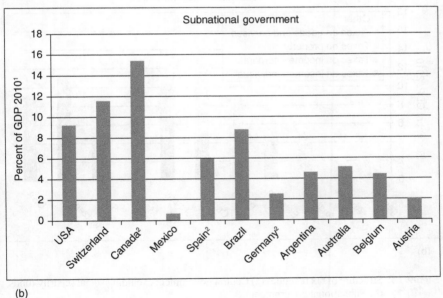

(b)

Figure 1.1 Allocation of tax revenues across levels of government (a) Central government excluding social security funds, (b) Subnational government

Source: OECD Revenue Statistics and own calculation.

[1]2009 for Argentina, Australia, Brazil, and Mexico.
[2]Shared revenue between SNGs and central government has been assigned to central government.

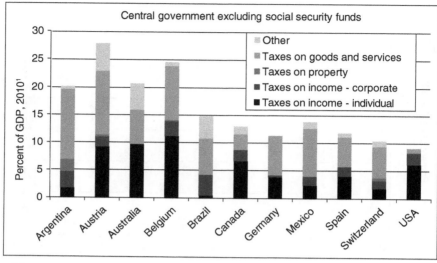

(a)

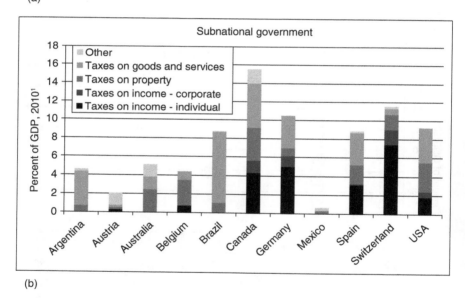

(b)

Figure 1.2 Structure of tax revenues (a) Central government excluding social security funds, (b) Subnational government

Source: OECD Revenue Statistics.

Note: Due to lack of information on shared taxes by instruments, shared taxes are assigned to SNGs as reported by OECD and national authorities.

[1]2009 for Argentina, Australia, Brazil, and Mexico.

Personal Income Tax (PIT)

All fiscal federations have a federal PIT. In addition, Canada, Switzerland, and the United States have SNG PITs (in SNGs that choose to have a PIT); Belgium and Spain provide for a regional surcharge to the central PIT, decided by the SNGs; and finally, in Germany, the federal government shares the central PIT revenue with states according to a pre-determined formula (Appendix A.1.2).

With the exception of the United States, most federations harmonize their SNG PIT systems to some degree. In the case of Canada, harmonization is de facto, although the constitution does not prescribe it. All provinces except Quebec use the federal tax base as their own and also have the federal government collect their PIT (Vaillancourt, 2012). In Switzerland, cantons must levy some personal income taxes, which cannot be regressive, but because rates are not bound by a minimum, these constraints are weak. The central and cantonal governments now use a common tax base and a common list of tax exemptions, but the amounts of deductions vary, and there is no formal harmonization requirement (Vaillancourt, 2012). In Spain and Belgium, the regional surtaxes use, to a large degree, the same base as the central PIT.

VAT and sales taxes

Most fiscal federations in the sample have a central VAT (Appendix A.1.2), with the exception of the United States, which has no federal general consumption tax. Indeed in most federations, the VAT is a key revenue source for the central government.

In contrast, few federations have regional VATs – possibly reflecting the efficiency, administration, and compliance costs associated with regional VATs. In India, a VAT-type tax is levied by the states, and a manufacturer's VAT by the central government, but with different bases. Brazil and six Canadian provinces have regional VATs in addition to the federal VAT. In the case of Canada, five provinces have adopted a regional VAT, the Harmonized Sales Tax (HST), which is highly (but not fully) harmonized among these provinces and the central VAT, the Goods and Services Tax (GST). The HST is collected by the central government (jointly with the central VAT), which redistributes the revenue back to the provinces according to a formula that approximates the provincial consumption tax bases (Rao, 2007). The HST system, however, requires complex inter-governmental arrangements and horizontal and vertical inter-governmental collaboration (Bird, 2010b and Perry, 2010). Quebec has a non-harmonized regional VAT, which is independently administered – Quebec also administers the national GST.

Most federations where all or part of the VAT revenue is allocated to the regions opt for a central VAT complemented by revenue-sharing arrangements. In Austria, Germany, Mexico, and Spain, the VAT is a unified central tax, but its revenue is shared between the central and subnational governments based on a formula. The Australian VAT (General Sales Tax) revenue is allocated to regions in full, with fiscal equalization objectives based on potential revenue capacity and expenditure needs (Blöchliger and Petzold, 2009).

Finally, forty-five states, the District of Columbia, Guam, and many local governments in the United States, and three Canadian provinces have final stage retail sales taxes, administered by the corresponding SNGs.

Other taxes

Custom duties are invariably central taxes in fiscal federations. Historically, in most federations, the centralization of these taxes was a key component in creating a unified integrated national market, eliminating restrictions and duties on inter-regional trade. Nowadays, import duties have become only a small component of the central government revenue in advanced economies.

Natural resource taxes are in principle a good candidate for central taxation due to volatility and uneven distribution of the base, but in practice SNGs of fiscal federations often have significant taxing powers over natural resources. While in Brazil natural resources are defined as federal resources, revenues are shared between all levels of government (Ter-Minassian, 2012). In the United States, both the federal and state governments impose natural resource taxes. In Canada resource royalties are provincial revenues. In Argentina, resource-rich provinces collect royalties from mining, oil, and gas with different regional rates (Artana et al., 2012). In Australia, states collect levies on the exploitation of some natural resources in their jurisdiction, while the central government also collects taxes on these activities.

Special financial sector taxation is already in place in some federations of emerging market economies (e.g., Brazil) and it is also being considered in some advanced European economies, typically in the form of financial transaction taxes (FTTs) or financial activity taxes (FATs) (International Monetary Fund, 2010). These taxes could be allocated to the central government to minimize distortions (e.g., double taxation), preserve financial market integration, and avoid base shifting. Also, since financial sector regulation and supervision is centralized in most countries, the central allocation of financial taxes would reduce administrative and monitoring costs. A FAT is essentially a tax on value added (profit plus labor costs) imposed on the basis of the company accounts. Thus, to some extent, this tax would be similar to the low-rate SNG taxes on businesses' payroll or value added taxes that already exist in some countries (e.g., Italy, Hungary). However, a FAT would presumably have a higher rate and a much more mobile base than these other existing taxes, making its decentralization problematic.

III. Centralization and harmonization of expenditure policies

A. *Distribution of spending responsibilities*

Traditional theoretical work on fiscal federalism (Musgrave, 1959) has focused on the potential benefits and costs of fiscal decentralization in three government functions with their associated expenditure areas: macroeconomic stabilization, redistribution, and resource allocation.[8]

Centralizing the macroeconomic stabilization function facilitates coordination of fiscal, monetary, and structural policies; leverages the financial capacity of the central government; allows for insurance against idiosyncratic regional economic shocks; and internalizes inter-regional spillovers. Expenditure programs aimed at redistribution across regions and regional equalization are also generally better managed by the center. In contrast, it is typically optimal to assign allocation-oriented expenditure policies to SNGs whenever possible, since they have better information about their residents' needs. Nevertheless, there is a role for the central government: to assume or coordinate key expenditure programs with large externalities or economies of scale. Thus, infrastructure projects with large network externalities (e.g., a national electricity grid or road network), national defense, and foreign affairs are generally centralized.

The decentralization pattern in the countries in our sample is broadly consistent with the normative theory of fiscal federalism. Figures 1.3 and 1.4 report cross-country averages of central government spending overall and for each of eight functional categories. Since social protection includes social assistance and unemployment insurance, it mainly falls in the stabilization and redistribution functions. In line with theory, spending on social protection is highly centralized. In contrast, spending is more decentralized for categories related to the allocation function – public order and safety, economic affairs, and environmental protection. Health care and education encompass both allocation and redistribution

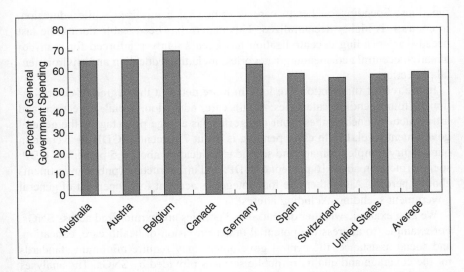

Figure 1.3 Spending by central government and social security institutions, latest year available

Sources: Australian Bureau of Statistics, European Commission, OECD.

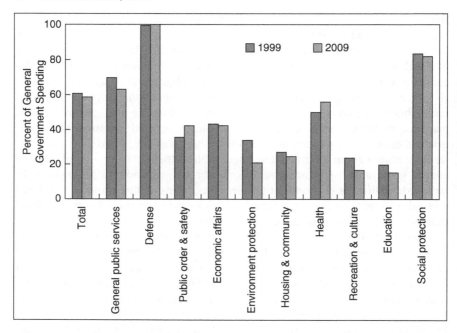

Figure 1.4 Spending by central government and social security institutions, 1999 and 2009.

Sources: Australian Bureau of Statistics, European Commission, OECD.

functions. Spending on health care is somewhat centralized while education, in contrast, is highly decentralized. This pattern has been stable during the last decade, as spending decentralization has been slightly reinforced for many of already-decentralized spending categories, including education and environmental protection.

In the rest of this section, we look in more detail at the degree of centralization of four spending categories: health care, education, social protection, and infrastructure. Each of these four categories has a large price tag: at the general government level, health care spending is about 7 percent of GDP on average in our country sample; primary and secondary education about 3.5 percent of GDP; social protection about 16 percent of GDP; and infrastructure (public investment) about 3 percent. Altogether, the four categories account for 70 percent of general government spending excluding interest.

We also examine whether decentralized policies are harmonized across SNGs. For example, to address the potential under-provision of health care, education, and social assistance, the central government may require minimum standards for the coverage and quality of public services provided by SNGs. The analyses below find that these harmonization policies are indeed common.[9] We also find that the central government often uses transfers to induce SNGs to implement harmonization policies.

B. Health care

The degree of centralization in health care policies differs significantly in our sample.[10] According to an index of decentralization developed by Joumard, André, and Nicq (2010), decision-making power on health care policy is most centralized in Belgium and most decentralized in Canada, Spain, and Switzerland, with Australia, Germany, and Mexico being in the middle of the spectrum (Appendix A.1.2). There are some regularities, though:

- In general, SNGs have oversight on the *provision* of health care. For example, they are responsible for hospital capacity planning as well as construction and maintenance of public hospitals in many of these countries (Paris et al., 2010).
- Health care *financing*, however, is generally centralized or outside the oversight of SNGs in many of the federal countries. Primary health care coverage is financed in the form of national social insurance in Belgium; central payroll tax in Germany; and general central taxation in Australia. In Switzerland, most beneficiaries must purchase insurance based on federal legislation. On the other hand, health care financing is decentralized in Canada and Spain. Centralized public programs offer limited coverage of health insurance in Mexico and the United States.

Decentralized health care policies are substantially harmonized through national requirements on health care benefits and eligibility (Appendix Table A.1.3). A tool frequently used to achieve harmonization is the establishment, by the central government, of a standard benefit package of health insurance that must be provided by the regions to all beneficiaries – for example, in Australia, Canada, Mexico, and Spain (Paris et al., 2010; Health Canada, 2011). U.S. States are also required to provide a minimum level of benefit package for low-income residents through the Medicaid program. In Switzerland, residents are obliged to purchase health insurance from competing private insurance companies, with the benefit package of insurance established by law (OECD and WHO, 2011). In some countries, the central government also places requirements on eligibility (Canada and the U.S. Medicaid Program) and offers subsidies on health insurance premiums for low-income individuals (Switzerland).

Central transfers play a key role in enforcing the implementation of harmonization policies across SNGs. In Canada, federal transfers account for about 20 percent of health expenditures of provincial and territorial governments. In the United States, federal matching transfers finance about two-thirds of total Medicaid costs. SNGs that violate national requirements face reductions in federal transfers.

C. Education

Public spending on education is highly decentralized in most federal countries (Figure 1.5).[11] Financing of education spending is also highly decentralized, as SNGs finance education spending largely from their own resources, except in

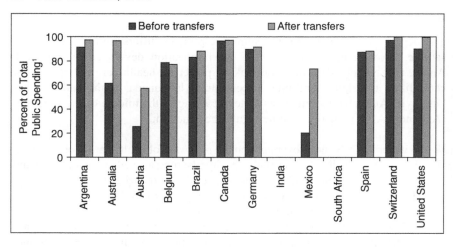

Figure 1.5 Subnational spending on primary and secondary education, 2009

Sources: OECD Education at a glance 2012.

[1]For Canada, data are in 2008. Data are not available for India and South Africa.

Australia, Austria, Mexico, and the United States. Moreover, decision-making powers over education policies are vested in subnational levels in Australia, Canada, Germany, Switzerland, and the United States (OECD, 2012). In multicultural countries such as Belgium and Spain, decentralization in education policies helps accommodate differences in official languages across jurisdictions.

Although decentralized, education policies are harmonized nationally in many federal countries. Harmonization is implemented through national education standards, for example on school curricula (e.g., education attainment goals by grade), minimum standards on schools and teachers, regulations on diplomas, and national examination standards and requirements. The coverage of national standards differs significantly by country (see a summary table in Appendix Table A.1.4).

National standards are established either by the central government or by a coordinating body among SNGs.[12] The central government approach is taken by Belgium, Brazil, Mexico, Spain, South Africa, and the United States (the No Child Left Behind program). Central government transfers play a key role in ensuring the implementation of the national standards in Mexico and the United States, but this is not the case in Spain. The coordination body approach is taken by Australia, Germany, and Switzerland. Agreements by the coordination body can be legally binding, as in Switzerland, and the implementation of the national standards is monitored and evaluated by independent institutions in Germany.

D. Social protection

Social protection spending consists of public pensions, unemployment insurance, and social and family assistance. Public pensions, especially if they are pay-as-you-go, may play a key role in redistribution between generations; unemployment insurance contributes to the macroeconomic stabilization function; and social assistance (e.g., minimum income and welfare programs) and family assistance aim at poverty reduction and redistribution.

The administration of public pensions and unemployment insurance is typically centralized (Appendix Table A.1.5): public pension plans are financed by national payroll taxes or central transfers (or both), with benefit levels determined regardless of where recipients live. The exception is Canada, where a separate pension plan for Quebec residents coexists with the national pension system. Similarly, the administration and financing of unemployment insurance is generally centralized, except in the United States, where state governments determine eligibility conditions, benefit levels, and employer contribution rates. However, the federal government contributes funding, including from a federal tax (FUTA), and special appropriations for extended coverage in recessions.

In the area of social and family assistance, the assignment of spending responsibilities differs significantly by country (see Appendix Table A.1.5). Centrally-administered social and family assistance programs exist in Australia, Austria, Belgium, and Germany, but this is not the case in Canada and Switzerland.[13] In Spain, the central government administers a family assistance program but does not provide social assistance, which is a responsibility of the regions. In the United States, family assistance is implemented by state governments, while some social assistance (e.g., the Supplementary Security Income (SSI) program) is centralized.

Decentralized social protection policies are generally harmonized to limit regional disparities, albeit to a varying degree (Appendix Table A.1.5). In Canada, the Quebec pension plan is de facto harmonized with the national plan (e.g., retirement eligibility age and replacement rate are similar to those for the national plan). In the United States, state unemployment insurance programs are partially harmonized through common principles of program design and requirements to extend benefit duration when unemployment worsens. Likewise, to harmonize state family assistance programs, the U.S. federal government sets minimum spending levels by state governments and maximum benefit durations. In both cases, federal transfers play a key role in ensuring harmonization. In Switzerland, the federal government establishes eligibility and the minimum benefit level of child allowance programs, while cantons administer and finance social assistance programs; a coordination body across cantons develops national standards for program design.

E. Infrastructure

The assignment of spending responsibilities on infrastructure in federal countries is largely consistent with the theoretical rationale. SNGs are generally responsible for projects that benefit local communities, such as local roads, water pipelines, and sanitary systems. The central government comes into play in designing and implementing national infrastructure projects whose economic benefits spread beyond local territories, such as inter-state highways and railway networks. The central government also plays an important role in promoting standards and harmonization across SNGs (Appendix Table A.1.6).

The central government often engages in infrastructure development as a counter-cyclical policy measure – giving it a stabilization dimension. In the federal country members of the OECD, although public investment is more decentralized than in unitary countries, the central government retains at least a quarter of total public investment, except in Canada (Figure 1.6). The size of the central government investment (including capital transfers) is at least 1 percent of GDP except in Canada, and exceeds 2 percent of GDP in Australia, Mexico, Spain, and the United States (Figure 1.7). In India and South Africa, the central government plays a proactive role in coordinating infrastructure projects to promote national economic growth.

As a harmonization policy, the central government often influences subnational choice of infrastructure projects through financial support, to promote projects of national priority or to alleviate disparities across regions. In Australia, Canada, Germany, and Switzerland, the central government encourages SNGs to implement infrastructure projects of national importance through earmarked transfers. In contrast, to equalize the quality of infrastructure across regions, the central governments in Mexico, Spain, and the United States support subnational infrastructure investment through formula-based infrastructure transfers.

Several countries have developed a national regulatory framework on private-public partnerships (PPPs), to guard against fiscal risks arising from subnational PPP projects. Such a framework exists in Australia, Brazil, and South Africa. In Spain, on the other hand, policies on PPPs are not harmonized as there is no central register of PPP projects, in contrast with many other European countries.

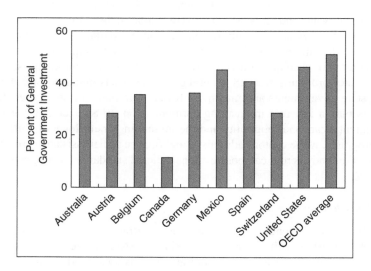

Figure 1.6 Central government public investment, 2009
Source: OECD.

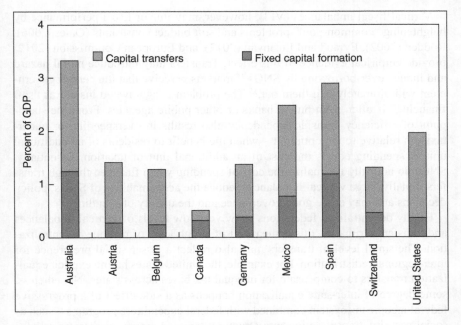

Figure 1.7 Central government public investment, 2009
Source: OECD.

IV. Transfers and vertical imbalances

A. Transfers: Rationale and modalities

Transfers to SNGs fulfill a number of objectives. First, fiscal decentralization in federations is generally more pronounced on the expenditure than on the revenue side, giving rise to SNG expenditure mandates that cannot be funded through SNG own revenue sources (Ter-Minassian, 1997). Indeed, spending decentralization in European fiscal federations, for instance, has outpaced revenue decentralization in the past 15 years (Escolano et al., 2012; European Commission, 2012). This mismatch ultimately translates into vertical transfers and revenue sharing arrangements on which SNGs rely to fund their budgets. Second, disparities in tax bases and hence in revenue-raising capacities across individual SNGs within countries give rise to horizontal inequalities. Transfers to address these disparities, in the form of equalization grants, are often an important inter-regional redistribution policy instrument. Third, inter-regional externalities from individual SNG spending programs may require central transfers to avoid over- or under-spending in certain categories. Finally, economy-wide and idiosyncratic shocks and policies across SNGs may require transfers from the central government to smooth economic cycles and provide a measure of risk-sharing.[14]

Vertical fiscal imbalances (VFI), however, may impair fiscal performance by heightening "common-pool" problems and soft budget constraints (Oates, 2006). Rodden (2002), Eyraud and Lusinyan (2012), and European Commission (2012) provide empirical evidence of this effect. Transfers may introduce moral hazard and induce over-borrowing by SNGs if markets perceive that the central government will ultimately bail them out.[15] The problem is aggravated insofar as "soft financing" is often from public banks or other public agencies. From the standpoint of efficiency, transfer dependency also results in overspending or under-taxation relative to the optimum – when the benefit to residents of an additional unit of spending equals the cost of an additional unit of taxation. Essentially, SNGs do not fully internalize the cost of spending when financed through transfers. Finally, large vertical imbalances reduce the accountability of SNGs' policy decisions and may erode good governance and the quality of spending.

Highly decentralized federations show very low levels of vertical imbalances and transfers. Primarily, this is the result of a high level of revenue decentralization. The small level of transfers may also reflect a lesser social preference for inter-regional redistribution. For example, the United States has no explicit equalization transfers to compensate for unequal tax bases across states. Nonetheless, some degree of inter-state equalization happens as a side-effect of a progressive federal income tax system combined with federal expenditure programs – such as social security, transportation infrastructure, targeted grants, or disaster relief – which benefit states across the country independently of their local tax capacity.

B. The extent of vertical fiscal imbalances

The literature has employed different measures of vertical fiscal imbalances (VFI). The most common definition of the VFI refers to transfer dependency: transfers received from the central government, either as a share of subnational total revenue (Rodden, 2002; Escolano et al., 2012) or expenditure (Jin and Zou, 2002). Others use the wedge (difference or ratio) between SNGs' own revenue and expenditure to calculate the size of vertical imbalances (Ahmad and Craig, 1997; Eyraud and Lusinyan, 2012; Bird and Tarasov, 2004). We use the former (transfer dependency) definition – that is, the proportion of SNG revenue that stems from central transfers – as a gauge of the potential moral hazard and "common pool" problems.[16] We also include shared taxes in the measure of transfers when computing the VFI index.[17] This is because, by and large, shared taxes in our sample are not primarily directly related to the tax collected in the region, nor typically do the SNGs have powers to independently change tax bases or rates of shared taxes in their jurisdictions (Perry, 2010; Eyraud and Lusinyan, 2012). Thus, as a first approximation, it appears appropriate to add shared tax revenue to transfers in the computation of the VFI if the latter is to be used as an indicator of the incentive distortion due to the dissociation of the cost of additional taxes from the benefits of the additional expenditure.

The size of vertical imbalances varies significantly within our sample of countries, with transfer dependency ranging from less than 15 percent in Canada to more than 80 percent in Mexico. This variation is a reflection of different institutional set ups adopted by fiscal federations (including the role of SNGs in the provision of public goods, the degree of externalities, the heterogeneity in revenue-raising capacity, and the weight of political and historical factors) and does not necessarily reflect just the level of decentralization. For instance, one finds countries with high levels of expenditure (and political) decentralization at the two ends of the spectrum in Figure 1.8: United States, Canada, and Switzerland with the lowest

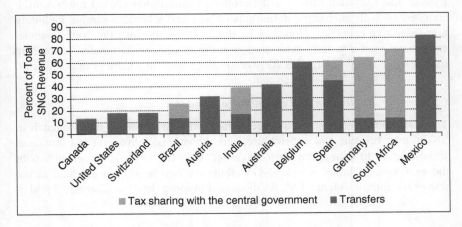

Figure 1.8a Transfers and vertical fiscal imbalance, 1995–2010 average

Sources: OECD, Brazilian National Treasury, Reserve Bank of India and South Africa Federal Reserve Bank.

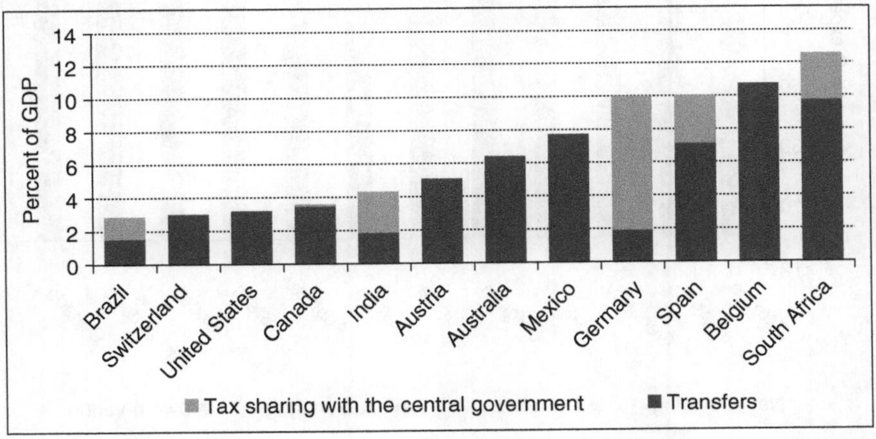

Figure 1.8b Transfers and vertical fiscal imbalance, 1995–2010 average

Sources: OECD, Brazilian National Treasury, Reserve Bank of India and South Africa Federal Reserve Bank.

VFIs and South Africa and Spain with some of the highest. VFIs are large in South Africa and Mexico, where a very centralized revenue system exists despite high expenditure decentralization.

While spending decentralization increased in most countries over the last two decades, vertical imbalances have not always worsened, reflecting *pari passu* decentralization of revenues and in some cases larger SNG borrowing. The average change in our measure of VFI between 1997 and 2007 is negative, even if more countries have seen an increase in transfer dependency than a decrease. Eyraud and Lusynian (2012) and European Commission (2012) reach similar conclusions with alternative definitions of VFI and a broader sample including non-federative countries. Nonetheless, the recent years since the 2008 financial crisis have seen a general deterioration at the margin, with transfers increasing their relative weight on total SNG revenue since 2007 in a number of countries.

C. Revenue distribution and expenditure mandates

Transfers and revenue sharing agreements fund a large part of the mismatch in SNGs' own revenue and expenditure, and subnational borrowing has remained small relative to their spending, on average, over the 1995–2010 period – with the exception of India, where SNG deficits are consistently larger than in the rest of the sample (Figure 1.9). As discussed in more detail in Chapters 3 and 5,

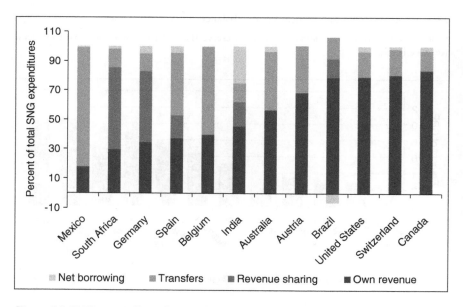

Figure 1.9 SNGs expenditure financing decomposition, average 1995–2010

Sources: OECD, Brazilian National Treasury, Reserve Bank of India, South African Reserve Bank, and Fund staff estimates.

sub-central borrowing is often constrained by institutional fiscal arrangements and, in some countries, by limited SNG market access.

For most OECD countries in the sample as well as South Africa, the distribution of central resources is designed keeping in mind a prospective balance between what needs to be spent by each level of government to guarantee minimum or standard services and the means to achieve them. This is generally accomplished with distribution formulas based on population and demographics (which proxy spending needs on health, education and social services), geographical, and economic variables (such as surface, unemployment, or infrastructure gaps). Earmarking is not widespread, although it is important in Belgium and Austria, applied in Canada for health and education, and used in the United States for a number of programs, including Medicaid.

Quite a few federations have established formal institutions (usually a council or a commission of experts) to advise the government or the legislature on the design and application of distribution formulas. These bodies are generally independent and often established in the constitution or by a special law. Distribution formulas are revised periodically, typically every five to seven years.

In most federations, transfer formulas attempt to minimize inter-regional gaps in revenue-raising capacity and are often also based on indicators of expenditure needs. Thus, the equalization component of transfers and revenue sharing is large in many countries (sizable in Germany and Spain, and high relative to total transfers in Australia and Switzerland). As mentioned, the United States has no explicit equalization transfers. In Brazil, India, and Mexico, the historical and political component of the transfer size is important, with less relation to spending mandates per se.

V. The European Union's budget

A. A brief history of the EU's budget

The first budget of the (then called) European Economic Community (EEC) was adopted by the European Council in 1958. It covered only administrative expenditure. As the EEC's objectives were translated into policy commitments, the budget grew to implement some of them, starting with the European Social Fund and the Common Agricultural Policy, which soon accounted for the bulk of the budget.

In the early years, revenue came from financial contributions from each of the six founding member states. But as expenditure grew to implement a more comprehensive set of policies (including the regional development policy, the common fisheries policy, the first research framework program, and the integrated Mediterranean programs) and with a growing number of member states, more stable sources of revenue were required. The first "financial perspective," setting binding multi-annual expenditure ceilings for each category of expenditure, was adopted for the period 1988–92.

Since then, the financial perspective served as a multiannual budget framework for the European Union.[18] It has incorporated the new range of policy initiatives that came with the 1992 Treaty of Maastricht (foreign affairs and security, justice, home affairs) as well as the Cohesion Fund created to invest in infrastructure in the poorest member states. It makes however for a relatively small central EU budget. The 1993–99 financial perspective set a ceiling of 1.27 percent of GNP, reduced to 1.24 percent of GNP for the period 2007–2013 and to roughly 1 percent of GNP for the period 2014–2020. The budget is based on the principle that expenditure must be matched by revenue (the European Union cannot issue debt).[19]

B. Revenues at the EU level

The EU budget is funded from three sources of revenues: (i) traditional own resources – mainly customs duties on imports from outside the EU and sugar levies, which are the only taxes integrally allocated to the central budget;[20] (ii) a standard percentage of the harmonized VAT base of each EU country[21]; and (iii) a specific contribution by each country based on its Gross National Income. This source of revenue was initially conceived to balance revenue and expenditure, but it has become the largest source of revenue of the EU budget.

As a consequence, the central budget of the European Union presents the unusual feature of a substantial reverse vertical fiscal imbalance. In contrast with established fiscal federations, transfers flow upwards from EU country members to the central EU budget. In 2011, about 18 percent of that total revenue came from traditional sources (customs duties, sugar levies, and other income such as fines and taxes on EU staff salaries). The rest, or about 82 percent of the total revenue, corresponded to two upward transfers: the VAT transfer (12 percent of total revenue) and the GNI contribution (70 percent of total revenue).

Historically, central government funding through upward transfers occurred in the early years of some federations, but was soon replaced by independent taxing powers. For example, in the early United States, the Articles of Confederation adopted by the Continental Congress in 1777 envisaged that transfers from the states would be the main funding means of the central government (Article 8 of the Articles of Confederation). However, this proved an unstable basis for the central public finances.[22] Eventually, the reforms introduced during 1789–95 by the first U.S. Secretary of the Treasury (Alexander Hamilton) and the new Constitution replaced upward transfers by central taxing powers (initially custom duties and some excises) and other independent revenue sources (e.g., land sales).

Thus, the European Union is the only contemporary case of a central budget stably funded primarily by upward transfers. Whether this system poses the same risks to fiscal discipline as the more common "downward" transfer dependency is an open question. However, the same underlying weakness appears to apply: the benefits associated with spending initiatives are not counterbalanced by the internalization by the same level of government of the costs associated with levying commensurate taxes.

In the past decade, the need to overcome this design failure and to alleviate the burden to major contributors has motivated discussion of new sources of EU revenues, either as a result of the partial centralization of existing taxes or through the creation of new tax instruments.[23] Recently, the European Commission proposed the creation of a Financial Transactions Tax. The proposal presented by the Commission in 2011 and approved later by the Parliament, was to harmonize the tax base and to set minimum rates for all transactions on (secondary) financial markets, once at least one EU party (financial institution) was involved in this transaction. According to the Commission's proposal, part of the tax would be used as an EU's own resource, which would partly reduce national contributions.[24]

C. EU's spending policies

In the EU context, expenditure allocation policies are largely the responsibility of member countries, although the center has some spending assignments with Union-wide synergies and network externalities, such as some infrastructure and research projects. The EU central budget also has responsibility for programs to reduce cross-country and regional disparities (e.g., cohesion and structural funds), but major redistributive policies remain with member countries. Regarding stabilization functions, macro-fiscal policy is largely decentralized at the member level, although the Fiscal Compact and the European Stability Mechanism are steps towards a greater coordination and stronger centralized surveillance.

In those policy areas designed and managed centrally by the European Union, spending is fully centralized (e.g., common agricultural policy). In other areas where policy making is shared with member countries, spending is earmarked and transferred directly to beneficiaries (without necessarily transiting through the national budgets). These include local or regional governments, companies, or individuals, according to a variety of criteria: for example, spending for cohesion policies is distributed as a function of relative income disparities, while funds for research and innovation are distributed competitively on the basis of each project's merits.

In the recently executed financial framework (2007–2013), spending by the EU was highly concentrated in two main categories: competitiveness and cohesion represented 45 percent of total spending (35 percent for structural and cohesion funds, including to reduce regional infrastructure disparities, and 10 percent for education exchange and research programs); while agriculture and environment represented 42 percent of total spending (34 percent for agricultural subsidies mainly paid to farmers and 8 percent for environmental policies). The reminder was divided among justice and security (1 percent of total spending), external relations and aid (6 percent of total spending) and administrative costs, including salaries, pensions and health insurance of EU civil servants (6 percent of total spending) (see Figure 1.10).

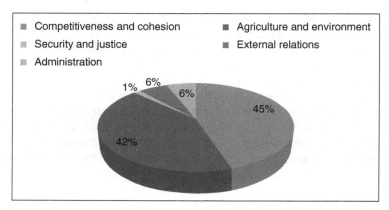

Figure 1.10 The distribution of EU's expenditures, 2007–2013

Source: Available at http://ec.europa.eu/budget/figures/fin_fwk0713/fwk0713_en.cfm (the European Stability Mechanism is not included in the budget).

VI. Conclusion

This chapter has discussed the distribution of the main budgetary functions (revenue, expenditure and inter-government transfers) across levels of government in the sample of fiscal federations.

On the revenue side, evidence shows that the central government accounts for slightly more than half of total government tax revenues, including in federal countries. Specifically, in our sample of fiscal federations, the share of the central government tax revenues (including shared taxes) in total general government revenues averages 55 percent – compared to 62 percent in non-fiscal federation OECD countries.[25] Even in the most decentralized fiscal federations in our sample (i.e., Canada, Switzerland, and the United States), the central government tax revenue represents almost 40 percent of total general government revenue.

Fiscal federations present some regularities in their central government tax assignments:

- Fiscal federations in the sample all have a central corporate income tax (CIT), sometimes complemented by regional CITs. This agrees with the counter-cyclical function of the central government, since the CIT revenue is highly pro-cyclical. Moreover, it contributes to market integration and provides a level field for competition. Finally, the regional CIT has a very tax-elastic base and may cause economic inefficiency if business location decisions are made for tax purposes. A central CIT minimizes these distortions.
- All fiscal federations also have a central personal income tax (PIT), but SNG PITs are also widespread – in the form of regional surcharges, piggybacking, or independent PITs, reflecting dissimilar preferences or revenue needs across regions. The PIT is a major source of central government revenue in

modern tax systems. A central progressive PIT is a key instrument for the counter-cyclical, redistributive, and inter-regional equalization roles of the central government.[26]

- Consumption taxation meets in principle most criteria for a good SNG tax, since its base is relative immobile and broadly distributed and has low volatility and pro-cyclicality. However, in practice, consumption taxes are rarely decentralized because of the technical difficulty of applying at the local level the most efficient form of consumption taxation, namely the VAT: unlike retail sales taxes, VAT is less subject to revenue leakage and cascading. As a consequence, VAT is the most generalized consumption tax and is typically centralized, while local consumption taxes are often retail sales taxes (e.g., in most U.S. States and municipalities and in some Canadian provinces).

On the expenditure side, evidence also shows that today, the central government, including in federal countries, often accounts for more than half of total government spending. Specifically, in our sample of fiscal federations, the share of the central government expenditure (including social security institutions) in total general government spending averages 60 percent – compared to 70 percent in non-fiscal federation OECD countries.[27] In fiscal federations in our sample, the central government expenditure represents at least 50 percent of total general government outlays, except for Canada.

In our sample, the central government plays an important role in social protection (e.g., public pensions) and redistributive policy programs. Spending categories pertaining to stabilization and redistribution functions, such as social insurance, are highly centralized. On the other hand, spending is highly decentralized for categories that can be classified under the resource allocation function, such as public order and safety, regional economic affairs (e.g., local transportation, housing, retail regulations), and regional environment protection (waste and water management, pollution abatement). Health spending is to some extent centralized, while education spending is highly decentralized.

Where spending is decentralized, governments have often effectively implemented harmonization policies in key areas – ensuring minimum provision levels while allowing SNGs wide discretion to allocate spending. For education, while provision and funding is decentralized in many countries, policies are partially harmonized through national education standards. For infrastructure, central transfers reduce regional disparities or encourage SNGs' contribution to national priority projects – while projects with important externalities or of national scope remain centralized.

Fulfilling central spending functions requires that the central government have the power to levy sufficient revenue and make spending decisions within its remit. Moreover, these functions also require the capacity to issue and service national debt reliably – underpinned by powers to mobilize revenue in appropriate amounts.

Historically, the allocation of taxing powers has followed the allocation of government expenditure responsibilities across levels of government, although in many cases with long lags and often only partly. Therefore vertical transfers (from the central government to lower levels of government) are an important component of SNG funding in many countries. Vertical transfers, however, play a relatively small role in the most decentralized federations.

The empirical evidence increasingly points to the risks for fiscal discipline posed by transfer dependency – the so-called vertical fiscal imbalance.[28] High transfer dependency can result in a softening of the budget constraint of SNGs and a deficit bias. This argues for an assignment of own revenues (including tax policy powers) commensurate to the spending responsibilities at each level of government. Indeed, the premise on which the efficiency gains from decentralization is predicated is that residents in a jurisdiction bear the full cost of raising the marginal dollar of tax revenue used to finance its public expenditure (Dahlby, 2001). Also, preponderance of own taxes tends to promote responsiveness to the electorate's preferences and democratic accountability (Blöchliger and Petzold, 2009). The same logic should also apply in the converse case of transfer dependency of the central government with respect to upward transfers from lower levels of government. Nevertheless, vertical transfers are difficult to avoid in countries with strong social preferences in favor of inter-regional equalization – which requires significant vertical transfers to compensate regions with low tax mobilization capacity. Also, achieving significant harmonization in expenditure policies may require vertical transfers. For example, national minimum standards in health care and social protection typically require equalization transfers.

While net transfers flow generally from central to subnational governments, the "reverse transfer dependency" case is of more than theoretical interest: it is currently the case of the relatively small EU budget. Today the EU derives most of its revenues from upward transfers and spends those funds on a series of policies aiming at increasing competitiveness and cohesion across Europe. In a future context of further European integration and growing spending demands, a key issue will be whether reverse transfers should remain the model for a future enlarged EU fiscal budget, or new sources of revenue would be developed at the European level.

Appendix A.1.1

Cross-country data on tax revenues

Appendix Table A.1.1a Tax revenues by levels of government 2010[1]

| | Total tax revenue, general government | Central government tax revenue (incl. shared taxes)[2] | Social security funds | SNG tax revenue (excl. shared taxes) | Shared taxes | Memorandum | |
						Central government tax revenues (excl. shared taxes)	SNG tax revenue (incl. shared taxes)
In percent of GDP							
Argentina	31.4	20.1	6.7	4.6	0.0	20.1	4.6
Australia	25.8	20.7	0.0	5.1	0.0	20.7	5.1
Austria	41.8	27.8	12.0	2.1	0.0	27.8	2.1
Belgium	43.9	25.4	14.1	4.4	0.0	25.4	4.4
Brazil	32.2	14.8	8.7	8.8	0.0	14.8	8.8
Canada	31.3	13.1	2.8	15.4	0.1	13.0	15.5
Germany	35.9	19.3	14.1	2.5	8.0	11.3	10.5
Mexico	17.4	13.9	2.9	0.7	0.0	13.9	0.7
Spain	32.7	14.8	12.0	5.9	3.0	11.8	8.9
Switzerland	28.6	10.4	6.7	11.5	0.0	10.4	11.5
USA	24.7	9.1	6.4	9.2	0.0	9.1	9.2
OECD[3]	33.8	21.0	8.3	4.4	0.8	20.2	5.2
In percent of total general government revenue							
Argentina		64.0	21.3	14.6	0.0	64.0	14.6
Australia		80.2	0.0	19.8	0.0	80.2	19.8
Austria		66.5	28.7	5.0	0.0	66.5	5.0
Belgium		57.9	32.1	10.0	0.0	57.9	10.0
Brazil		46.0	27.0	27.3	0.0	46.0	27.3
Canada		41.9	8.9	49.1	0.4	41.5	49.5
Germany		53.8	39.3	7.0	22.3	31.5	29.2
Mexico		79.9	16.7	4.0	0.0	79.9	4.0
Spain		45.3	36.7	18.0	9.2	36.1	27.2
Switzerland		36.4	23.4	40.2	0.0	36.4	40.2
USA		36.8	25.9	37.2	0.0	36.8	37.2
OECD[3]		62.1	24.5	13.1	2.3	59.8	15.4

Source: OECD revenue statistics and fund staff estimates.

[1]2009 for Argentina, Australia, Brazil, and Mexico.
[2]Central government excluding social security funds.
[3]Unweighted average.

Appendix Table A.1.1b Structure of central and SNG tax revenue,[1] 2010[2]

	Taxes on income			Taxes on payroll and workforce	Taxes on property	Taxes on goods and services				Other
	Total	Individual	Corporate			Total	VAT	Sales tax	Excises	
Central government, excluding social security funds, in percent of total central government tax revenue										
Argentina	24.7	8.5	14.8	0.0	10.9	63.3	36.9	0.0	8.5	1.1
Austria	41.6	33.0	6.8	7.2	1.1	41.5	28.6	0.0	8.5	8.6
Australia	70.0	46.7	0.2	0.2	0.0	29.8	17.4	0.5	9.5	0.0
Belgium	56.6	45.5	11.0	0.0	1.0	39.6	28.9	0.0	8.7	2.8
Brazil	49.3	2.9	25.5	5.3	0.1	44.4	5.8	29.6	1.0	0.9
Canada	70.1	51.5	15.8	0.0	0.0	21.6	14.8	0.0	4.7	8.3
Germany	37.0	33.7	3.4	0.0	0.0	63.0	34.1	0.0	22.2	0.0
Mexico	35.9	17.0	11.6	0.0	0.0	62.8	24.7	0.0	4.2	1.3
Spain	51.2	34.0	14.5	0.0	0.2	45.3	35.0	0.0	8.3	3.3
Switzerland	41.0	17.4	14.1	0.0	4.9	54.1	34.4	0.0	13.8	0.0
USA	90.7	67.5	23.2	0.0	1.2	8.1	0.0	0.0	4.5	0.0
Subnational government in percent of total SNG tax revenue										
Argentina	0.0	0.0	0.0	0.0	15.4	79.1	0.0	0.0	0.0	5.5
Austria	15.3	13.2	2.0	44.5	10.8	11.0	0.0	0.0	0.0	18.5
Australia	0.0	0.0	0.0	25.4	48.2	26.4	0.0	0.0	0.1	0.0
Belgium	17.3	17.3	0.0	0.0	62.4	19.4	0.0	0.0	0.0	0.9
Brazil	0.0	0.0	0.0	0.0	12.4	86.8	78.9	0.0	0.0	0.9
Canada	36.1	27.8	8.4	4.3	22.8	31.2	9.9	6.0	5.8	5.6
Germany	58.5	47.7	10.8	0.0	8.0	33.4	32.2	0.0	0.3	0.0
Mexico	0.0	0.0	0.0	41.4	45.9	5.8	0.0	0.0	0.0	6.9
Spain	37.2	35.2	1.3	0.0	22.5	38.7	16.3	0.0	13.8	1.6
Switzerland	80.7	64.3	14.0	0.0	14.0	5.3	0.0	0.0	0.0	0.0
USA	26.2	19.7	6.6	0.0	33.6	40.2	0.0	21.7	6.7	0.0

Source: OECD revenue statistics.

[1] Due to lack of information on shared taxes by increments, shared taxes are assigned to SNGs as separate U…OECD-and-national-estimate…

Appendix A.1.2
Main features of different tax arrangements

Appendix Table A.1.2a. Tax arrangements in selected countries

	CIT	PIT	Consumption taxes (VAT, sales, excise)	Wealth taxes (property, inheritance, etc.,)	Other business tax	Other state/provincial taxes
Argentina	Federal, shared with states	Federal, shared with states	Federal, shared with states	Provincial property tax	Provincial turnover tax	Some provinces tax labor or sales of utilities, and the 12 provinces that did not transfer their pay-as-you-go pension system collect labor taxes on public employees. Resource-rich provinces collect royalties from mining, electricity, and the production of crude oil and natural gas.
Australia	Federal	Federal	Federal VAT shared with states, possible piggyback on excise	State stamp tax on property transfer, motor vehicle tax, land tax		State payroll tax, limited natural resource royalty revenues, gambling tax, insurance tax
Belgium	Federal	Federal, municipalities can impose surcharge	Federal	Regional real estate tax, inheritance tax, but federal level has some control over tax base		Other local taxes, like waste, leisure (amusement, gambling) tax

(Continued)

Appendix Table A.1.2a (Continued)

	CIT	PIT	Consumption taxes (VAT, sales, excise)	Wealth taxes (property, inheritance, etc.,)	Other business tax	Other state/provincial taxes
Brazil	Federal	Federal	Federal VAT, state VAT	State taxes on property transfer, taxes on vehicle, taxes on inheritance and gifts		Federal natural resource revenues (royalties and special rents) shared with states
Canada	Both central and provincial CIT, but many provinces have federal government collect their CIT	Both central and provincial PIT, but many provinces use federal PIT as tax base and have federal government collect it for them	Provincial (QST or HST), with some provinces using own rate and collection, some using the federal government to collect for them, state excises			Payroll taxes, resource royalties (both deductible from federal CIT)
Germany	Federal, shared with states	Federal, shared with states	Federal, shared with states	State inheritance tax, motor vehicle tax		Gambling tax
India	Federal	Federal, except state tax on agricultural income	State VAT, but rate set by the federal government, federal sales tax, federal excises, except alcohol (state), federal VAT that is in effect a duty of excise	State taxes on land and buildings, vehicle tax	State business tax	A fixed proportion of overall central tax revenues is shared with states, tax on mineral rights

Mexico	Federal, shared with states	Federal, shared with states	Federal, VAT shared with states	State tax on vehicle ownership, tax on acquisition of used motor vehicles		Payroll tax, lodging tax, tax on lotteries, entertainment tax
South Africa	Federal	Federal	Federal			Motor vehicle license, gambling tax, liquor licenses
Spain	Central except in Basque Country and Navarra	Central except in Basque Country and Navarra, shared with regions	Central shared with regions. No applied VAT in Canary Islands.	Wealth tax, gifts and inheritance tax, tax on vehicles	Tax on building works, tax on the increase of urban land value	Tax on gambling
Switzerland	Both federal and cantonal CIT and tax on capital, tax base harmonized	Cantonal PIT and net wealth tax, tax base harmonized but social deductions may differ among cantons.	Federal	Cantonal real estate tax, capital gains tax, capital transfer tax, inheritance and gift tax		
United States	Both state and federal CIT	Both state and federal PIT	State sales tax, federal and state excise tax	Property tax usually local tax, but states set rules; inheritance tax; federal estate tax		Payroll tax, taxes on natural resources

Source: Staff research based on various publications.

Appendix Table A.1.2b Main features of corporate income tax arrangements

	Central/ SNG tax	Who defines tax base	Who sets tax rate	Actual range of SNG tax rates	Tax sharing arrangements	Who administers the tax
Argentina	Central				Yes	Central
Australia	Central				No	
Belgium	Central				No	Central
Brazil	Central				Yes	
Canada	Both central and provincial CIT	Province, but de facto tax base harmonization	Province	10–18%	No	Central for most provinces
Germany	Central				Yes	State tax authorities
India	Central				No	
Mexico	Central				Yes	
South Africa	Central				No	
Spain	Central, except in Navarra and Basque Country				No	Central
Switzerland	Both central and cantonal CIT	Tax base harmonized, but cantons can give certain exemptions	Canton	4–14%	No	Cantons (even for federal CIT)
United States	Both federal and state CIT	State	State	1–12% (four states have no CIT)	No	States

Source: Staff research based on various publications.

Appendix Table A.1.2c Main features of PIT tax arrangements

	Central/ SNG tax	Who defines tax base	Who sets tax rate	Actual range of SNG tax rates	Tax sharing arrangements
Argentina	Central				Yes
Australia	Central				No
Belgium	Central		Regions can vary slightly the PIT rate but without changing the overall progressivity		No
Brazil	Central				Yes
Canada	Both central and provincial PIT	Province, but de facto tax base harmonization	Province	Different progressive schemes by provinces	No
Germany	Federal				Yes
India	Central, except state tax on agricultural income			Agricultural income is taxed in only a few states	No
Mexico	Central				Yes
South Africa	Central				No
Spain	Central, except in Navarra and Basque Country	Central government, but ACs can modify tax base to some extent	ACs can set the tax rate on 50% of tax base		Yes, 50%
Switzerland	Both federal and cantonal CIT	Canton, tax base harmonized	Canton	4–14%	No
United States	Both federal and state CIT	State	State	0.36–11% (seven states have no PIT)	No

Source: Staff research based on various publications.

Appendix Table A.1.2d Main features of VAT/sales tax arrangements

	Central/ SNG tax	Who defines tax base	Who sets tax rate	Actual range of SNG tax rates	Tax sharing arrangements
Argentina	Central				Yes
Australia	Central				Yes
Belgium	Central				No
Brazil	Both federal and state VAT	Central government	Central government	7–25%	Central VAT shared
Canada	Both federal and provincial VAT	Province, some provinces have harmonized tax base with federal VAT	Province	0–10%	No
Germany	Central	Central government	Central government		Yes
India	State VAT, central sales tax	State for state VAT	Central government	4% and 12.5%	No
Mexico	Central				Yes
South Africa	Central				No
Spain	Central				Yes, 50%
Switzerland	Federal				No
United States	State	State	State	2.9–7% (five states have no sales tax)	No

Source: Staff research based on various publications.

Appendix Table A.1.3 Health care decentralization and harmonization

	Health care decentralization rank/index[1]	Characteristics of health care systems	Medical procedure benefits defined at the central level (Y/N)
Australia	9	Universal health care coverage is established at the central level, administered by the federal government, and financed mostly by general taxation. Subnational governments are responsible for planning hospital capacities. Both central and subnational governments finance construction and maintenance of public hospitals.	Yes (positive list)
Belgium	21	Universal health care coverage is established at the central level, administered by social security institutions, and financed by payroll taxes. Both central and subnational governments are responsible for planning hospital capacities and financing construction and maintenance of public hospitals.	Yes (positive list)
Canada	2	Universal health care is established at the level of subnational governments (provinces and territories). Public health spending is financed by subnational taxes as well as earmarked federal transfers for health. Subnational governments are responsible for planning hospital capacities and financing construction and maintenance of public hospitals.	Yes. The Canada Health Act mandates provincial and territorial governments to offer health insurance for specific health services universally and equitably.
Germany	16	Universal health care coverage is established at the central level, administered by social security institutions, and financed by payroll taxes. Subnational governments are responsible for planning hospital capacities. Subnational governments and social security institutions finance construction and maintenance of public hospitals.	Yes (negative list)

(Continued)

Appendix Table A.1.3 (Continued)

	Health care decentralization rank/index[1]	Characteristics of health care systems	Medical procedure benefits defined at the central level (Y/N)
Mexico	14	More than half of the population is covered under social security. Another 20 percent of the population is covered under a publicly-subsidized voluntary health program. Both central and subnational governments are responsible for planning hospital capacities. Central government, subnational governments, and social security institutions finance construction and maintenance of public hospitals.	Yes (positive list)
Spain	1	Universal health care coverage is established at the level of subnational governments (regions), financed mostly by general taxation. Subnational governments are responsible for planning hospital capacities and financing construction and maintenance of public hospitals.	Yes (positive list)
Switzerland	4	Universal health care coverage is established at the central level. Residents are required to purchase health insurance, which is offered by competing private health insurance companies. Subnational governments are responsible for planning hospital capacities and financing construction and maintenance of public hospitals.	Yes (negative list)

Source: Joumard, Andre and C. Nicq (2010).

Note: Information for the United States is not available.
[1]The index ranks the degree of decentralization in decision making over key health policy issues for 28 OECD countries.

Country	Responsibilities of central and subnational governments	Policies to ensure harmonization across subnational governments
Argentina	Primary education has been the responsibility of provinces, and secondary education was transferred from the federal government to the provincial government in the early 1990s.	The federal government coordinates with provincial and municipal government on the regulation of primary and secondary education.
Australia	Each state government manages its own primary and secondary school system and is responsible for financing and regulation.	Regional governments and the federal government coordinate through an inter-government council for primary and secondary education. The federal government is currently formulating a national curriculum in some subjects for primary and secondary education.
Belgium	The three communities (Flemish, French and German language) are responsible for their own educational systems. The communities finance over 80 percent of public educational spending, while the federal government provides financial transfers to them based on the number of pupils aged between six and 17 years old.	The federal government sets national standards on the compulsory education period, minimum requirements for awarding diplomas, and teacher pension scheme.
Brazil	The educational system is a collaborative organization between federal, state, and municipal government organizations. Each year the federal government is mandated to apply no less than 18 percent of public expenditures on education. The federal district, states, and municipalities must apply at least 25 percent of their tax revenues, including transfer revenue from the federal government.	The federal government legislates on guidelines for national education and provides technical and financial assistance to state and local governments. The states can legislate on regional educational issues, provided that the federal legislation is respected.
Canada	Regional governments are responsible for elementary and secondary education in their own regions. Regional and local governments finance over 95 percent of total public spending on education.	There is no federal department of education or integrated national system of education. The Council of Ministers of Education provides a forum for provincial and territorial education ministers to discuss and coordinate on educational issues.
Germany	Education is primarily the responsibility of the states (Länder), which finance over 90 percent of public education expenditure. Within the states, the state governments are responsible for teaching staff payroll in public primary and secondary schools, while local authorities bear the costs of non-teaching staff and the material costs.	A regional coordinating body called the Standing Conference of the Ministers of Education and Cultural Affairs sets national educational standards for quality assurance. The schools in each state are evaluated by external agencies against the national standards.

(Continued)

Appendix Table A.1.4 (Continued)

Country	Responsibilities of central and subnational governments	Policies to ensure harmonization across subnational governments
India	Both the states and the federal governments can enact legislation in education. State governments provide most educational funding, although, since independence, the central government has increasingly assumed the cost of education under the national five-year plans.	N/A
Mexico	Financing of education spending is highly centralized. The central government provides over 80 percent of funding, based on a formula in proportion to the number of teachers and schools that had been supported by the federal education ministry as of 1992.	The central government sets requirements on curriculum and textbooks for primary education, which states must adhere to. States can choose from an approved list of textbooks for lower secondary education.
South Africa	Public spending on primary and secondary education is split between the national and provincial governments.	The Ministry of Education sets national policy, which is implemented by provincial governments.
Spain	The responsibility of education has been divided by law between the central and regional governments (Autonomous Communities). Regional governments contribute over 95 percent of total public education funding. Regional governments are also responsible for teaching their own co-official language, such as Aranese, Catalan, Valencian, Galician, and Basque.	The Ministry of Education of the central government sets basic educational standards and regulation of academic diplomas. Regional governments are responsible for the implementation of such basic national standards and the regulation of non-basic aspects of the education system.
Switzerland	The nine-year compulsory primary and lower secondary education are responsibilities shared between the cantons and their municipalities, which finance about 87 percent of total public spending on education.	Switzerland does not have a federal ministry of education. The 26 members of the Swiss Conference of Cantonal Ministers of Education ensure the coordination of the primary and secondary education system across cantons.
United States	Education is primarily a responsibility shared by the state and local governments. The ages and achievement standards for compulsory education vary by state. The federal government contributes about 11 percent of total spending on elementary and secondary education, mainly targeted at economically disadvantaged and disabled students through the federal program "No Child Left Behind" (NCLB) launched in 2001.	NCLB requires annual tests of reading and mathematics proficiency of students in selected grades of all public schools (not just those receiving the funds) in participating states. The states are responsible for monitoring students' progress and collecting data.

Source: Staff research based on various publications.

	Public pension centralized (Y/N)	Unemployment insurance centralized (Y/N)	Centrally-administered family assistance program (Y/N)	Centrally-administered social assistance program (Y/N)
Argentina	Yes	Yes	N/A	N/A
Austria	Yes	Yes	Yes	Yes
Australia	Yes	Yes	Yes	Yes
Belgium	Yes	Yes	Yes	Yes
Brazil	Yes	Yes	Yes	N/A
Canada	No. The Canadian province Quebec decided to opt out of the federal pension plan and implemented its own pension plan in the 1960s.	Yes	Yes. Family assistance programs in Canada comprise federal tax credit as well as the National Child Benefit Supplement program provided by a partnership of federal, provincial, and territorial governments.	No. Social assistance programs are governed by the provinces and territories.
Germany	Yes	Yes	Yes	Yes
Mexico	Yes	Yes	Yes	N/A
Switzerland	Yes	Yes	No. Child allowances are financed and administered by cantons and municipalities. However, the federal government establishes a minimum monthly benefit.	No. Social assistance programs are administered and financed by the cantons.
Spain	Yes	Yes	Yes	No. The minimum income scheme "Ingreso Mínimo/Renta Mínima de Inserción" is governed by the regional governments.
United States	Yes	No. Unemployment benefit schemes are designed and administered by state governments.	No. The Temporary Assistance for Needy Families (TANF) program is administered and implemented by the states.	Yes

Sources: International Social Security Association and OECD country database on benefits and wages.

"N/A" indicates that information is not available from the sources.

Appendix Table A.1.6 Infrastructure spending centralization, decentralization, and harmonization

Country	Responsibilities of central and subnational governments	Policies to ensure harmonization across subnational governments
Argentina	The delivery and financing responsibilities for roads are shared by the federal, provincial, and municipal governments. Sea transport infrastructure is the federal government's exclusive responsibility, while provincial governments are responsible for delivering airports and passenger rail infrastructure.	N/A
Australia	Land transport infrastructure is a responsibility shared by the central and state governments. The states are responsible for most of the nation's road construction and maintenance works.	The Australian central government is delivering the National Building Program based on projects of national and regional importance. On public-private partnerships (PPPs), the national PPP guideline endorsed by the Council of Australian Governments applies to PPP projects at both national and subnational levels.
Belgium	Regions are typically responsible for public transport infrastructure excluding the state-owned railway company. However, infrastructure projects in the Brussels-Capital Region are financed by a special program of the federal government to promote Brussels as a major international city and urban agglomeration.	N/A
Brazil	Infrastructure is a shared responsibility by the federal, state, and municipal governments. The federal government is responsible for national matters, the municipalities are responsible for local issuers, and the states have residual responsibilities. A federal levy on the importation and sale of fuel products is shared with the states and municipalities to finance investment in transport infrastructure and other projects.	Federal laws on concessions and PPPs set general rules on subnational PPPs. Subnational laws must be consistent with the federal law, and the federal government can withhold transfers in the event of noncompliance.
Canada	Municipalities play a leading role in managing and operating infrastructure and own about 65 percent of public capital stocks. Provincial and territorial governments own 31 percent, and the federal government owns the rest. In recent years, the federal government has provided infrastructure funding for provincial and municipal governments, mainly through Infrastructure Canada.	Infrastructure Canada provides federal transfers to subnational governments to support regional infrastructure priorities, finance strategic investments of national and regional benefit, and provide short-term economic stimulus.

Germany	The federal government is responsible for federal roads, railways and inland waterways, while state governments administer federal roads by carrying out the project on behalf of the federal government. State governments are responsible for airports and seaports, but their connections to the surface transport modes are covered by the federal government. The states are also responsible for state trunk roads within their own jurisdiction. The federal government invests in infrastructure through both the on-budget federal infrastructure master plan and a toll-financed fund for off-budget projects.	The 2011–15 Framework Investment Plan abandoned a quota system and stressed the importance of developing the federal trunk roads nationwide. This has been a policy shift because the federal infrastructure master plan had relied on a quota system to ensure a fair distribution of investments between subnational governments until 2006. Subnational governments coordinate their transportation infrastructure policies through a cross-regional committee, for which the federal ministry is a guest.
India	Both the central government and state governments are actively utilizing PPPs for infrastructure projects. The central government provides grants up to 20 percent of the total capital cost to PPP projects undertaken by any state government, local body, central ministry, or statutory entity.	The central government outlines major infrastructure projects in its five-year plans.
Mexico	The central government is responsible for federal highway construction and maintenance, rural road financing; state governments are responsible for some airports, state feeder roads, maintenance of secondary feeder roads, implementation of rural road development, and municipal governments are responsible for local public transportation and local streets.	The Ministry of Social Development coordinates the central government's matching grants for water, electricity, and rural roads targeted to isolated indigenous communities.
South Africa	The central government has been working on a national primary road network in the past decade, by consolidating national and provincial roads and promoting the user-pay principle. In principle, the national system and urban arterials are financed by tolling and central government borrowing, provincial roads by fuel levies, and purely access roads by general taxes such as environment tax.	The central government conducts its road policy mainly through a state-owned enterprise. The central government has the oversight and approval responsibilities for PPPs developed in local governments.

(Continued)

Appendix Table A.1.6 (Continued)

Country	Responsibilities of central and subnational governments	Policies to ensure harmonization across subnational governments
Spain	The central government is responsible for national infrastructure including commercial ports and airports; regional governments (autonomous communities) are responsible for regional infrastructure including sport ports and sport airports; municipalities are responsible for local infrastructure. Although the first few PPP projects in Spain were contracted with the central government in the 1990s, PPP activity has decentralized and accelerated at regional and local levels since then.	The central government uses a regional solidarity fund to provide infrastructure funds to poor regions. To qualify, per capita GDP in the region must be below 75 percent of the European average. There is no central register of PPP projects or PPP unit in the central government.
Switzerland	Transport infrastructure is a shared responsibility among the federal, cantonal, and municipal governments based on the beneficiaries-pay principle. Earmarked revenues, including federal fuel taxes, cantonal vehicle taxes, and various municipal fees, are used to finance road expenditures. Federal-cantonal and cantonal-municipal transfers are also used to finance the funding gaps at the subnational level.	The federal government provides earmarked grants to the cantons for major road constructions, natural disaster prevention, or environmental protection.
United States	The federal government finances about one quarter of highway and mass transit infrastructure expenditure through grants to state governments from the Federal Highway Trust Fund (FHTF). The FHTF is funded by the federal motor fuel tax. About 90 percent of the fund is allocated to states based on a formula and the remaining is discretionary.	The federal government sets the criteria for FHTF qualifying projects, such as interstate highway maintenance or national highway construction.

Source: Staff research based on various publications.

Notes

1 For the sample definition, see the Introduction and Overview chapter of this book. Some countries may not be included because of lack of data. As mentioned earlier in this book, "central government" refers to the highest national government level (e.g., the federal government), and "subnational government" (SNG) refers to all levels of government below the central government. In fiscal federations (and highly decentralized countries) the SNG level usually comprises state or regional governments and local or municipal governments. The term "general government" refers to the consolidation of central government and SNGs – that is, the government sector as a whole.

2 According to Weingast, 2014: "The first generation fiscal federalism assumption of benevolent maximizers of social welfare ignores the actual goals of political officials who typically must run for reelection. This perspective also ignores the problem of how federal systems remain stable given the incentives of officials at the different levels to cheat on the rules; for example, by encroaching on power and prerogatives of another level." See also Oates, 2005.

3 For example, a tax cut by the central government to stimulate an economic activity may be offset by SNGs trying to use the opportunity to raise their tax rates on the same base.

4 Keen and Kotsogiannis (2004) show, for example, that lower-level tax competition can be welfare reducing either because it makes low subnational taxes even lower *or* because it makes excessively high subnational taxes even higher. For a review of the literature on tax harmonization, coordination, and competition see e.g., Keen and Konrad (2013).

5 See Appendix A.1.1 for cross-country data on tax revenues. Central government tax revenue also represents a low share of GDP in Mexico, although this reflects the small overall size of general government tax revenue in Mexico relative to the rest of the sample.

6 Whenever the available information allows, shared revenue has been assigned to the central government, in line with the fact that SNGs have generally little control over such revenue (the tax rate, its coverage, or the distribution of the revenues). Hence, their exclusion is appropriate if the classification is to be used as an indicator of the degree to which SNGs (and residents in their jurisdictions) internalize the tax impact of their spending decisions.

7 See Appendix A.1.2 for the distinctive features of tax arrangements (including CIT, PIT, and VAT)

8 See also Tiebout (1956), Oates (1972, 2005), McLure and Martinez-Vazquez (2000), and International Monetary Fund (2009). More recent (second generation) theoretical work on fiscal federalism emphasizes the political and institutional conditions under which greater fiscal decentralization may enhance or undermine efficiency. See Oates (2005) and International Monetary Fund (2009) for a brief review. For the macroeconomic implications of federation's design, see Fedelino (2009).

9 Within the European Union, when SNGs have responsibilities in the areas of health care, education, and social protection, they are to a large extent bound by national rules and guidelines (European Commission, 2012).

10 Owing to availability of detailed information, this discussion of health care spending is based on a reduced sample of fiscal federations comprising Australia, Belgium, Canada, Germany, Mexico, Spain, Switzerland, and the United States.

11 This subsection focuses on primary and secondary education and does not address tertiary education.

12 See Appendix Table A.1.4 for descriptions of harmonization policies in education in Germany, Mexico, Spain, Switzerland, and the United States.

13 In Canada, a child benefit program is implemented through a partnership among federal, provincial, and territorial governments.

14 Chapter 2 discusses the role of transfers in smoothing regional shocks.

15 Moral hazard and financing issues are discussed at more length in Chapters 3, 5, and 6.
16 Main conclusions and comparative rankings are not materially affected by the measure employed, however. The underlying data source is the OECD Fiscal Federalism Network (http://www.oecd.org/ctp/fiscalfederalismnetwork/).
17 The VFI is therefore computed as net transfers and shared taxes received as a share of subnational total revenue.
18 For the influence of the European budget framework and rules and national fiscal rules, see Debrun et al. (2008).
19 Every multiannual budget framework has built-in schemes to compensate certain EU countries. The three major compensation schemes are: (i) The "UK rebate," by which the UK is reimbursed by 66% of the difference between its contribution and what it receives back from the budget (the calculation is based on the U.K. GNI); (ii) VAT lump-sum payments to the Netherlands and Sweden; (iii) and reduced VAT contribution rates for the Netherlands, Sweden, Germany, and Austria.
20 EU members keep 25 percent of the revenue to cover the cost of collection (http://ec.europa.eu/budget/explained/budg_system/financing/fin_en.cfm).
21 The harmonized VAT base to be taxed is capped at 50 percent of GNI for each country. This rule is intended to prevent less prosperous countries having to pay a disproportionate amount (in such countries consumption – and so, the notional harmonized VAT – tends to account for a higher percentage of national income). For an original discussion of VAT in the EU, see Keen and Smith (1996).
22 Bordo et al. (2011), Henning and Kessler (2012), Hall and Sargent (2013).
23 On several occasions since 2001, the European Union has discussed a Common Corporate Income Tax (CIT), which could partially contribute to the European budget. But not much progress has been made, beyond considering the possibility of starting with a Common Consolidated Corporate Tax Base. According to the most recent proposal by the Commission, a common tax base would be apportioned among Member States based on a formula, which would be common across all members, but tax rates could vary across jurisdictions. The purpose of this common tax base would be to minimize distortions and reduce compliance costs for companies operating across the European Union. For more information, see: European Commission (2001, 2007, and 2011). For a summary and current status, see http://ec.europa.eu/taxation_customs/taxation/company_tax/common_tax_base/index_en.htm
24 The minimum tax rates foreseen were 0.1% for the trading in shares and bonds, and 0.01% for derivative agreements such as options, futures, contracts for difference, or interest rate swaps. For a summary of this proposal, see http://ec.europa.eu/taxation_customs/taxation/other_taxes/financial_sector/index_en.htm and http://europa.eu/rapid/press-release_IP-11-1085_en.htm
25 Simple average for 1995–2010. Own expenditure excludes transfers to SNGs.
26 Even a central proportional tax would be equalizing if spent across regions roughly in proportion to their population.
27 Simple average for 1995–2010. Own expenditure excludes transfers to SNGs.
28 Eyraud and Lusinyan (2012) and European Commission (2012) find evidence that transfer dependency is associated with lower general government balances in the OECD and the European Union respectively. Escolano et al. (2012) find that decentralization has a positive effect on the fiscal performance of the general government but significantly less so if it is accompanied by high transfer dependency. Regarding earlier empirical studies with a somewhat less negative view of transfers, but based on more limited data, De Mello (2000) finds that among OECD countries transfers may have been used by the central government to instill fiscal discipline in SNGs. Similarly, Darby et al. (2005) argue that in OECD countries central governments make use of grants to effectively control subnational expenditure, acting as counterweight to the "common-pool" problem. Finally, Baskaran (2010) finds the effect of transfers statistically insignificant.

References

Ahmad, Ehtisham and Jon Craig, 1997, "Intergovernmental Transfers," in *Fiscal Federalism in Theory and Practice*, edited by T. Minassian (Washington: International Monetary Fund).

Artana, Daniel, et al., 2012, "Sub-National Revenue Mobilization in Latin American and Caribbean Countries: The Case of Argentina," IDB Working Paper Series No. 297 (Washington: Inter-American Development Bank).

Baskaran, T., 2010, "On the Link between Fiscal Decentralization and Public Debt in OECD Countries," *Public Choice*, Vol. 145 (December), pp. 351–78.

Bird, Richard, 2010a, "Taxation and Decentralization," Economic Premise No. 38 (Washington: World Bank), available at http://siteresources.worldbank.org/INTPREMNET/Resources/EP38.pdf

————, 2010b, "Subnational Taxation in Developing Countries: A Review of the Literature," Policy Research Working Paper No. 5450 (Washington: World Bank).

Bird, Richard, 2012, "Subnational Taxation in Large Emerging Countries: BRIC Plus One," IMFG Paper on Municipal Finance and Governance No. 6 (Toronto: Institute on Municipal Finance and Governance).

Bird, Richard, and Michael Smart, 2010, "Assigning State Taxes in a Federal Country: The Case of Australia," in *Melbourne Institute – Australia's Future Tax and Transfer Policy Conference: Proceedings of a Conference* (Melbourne: Melbourne Institute of Applied Economic and Social Research).

Bird, Richard, and Andrey Tarasov, 2004, "Closing the Gap: Fiscal Imbalances and Intergovernmental Transfers in Developed Federations," *Environment and Planning C: Government and Policy*, Vol. 22 (February), pp. 77–102.

Blöchliger, Hansjörg, and Oliver Petzold, 2009, "Finding the Dividing Line between Tax Sharing and Grants: A Statistical Investigation," OECD Working Paper on Fiscal Federalism No. 10 (Paris: Organisation for Economic Cooperation and Development).

Blöchliger, Hansjörg, and Josette Rabesona, 2009, "The Fiscal Autonomy of Sub-Central Governments: An Update," OECD Working Paper on Fiscal Federalism No. 9 (Paris: Organisation for Economic Cooperation and Development).

Bordo, Michael D., Agnieszka Markiewicz, and Lars Jonung, 2011, "A Fiscal Union for the Euro: Some Lessons from History," NBER WP No. 17380 (Cambridge, MA).

Dahlby, Bev, 2001, "Taxing Choices: Issues in the Assignment of Taxes in Federations," *International Social Science Journal*, Vol. 167 (March), pp. 93–101.

Darby, Julia, Anton Muscatelli, and Graeme Roy, 2005, "How Do Sub-Central Government React to Cuts in Grants Received from Central Governments. Evidence from a Panel of 15 OECD Countries," CPPR Discussion Paper, No. 1.

Debrun, Xavier, et al., 2008, "Tied to the Mast? National Fiscal Rules in the European Union," *Economic Policy*, Vol. 23 (April), pp. 297–362.

De Mello, Luiz R., 2000, "Can Fiscal Decentralization Strengthen Social Capital?" IMF Working Papers 00/129 (Washington: International Monetary Fund).

Escolano, Julio, et al., 2012, "Fiscal Performance, Institutional Design and Decentralization in European Union Countries," IMF Working Paper 12/45, available at http://www.imf.org/external/pubs/ft/wp/2012/wp1245.pdf

European Commission, Economic and Financial Affairs, 2012, "2012 Report on Public Finances in EMU," *European Economy*, Vol. 4 (Brussels).

Eyraud, Luc, and Lusine Lusinyan, 2012, "Vertical Fiscal Imbalances and Fiscal Performance in Advanced Economies," paper presented at the 80th Meeting of the Carnegie-Rochester-NYU Conference on Public Policy, Pittsburgh, November.

Fedelino, Annelisa, 2009, "Macro Policy Lessons for a Sound Design of Fiscal Decentralization," IMF Board Paper SM/09/208 (Washington: International Monetary Fund).

Gichiru, Wangari, et al., 2009, "Sub-Central Tax Competition in Canada, the United States, Japan, and South Korea," paper prepared for the Fiscal Federalism Network, Organisation for Economic Cooperation and Development (Madison: University of Wisconsin-Madison).

Hall, George J., and Thomas J. Sargent, 2013, "Fiscal Discriminations in Three Wars," NBER WP No. 19008 (Cambridge, MA).

Health Canada, 2011, Canada Health Act Annual Report 2010–11, Available at: http://www.hc-sc.gc.ca/hcs-sss/pubs/cha-lcs/2011-cha-lcs-ar-ra/index-eng.php

Henning, C. Randall, and Martin Kessler, 2012, "Fiscal Federalism: US History for Architects of Europe's Fiscal Union," Bruegel Essay and Lecture Series (Brussels), available at http://www.bruegel.org

International Monetary Fund, 2009, "Macro Policy Lessons for a Sound Design of Fiscal Decentralization," IMF Departmental Paper (Washington: International Monetary Fund). Available at: http://www.imf.org/external/np/pp/eng/2009/072709.pdf

———, 2010, "A Fair and Substantial Contribution by the Financial Sector: Final Report for the G-20," (Washington: International Monetary Fund), available at http://www.imf.org/external/np/g20/pdf/062710b.pdf

Jin, Jing, and Heng-Fu Zou, 2002, "How Does Fiscal Decentralization Affect Aggregate, National, and Subnational Government Size?" *Journal of Urban Economics*, Vol. 52 (September), pp. 270–93.

Joumard, Isabelle, Christophe André, and Chantal Nicq, 2010, "Health Care Systems: Efficiency and Institutions," OECD Economics Department Working Paper No. 769 (Paris: Organisation for Economic Cooperation and Development).

Keen, Michael, and Kai A. Konrad, 2013, "The Theory of International Tax Competition and Coordination," in *Handbook of Public Economics*, edited by Alan J. Auerbach, Raj Chetty, Martin Feldstein, and Emmanuel Saez, *Elsevier*, Vol. 5, pp. 257–328.

Keen, Michael, and Christos Kotsogiannis, 2004, "Tax Competition in Federations and the Welfare Consequences of Decentralization," *Journal of Urban Economics*, Vol. 56 (November), pp. 397–407.

Keen, Michael, and Stephen Smith, 1996, "The Future of Value Added Tax in the European Union," *Economic Policy*, No. 23 (October), pp. 373–420.

McLure, Charles E., and Jorge Martinez-Vazquez, 2000, "The Assignment of Revenues and Expenditures in Intergovernmental Fiscal Relations" (unpublished; Washington: World Bank Institute).

Musgrave, Richard Abel, 1959, *The Theory of Public Finance: A Study in Public Economy* (New York: McGraw-Hill).

———, 1983, "Who Should Tax, Where, and What?" in *Tax Assignment in Federal Countries*, edited by Charles E. McLure, Jr. (Canberra: Centre for Research on Federal Financial Relations, The Australian National University).

Oates, Wallace E., 1972, *Fiscal Federalism* (New York: Harcourt Brace Jovanovich).

———, 2005, "Toward a Second-Generation Theory of Fiscal Federalism," *International Tax and Public Finance*, Vol. 12 (August), pp. 349–73.

———, 2006, "On Theory and Practice of Fiscal Decentralization," IFIR Working Paper Series, 2006–05 (Lexington: Institute for Federalism & Intergovernmental Relations).

OECD (Organisation for Economic Cooperation and Development), 2012, *Education at a Glance 2012: OECD Indicators* (Paris).

————, and WHO (World Health Organization), 2011, *OECD Reviews of Health Systems: Switzerland 2011* (Paris: Organisation for Economic Cooperation and Development), available at http://dx.doi.org/10.1787/9789264120914-en

Paris, Valérie, Marion Devaux, and Lihan Wei, 2010, "Health Systems Institutional Characteristics: A Survey of 29 OECD Countries," OECD Health Working Papers, No. 50 (Paris: Organisation for Economic Cooperation and Development)., available at http://dx.doi.org/10.1787/5kmfxfq9qbnr-en

Perry, Victoria J., 2010, "International Experience in Implementing VATs in Federal Jurisdictions: A Summary," *Tax Law Review*, Vol. 63 (August), pp. 623–38.

Rao, M. Govinda, 2007, "Resolving Fiscal Imbalances: Issues in Tax Sharing," in *Intergovernmental Fiscal Transfers: Principles and Practice*, edited by Robin Boadway and Anwar Shah (Washington: World Bank).

Rodden, Jonathan, 2002, "The Dilemma of Fiscal Federalism: Grants and Fiscal Performance around the World," *American Journal of Political Science*, Vol. 46 (July), pp. 670–87.

Ter-Minassian, Teresa, 1997, *Fiscal Federalism in Theory and Practice* (Washington: International Monetary Fund).

————, 2012, "Reform Priorities for Sub-National Revenues in Brazil," Policy Brief No. IDB-PB-157 (Washington: Inter-American Development Bank).

Tiebout, Charles M., 1956, "A Pure Theory of Local Expenditures," *Journal of Political Economy*, Vol. 64 (October), pp. 416–24.

Vaillancourt, François, 2012, "Own Revenues in Federations: Tax Powers, Tax Bases, Tax Rates and Collection Arrangements in Five Federal Countries," *eJournal of Tax Research*, Vol. 10 (February), pp. 65–87.

Vanistendael, Frans, 2011, "The European Union," in *Tax Aspects of Fiscal Federalism, A Comparative Analysis*, edited by Gianluigi Bizioli and Claudio Sacchetto (Amsterdam: International Bureau of Fiscal Documentation).

Weingast, Barry R., 2014, "Second Generation Fiscal Federalism: Political Aspects of Decentralization and Economic Development," *World Development*, Vol. 53, issue C, pp. 14–25.

2 The role of fiscal transfers in smoothing regional shocks

Tigran Poghosyan, Abdelhak Senhadji, and Carlo Cottarelli

I. Introduction

This chapter analyses the role of net fiscal transfers in mitigating the impact of regional shocks on subnational public finances in federations. As discussed in Chapter 1, fiscal transfers play different roles, including closing vertical imbalances, achieving redistribution goals, and insuring states or provinces against macroeconomic shocks. The latter role in turn could be subdivided into insurance against *idiosyncratic* macroeconomic shocks hitting individual states (*risk-sharing*) and insurance against *common* shocks hitting all states simultaneously (*stabilization*). This chapter focuses on the extent of risk-sharing – an issue that has figured front and center in the discussion regarding euro area institutions in recent years – and, relatedly, whether a federal system with a central budget – or equivalent risk-sharing mechanisms – would achieve better insurance against macroeconomic shocks than a system without it.

Disentangling the respective roles of redistribution, stabilization, and risk-sharing is complicated as in most federations fiscal transfers play them simultaneously.[1] Ideally, measuring risk-sharing would require conducting a counterfactual analysis and comparing the magnitudes of insurance in existing federations before and after a central budget had been established. In practice, conducting such analysis is not possible given the difficulty of finding data on federations before the establishment of a central budget (i.e., the counterfactual), as almost all existing federations have been functioning with centralized fiscal systems for decades now. Therefore, we follow an alternative route. First, drawing on the literature, we discuss the relative effectiveness of centralized versus decentralized fiscal systems in offsetting the impact of macroeconomic shocks. Second, we assess empirically the importance of risk-sharing in three large fiscal federations (Australia, Canada, and the U.S.), and the mechanisms through which this risk-sharing occurs.[2]

This chapter also offers some methodological refinements in the estimation of risk-sharing and redistribution motives of fiscal transfers. It starts with the standard two-step approach that has been used in the literature – where redistribution and risk-sharing motives are estimated separately – and proposes a new, more efficient one-step approach. It also proposes an alternative approach which allows one to assess separately the extent to which individual components of net fiscal transfers contribute to risk-sharing (and redistribution).

The remainder of this chapter is structured as follows: Section II summarizes the theoretical arguments on whether a central budget in federations could enhance insurance against macroeconomic shocks. Section III reviews existing empirical approaches for measuring the impact of fiscal transfers on redistribution and insurance and summarizes the evidence from the previous literature. Section IV introduces an efficient one-step empirical methodology to estimate fiscal risk-sharing and redistribution. Section V describes the data and provides summary statistics. Section VI presents estimates from two empirical methodologies: the standard two-step approach used in previous studies and our new more efficient methodology. Section VII introduces a third empirical approach which allows us to assess separately the role of individual gross components of net fiscal transfers in dampening the impact of shocks through fiscal transfers. The last section concludes.

II. Does a central budget enhance insurance against macroeconomic shocks? Review of main theoretical arguments

Members of a fiscal federation benefit from insurance against income shocks in the same way that individuals do – it enables them to buffer their consumption path in the face of such shocks. The logic of consumption-smoothing was famously articulated by Friedman (1957) in his treatise on the permanent income hypothesis. He demonstrated how consumers with access to credit markets would save and borrow to make their consumption path smoother than their income path.

In addition to saving and borrowing in credit markets, risk-sharing across members of a federation can also help smooth the consumption path at the state level – states that do better than usual at a certain period in time help insure states that are doing worse than usual. Over time, the benefits of this arrangement are expected to be shared across members of a federation, as no state should perform consistently better or worse than the average one.

Various studies discuss how fiscal centralization can, in theory, enhance the extent of insurance against macroeconomic shocks (for more detailed discussions, see the surveys in Beetsma and Debrun, 2004 and Beetsma and Giuliodori, 2010):

- **Risk-sharing (interregional insurance):** A centralized fiscal system allows states to pool risks emanating from idiosyncratic shocks. This interregional insurance works on top of the stabilization function (or intertemporal insurance). Some commentators justify the importance of risk-sharing in federations with the fact that in the absence of state-specific exchange rates, shocks hitting individual states and provinces cannot be cushioned through changes in terms of trade due to price stickiness. In addition, households will have limited capacity to smooth regional shocks if markets for production inputs (labor and capital) are not mobile enough or if private credit markets do not function properly.[3]
- **Scale economies:** Another argument in favor of centralizing countercyclical fiscal policies is related to scale economies benefiting central governments in

performing their stabilization function. An important factor here is the ability of the central government to borrow at better terms from markets than can individual states. This is vividly illustrated in the case of the U.S., where states pay a risk-premium over Treasury bond yields to borrow from markets.

- **Fiscal spillovers and fiscal policy coordination:** Some studies argue that fiscal stabilization is of a "public good" nature. They point out that highly integrated neighboring states are likely to benefit from stabilization measures carried out by one of them, since the impact of these measures is likely to leak out to other states through interstate trade spillovers. As a result, a "free-riding" problem emerges making decentralized policies excessively passive. In particular, uncoordinated state-specific fiscal policies may not be as effective as coordinated policies run at the central level that internalize these spillover effects (Hamada, 1985). Some have underscored the efficacy of a centralized fiscal policy in the particular case where monetary policy reaches its lower bound.

- **Ricardian equivalence:** In the presence of (even partly) Ricardian households, the stabilization function of state fiscal policies in a fully decentralized fiscal system can be hampered by the decision of households to increase savings in periods of fiscal expansion in anticipation that higher deficits will need to be financed through higher taxes in a later period. In other words, fiscal multipliers in a fully decentralized system with Ricardian households will be very weak. By contrast, Ricardian effects tend to have a smaller impact on fiscal multipliers in centralized fiscal systems, since households in states running deficits may expect that the financing of those deficits will be shared with households living in other states. For instance, Bayoumi and Masson (1998) find that in Canada a non-liability creating stabilization would be two to three times more effective than decentralized stabilization financed through the increase in the local public debt.

However, there are also arguments against the centralization of fiscal policy in the context of stabilization and risk-sharing:

- **Design issues:** The arguments above for centralization of fiscal policy ignore issues related to the design of an efficient tax and transfer system necessary to achieve a well-coordinated stabilization policy and efficient risk-sharing. In particular, it is difficult to design a federal fiscal system that would exclusively minimize the variability of regional income without leading to a systematic redistribution of income from rich to poor regions. Indeed, empirical evidence suggests that the former consistently pay higher federal taxes and receive lower federal transfers on average (Goodhart and Smith, 1993).

- **Moral hazard issues:** Implicit bailout guarantees offered by the centralized fiscal arrangement may decrease incentives for good policies. This classic moral hazard problem could worsen the fiscal position of states and increase their vulnerability to macroeconomic shocks. The moral hazard argument has been put forward by the Eurobond skeptics arguing that Eurobonds would weaken market discipline and lead individual governments to postpone long-overdue reforms (Chapter 3 discusses moral hazard issues in federations in greater detail). The moral argument could also be used for other types of insurance schemes, such as the one that is the focus of in this paper, whereby the central government provides member states transfers to offset the impact of shocks.

Overall, given these contrasting theoretical arguments, the issue is how much, in practice, central budgets help cushion the impact of regional shocks.

III. Redistribution and risk-sharing in existing federations: Empirical approaches and evidence from previous studies

As mentioned earlier, fiscal transfers in federations have two important effects on regional incomes: (i) *redistribution*, or permanent transfer of funds from richer to poorer regions to help convergence of regional living standards to the national average, and (ii) *insurance* against macroeconomic shocks, or temporary transfer of funds to smooth out the impact of idiosyncratic regional (*risk-sharing*) and common (*stabilization*) shocks.[4]

More specifically, insurance measures the extent to which fiscal transfers off-set regional disposable incomes from temporary shocks to regional outputs. For instance, a level of insurance of 10 percent implies that the disposable income of a given region would fall by 90 cents in response to a temporary decline in its output by $1. This temporary decline in output could be either relative to the national average output (risk-sharing) or a simultaneous decline in output across all regions (stabilization). Similarly, the magnitude of the redistribution effect measures the extent to which fiscal transfers flow from the relatively rich regions to the poor ones. For example, a redistribution effect of 20 percent would imply that a region with a $1 permanently lower output relative to the national average (as a result of a permanent shock) would have a disposable income that is only 80 cents below the national average, with the remaining 20 cents being covered by the permanent transfer of funds from richer regions.

The literature uses three empirical approaches to quantify the effect of fiscal transfers in the U.S. and other federations (Appendix A.2.1 provides a technical review of these approaches, and Table 2.1 summarizes the results).

- The *first* approach, pioneered by Sachs and Sala-i-Martin (1992), assesses the overall impact of fiscal transfers on redistribution and risk-sharing, without distinguishing between the two. Using data on nine U.S. regions for the period 1970–80, the authors estimate a combined cushioning effect of net fiscal transfers in the range of 33–40 percent of the initial shock and conclude that the U.S. federal fiscal system substantially smoothes regional income shocks. Masson and Taylor (1993) adopt the same methodology to study fiscal transfers in Canada during 1965–1988. They find that the effect of net fiscal transfers is only 13 percent and that federal taxes play a more important

Table 2.1 Empirical estimates of redistribution and risk-sharing from previous studies

Study	Country	Sample period	Federal fiscal flows	
			Redistribution	Risk-sharing
Sachs and Sala-i-Martin (1992)	USA	1970–80		33–40
Masson and Taylor (1993)	Canada	1965–88		13
Andersson (2004)	Sweden	1983–2001		7–22
von Hagen (1992)	USA	1981–86	47	10
Goodhart and Smith (1993)	Canada	1966–88	15	17
	UK	1984–87	21	21
	USA	1982–86	13	11
Bayoumi and Mason (1995)	Canada	1969–86	39	31
	USA	1969–86	22	17
Decressin (2002)	Italy	1970–95	25–35	10–15
Melitz and Zumer (2002)	Canada	1965–88	16	10–15
	France	1973–89	38	20
	UK	1971–93	26	20
	USA	1977–92	16	20
Obstfeld and Peri (1998)	Canada	1971–95	53	13
	Italy	1979–93	8	3
	USA	1969–85	19	10

Source: Authors, based on the literature search.

Note: Numbers in the middle of the redistribution and risk-sharing columns refer to the combined effect of the two for studies that do not separate them.

role in cushioning the impact of regional shocks (4 to 22 percent, averaging 12 percent when weighted by population) compared to gross fiscal transfers (−26 to 10 percent, averaging close to zero when weighted by population). Using Swedish data for the period 1983–2001, Andersson (2004) concludes that net fiscal transfers absorb between 7 and 22 percent of an initial shock to personal income. Similar to Masson and Taylor, her results indicate that taxes play a more important role than do gross fiscal transfers.

• The *second* approach was proposed by Von Hagen (1992). As mentioned above, the issue with Sachs and Sala-i-Martin's approach is that it does not distinguish between redistribution and insurance motives. Von Hagen uses an alternative specification that disentangles risk-sharing from redistribution. Because this specification relies on two separate regressions – one for risk-sharing and another for redistribution – this approach will be referred to as the *two-step approach*. Using data on 48 states of the U.S. during 1981–86, Von Hagen obtains a much smaller estimate of insurance against regional shocks, amounting to 10 percent. However, he finds a large redistribution effect of 47 percent. Von Hagen's two-step methodology was adopted by Goodhart and Smith (1993) to study the role of fiscal transfers in a wider set of countries, including the U.S. (1982–86), Canada (1965–88), and the

United Kingdom (1983–87). The results on risk-sharing for the U.S. (11 percent) are comparable to those in Von Hagen; however they find a smaller redistribution effect (13 percent).[5] In Canada and the U.K., the impact of fiscal transfers on risk-sharing (17 and 21 percent, respectively) and redistribution (15 and 21 percent, respectively) was found to be relatively larger compared to the respective estimates for the U.S.

• The *third* approach was outlined in Bayoumi and Masson (1995). Similar to Von Hagen's, this is a two-step approach, but unlike Von Hagen's, it does not separately identify the effects of federal taxes and of gross fiscal transfers. Using data on states in the U.S. and Canadian provinces during 1969–1986, Bayoumi and Masson find a stronger redistributive effect of net fiscal transfers in Canada (39 percent) relative to the U.S. (22 percent). By contrast, the risk-sharing effect of net fiscal transfers is found to be larger in the U.S. (31 percent) compared to Canada (17 percent). Using Bayoumi and Masson's approach and focusing on shocks to regional personal income, rather than regional GDP, Melitz and Zumer (2002) find that risk-sharing between regions in France and in the U.K. is similar in magnitude to that in the U.S. (20 percent). Redistribution, however, is larger in France (38 percent) and in the U.K. (26 percent) than in the U.S. and Canada (16 percent). Obstfeld and Peri (1998) use a dynamic version of Bayoumi and Masson's two-step approach by specifying a bivariate vector autoregression (VAR) model on demeaned regional incomes to analyze the impact of net fiscal transfers in the U.S., Canada, and Italy. They find a first year risk-sharing effect of 10–13 percent for the U.S. and Canada, comparable to previous estimates, but the magnitude is much smaller for Italy (3 percent). The long-run redistribution effect is the strongest in Canada (53 percent), followed by the U.S. (19 percent) and Italy (8 percent). Decressin (2002) repeats this exercise for the case of Italy using the period 1970–95 and finds much larger risk-sharing (10–15 percent) and redistribution (25–35 percent) effects.

Overall, the evidence from the reviewed studies suggests that risk-sharing and redistribution estimates vary widely across countries, sample periods, and estimation methods (Table 2.1). For instance, using the same methodology, Sachs and Sala-i-Martin, Masson and Taylor, and Andersson find substantially different estimates for the U.S., Canada, and Sweden, respectively. Nevertheless, a common pattern emerges: the redistributive motive is generally stronger than the risk-sharing motive. For instance, in the U.S. the average estimate of risk-sharing (14 percent) is about half of the average estimate of redistribution (23 percent). However, these studies use relatively old data sets and an arbitrary two-step procedure. In addition, they do not separate the impact of automatic transfers (arising from the operation of centralized automatic stabilizers) from that of discretionary transfers. The following sections attempt to address these issues using more recent data on three federations and three empirical methodologies – the conventional two-step approach, a new one-step procedure, and separate estimates for different types of transfers.[6]

IV. New one-step estimation method

As discussed in the previous section, the existing literature uses a two-step approach for measuring the relative magnitudes of fiscal risk-sharing and redistribution. The redistribution effect is typically measured using a cross-sectional regression on average levels of regional variables (equation A.2.6 in Appendix A.2.1), while the risk-sharing effect is measured using panel data regressions on changes of regional variables (equation A.2.7). To ensure the robustness of results, we complement the two-step methodology used in previous studies with a new methodology that assesses the effect of redistribution and risk-sharing in one step. While this methodology mirrors the two-step approach (with a one-to-one mapping of the coefficient estimates as shown below), it is more efficient because it combines the high and low frequency information in the data. In particular, it accounts for the dynamic effects of fiscal transfers highlighted in Obstfeld and Peri (1998) by introducing a short-run adjustment of disposable income to its long-run equilibrium level.

More specifically, we apply the Pooled Mean Group (PMG) estimator of Pesaran et al. (1999), which is a panel data version of the error-correction model. The empirical specification takes the following form:

$$\Delta\left(\frac{YD_{it}}{\overline{YD}_t}\right) = \phi_i\left[\frac{YD_{it-1}}{\overline{YD}_{t-1}} - \alpha - \beta\frac{Y_{it-1}}{\overline{Y}_{t-1}}\right] + \delta_i\Delta\left(\frac{Y_{it}}{\overline{Y}_t}\right) + \mu_i + \varepsilon_{it} \qquad (2.1)$$

where i and t indices denote state and time, Y_{it} is the state-level real per capita GDP, YD_{it} is the state-level real per capita disposable income after accounting for net fiscal transfers, $\overline{YD}_t$ and $\overline{Y}_t$ are national averages of respective variables in period t,[7] μ is the state-specific fixed effect, and ε is an *i.i.d.* error term. The term enclosed in brackets is the error-correction term measuring the extent of the deviation of the relative disposable income from its long-run equilibrium value (determined by the relative GDP).

The coefficients in specification (2.1) can be directly mapped to those in the two-step methodology of Bayoumi and Masson (1995) described in Appendix A.2.1. The coefficient β measures the *redistribution* effect of fiscal transfers (the equivalent of β_{redist} in equation A.2.6). More specifically, it indicates the long-run response of relative disposable income to a permanent change in relative GDP.[8] Similarly, the coefficient δ measures the risk-sharing effect of fiscal transfers (the equivalent of $\beta_{risk\text{-}sharing}$ in equation A.2.7) given by the short-run response of changes in relative disposable income to transitory changes in relative GDP. The coefficient ø is the speed of adjustment of the relative disposable income to its long-run equilibrium value. The magnitude of this coefficient illustrates the dynamic effect of fiscal transfers: the larger is the absolute value of this coefficient, the faster is the adjustment of the relative disposable income to its long-run equilibrium value facilitated by the fiscal transfers. Finally, the specification includes state-specific fixed effects μ_i to capture unobserved heterogeneity of relative disposable income growth rates across states.

The one-step PMG specification has several advantages relative to the two-step approach employed in the previous literature.[9] First, by combining the level and first difference regressions in one step, the PMG provides more efficient estimates of redistribution and risk-sharing.[10] Second, the PMG estimator is more flexible and allows state-specific variation in short-run coefficients (δ_i) measuring the degree of risk-sharing. The difference in the magnitude of fiscal risk-sharing across states reflects differences in the ability of individual states to insure against idiosyncratic shocks through private markets and reallocate production factors (labor and capital). In contrast, the PMG estimator pools long-run slope coefficients into a common coefficient (β). This is consistent with the fact that redistribution formulas aiming to smooth long-run divergences of income across states are not expected to vary widely from state to state. Finally, the PMG specification can be tested against a more flexible Mean Group (MG) estimator that allows for both redistribution and risk-sharing coefficients to vary across states using the Hausman test.[11] If the homogeneity assumption is rejected, the MG results could be used to analyze redistribution and risk-sharing.

V. Data

We use data on three federations – Australia, Canada, and the U.S. For these federations, we collect information on total transfers from the federal government to state budgets (both earmarked transfers and block grants); these are based on pre-determined formulas that are not directly linked to the regional cyclical fluctuations. In addition, we obtain state-level information on gross federal transfers to individuals (including retirement, medical and income maintenance benefits, education and training assistance, unemployment insurance compensation) and taxes (including personal and corporate income taxes) that are largely driven by automatic stabilizers and are more closely related to regional cycles.[12] For Australia and the U.S. the sample period spans from 1998 to 2010 (13 years), while for Canada from 1992 to 2009 (18 years). The length of the time series is comparable to those used in previous studies surveyed in Table 2.1 (averaging 16 years).[13] Appendix A.2.2 contains detailed information on data sources and sample periods.

A. Descriptive statistics

Figures 2.1–2.3 show the magnitude of fiscal transfers in Australia, Canada, and the U.S. In all three countries fiscal transfers are sizeable. Federal tax revenues range between 15 and 20 percent of state GDP, while gross fiscal transfers range between 5 and 15 percent. The cyclical effect of gross fiscal transfers and taxes is clearly illustrated in the case of the U.S., where federal tax revenues have declined markedly and outlays increased significantly in 2009–2010. Federal taxes have also seen a sharp decline in the aftermath of the crisis in Canada and Australia while spending was somewhat less responsive than in the U.S. (except in Australia in 2009).

The figures also show that in all three countries, net transfers from the federal government have increased following the global financial crisis. This increase

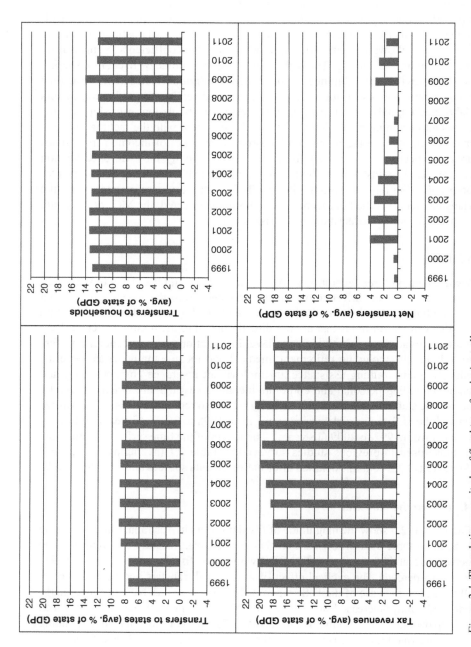

Figure 2.1 The relative magnitude of fiscal transfers in Australia

Source: Australia – Bureau of Statistics, Canada – Department of Finance, and U.S. – Census Bureau

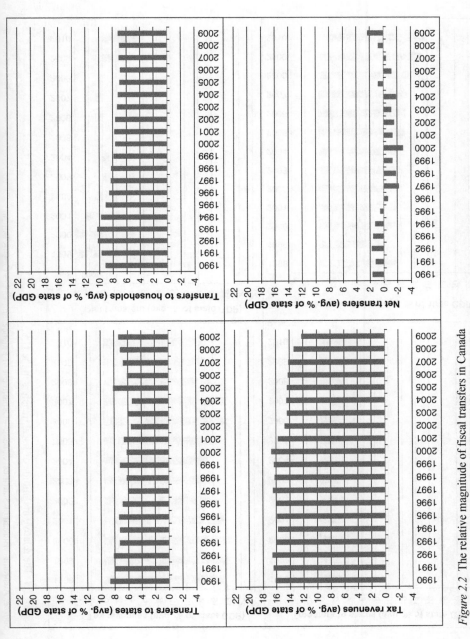

Figure 2.2 The relative magnitude of fiscal transfers in Canada

Source: Australia – Bureau of Statistics, Canada – Department of Finance, and U.S. – Census Bureau.

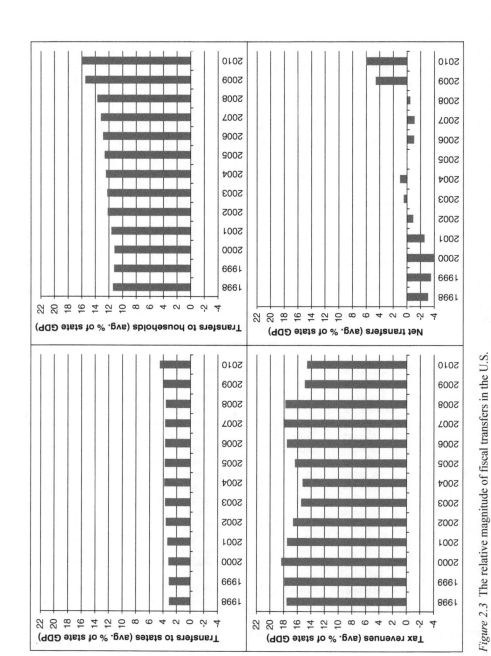

Figure 2.3 The relative magnitude of fiscal transfers in the U.S.

Source: Australia – Bureau of Statistics, Canada – Department of Finance, and U.S. – Census Bureau.

reflects a combination of automatic stabilizers and discretionary stimulus packages enacted to smooth out the impact of the crisis.

B. Preliminary evidence on redistribution

Figures 2.4a–2.4c present graphical evidence on redistribution through fiscal transfers. For each country, they show the interquartile range of net fiscal transfers over the sample period under consideration in each state. The box plots show clear evidence of redistribution in all three countries. For example, in the U.S. (Figure 2.4a), West Virginia, Mississippi, Maine, and several other states were permanent net recipients of net fiscal transfers during 1998–2010. In West Virginia, the median annual net fiscal transfer amounted to slightly less than 20 percent of state GDP. On the opposite side of the spectrum, Minnesota, Delaware, and Connecticut (among others) were net contributors. For instance, in Minnesota the median net fiscal transfer amounted to about 15 percent of state GDP. A similar picture emerges when considering Canada and Australia. In Canada (Figure 2.4b), Newfoundland and Labrador were the largest net recipients (with a median of 10 percent of state GDP), while Ontario was the largest net contributor (with a median of –10 percent of state GDP). Similarly, in Australia (Figure 2.4c), Northern Territory was the largest net recipient state (with a median of 15 percent of state GDP), while Australian Capital Territory was the largest net contributor (with a median of –5 percent of state GDP).

It is important to note that notwithstanding the similarity in terms of magnitude, redistribution in these three countries is driven by different considerations. In Canada and Australia, redistribution is an explicit objective of the federal government enshrined in the constitution, while in the U.S. redistribution takes place as a byproduct of revenue and spending centralization, including their progressive features. This element is further discussed below.

VI. Estimates

This section presents estimates based on equation (2.1) using the Pooled Mean Group estimator. For comparison purposes, we also report results based on the Bayoumi and Masson (1995) two-step approach.

A. Bayoumi and Masson (1995): Two-step approach

Table 2.2 reports estimates based on the Bayoumi and Masson (1995) two-step approach. The purpose of this exercise is to update empirical evidence using a conventional approach used in previous studies before moving to a new and more efficient approach. Panel A shows redistribution estimates based on cross-sectional regressions between state-specific mean values of regional incomes relative to the national average (equation A.2.6). The magnitude of redistribution ($1 - \beta_{redist}$) is 28 percent and 31 percent for the U.S. and Canada, respectively. The U.S. estimate is somewhat larger than the 22 percent reported in Bayoumi and

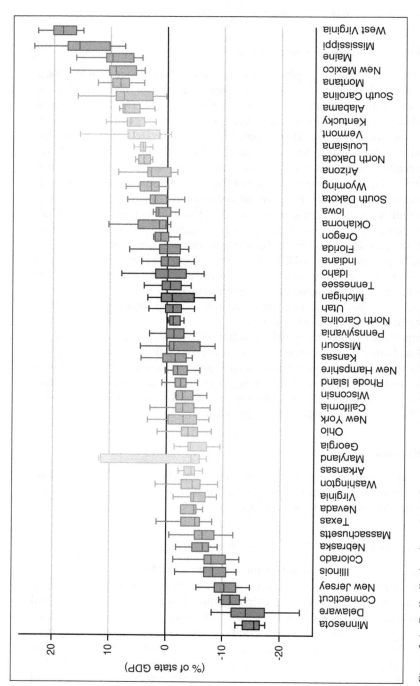

Figure 2.4a Redistribution through net fiscal transfers in the U.S. (1998–2010)

Source: Australia – Bureau of Statistics, Canada – Department of Finance, and U.S. – Census Bureau.

Note: The whiskers of the plot denote the minimum and maximum values of variables for each state within a country. The edges of the box denote 25th and 75th percentiles of the distribution. The line splitting the box denotes the median.

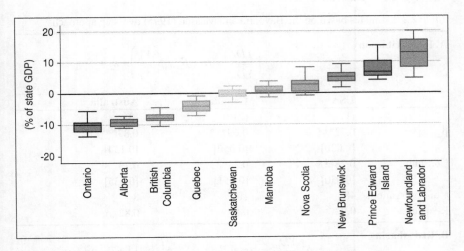

Figure 2.4b Redistribution through net fiscal transfers in Canada (1992–2009)

Source: Australia – Bureau of Statistics, Canada – Department of Finance, and U.S. – Census Bureau.

Note: The whiskers of the plot denote the minimum and maximum values of variables for each state within a country. The edges of the box denote 25th and 75th percentiles of the distribution. The line splitting the box denotes the median.

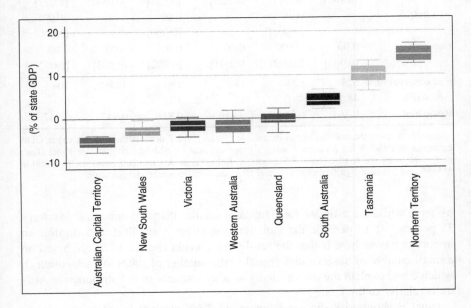

Figure 2.4c Redistribution through net fiscal transfers in Australia (1998–2010)

Source: Australia – Bureau of Statistics, Canada – Department of Finance, and U.S. – Census Bureau.

Note: The whiskers of the plot denote the minimum and maximum values of variables for each state within a country. The edges of the box denote 25th and 75th percentiles of the distribution. The line splitting the box denotes the median.

Table 2.2 Estimates based on the Bayoumi and Masson (1995) two-step approach

A. Redistribution

$$\left(\frac{\overline{YD_i}}{\overline{YD_t}}\right) = \alpha - \beta_{redist}\left(\frac{\overline{Y_i}}{\overline{Y_t}}\right) + \varepsilon_i$$

	USA	Canada	Australia
	(1)	(2)	(3)
$\beta_{\_redist}$	0.72***	0.69***	0.87***
	[0.030]	[0.050]	[0.154]
Constant	0.28***	0.31***	0.13
	[0.030]	[0.051]	[0.135]
# of observations	48	10	8
R-squared	0.92	0.87	0.82

B. Risk-sharing

$$\Delta\left(\frac{YD_{it}}{YD_t}\right) = \alpha_i + \beta_{risk-sharing}\Delta\left(\frac{Y_{it}}{Y_t}\right) + \gamma Trend + \upsilon_{it}$$

	USA		Canada		Australia	
	(1)	(2)	(3)	(4)	(5)	(6)
$\beta_{\_risk\text{-}sharing}$	0.95***	0.95***	0.92***	0.92***	0.95***	0.95***
	[0.107]	[0.107]	[0.020]	[0.021]	[0.034]	[0.037]
γ (trend)		0.00		0.00		−0.00
		[0.001]		[0.000]		[0.000]
Constant	0.00	−0.00	0.00	0.00	0.00	0.00
	[0.007]	[0.002]	[0.001]	[0.002]	[0.003]	[0.002]
# of observations	624	624	180	180	104	104
# of states	48	48	10	10	8	8
R-squared	0.364	0.364	0.816	0.816	0.947	0.947

Notes: YD denotes the real per capita disposable income, and Y denotes the real per capita GDP. Estimates in Panel A are performed using a cross-sectional OLS, while estimates in Panel B are performed using the fixed-effects OLS estimator. Robust clustered standard errors are in brackets. ***, **, and * denote significance at 1, 5, and 10 percent confidence level, respectively.

Masson, while the estimate for Canada is smaller than Bayoumi and Masson's 39 percent. At 13 percent, the redistribution effect is smallest in Australia. An important caveat here is that the results for Canada and Australia are based on a small number of observations (equal to the number of states in each country), which could explain the unexpectedly smaller estimate of redistribution in Australia relative to the U.S.

Panel B shows risk-sharing estimates (1-βrisk-sharing) based on panel data regressions between changes in demeaned income variables (equation A.2.7) using the baseline and trend-augmented specifications. For the U.S. and Australia, the risk-sharing estimate is approximately 5 percent, while it is slightly higher for Canada (8 percent). Interestingly, our risk-sharing estimates for the U.S. and

Canada over 1998–2010 are much smaller than those obtained in Bayoumi and Masson for the earlier sample period (1969–1986). This could be due to the fact that with an increased harmonization of regional business cycles and better functioning cross-regional financial markets, the scope for risk-sharing in these federations has declined over time.

B. Pooled mean group estimator: One-step approach

Table 2.3 reports estimates based on the PMG estimator. Columns (1) and (2) display the estimates for the U.S. using the baseline and trend-augmented specifications, respectively. In both specifications, the magnitude of redistribution is 13 percent, which is smaller than the average 26 percent found in

Table 2.3 Estimates based on the Pooled Mean Group (PMG) Estimator

$$\Delta\left(\frac{YD_{it}}{\overline{YD_t}}\right) = \phi_i\left[\frac{YD_{it-1}}{\overline{YD_{t-1}}} - \alpha - \beta\frac{Y_{it-1}}{\overline{Y}_{t-1}} - \gamma Trend\right] + \delta_i\Delta\left(\frac{Y_{it}}{\overline{Y}_t}\right) + \mu_i + \varepsilon_{it}$$

	USA		Canada		Australia	
	(1)	(2)	(3)	(4)	(5)	(6)
Long-run coefficient						
β (redistribution)	0.87***	0.87***	0.82***	0.80***	0.78***	0.76***
	[0.01]	[0.01]	[0.02]	[0.02]	[0.03]	[0.02]
γ (trend)		0.00***		0.00		−0.00***
		[0.00]		[0.00]		[0.00]
Speed of adjustment	−0.70***	−0.70***	−0.57***	−0.56***	−0.31***	−0.38***
	[0.04]	[0.04]	[0.08]	[0.08]	[0.06]	[0.09]
Short-run coefficient						
δ (risk-sharing)	0.89***	0.89***	0.96***	0.96***	0.96***	0.96***
	[0.04]	[0.04]	[0.03]	[0.02]	[0.03]	[0.03]
# of observations	624	624	180	180	104	104
# of states	48	48	10	10	8	8
Hausman test (p – value)	0.39	0.88	0.34	0.85	0.11	0.76

Note: In the equation, YD denotes the real per capita disposable income, and Y denotes the real per capita GDP. Estimations are performed using the PMG estimator of Pesaran et al. (1999). Estimates include province-specific fixed effects. Robust clustered standard errors are in brackets. Reported short-term and speed of adjustment coefficients represent averages of state-specific estimates. Intercept is included in the long-run specification but not reported. Sample periods are: Australia (1998–2010), Canada (1992–2009), and USA (1998–2010). ***, **, and * denote significance at 1, 5, and 10 percent confidence level, respectively.

studies reported in Table 2.1 as well as the 28 percent found with the two-step methodology and more recent data. In contrast, the magnitude of risk-sharing at 11 percent is comparable to the 14 percent average found in previous studies and larger than the 5 percent number based on the two-step methodology. Compared to individual studies, our risk-sharing estimate is close to that of Von Hagen (1992), Goodhart and Smith (1993), and Obstfeld and Peri (1998) but much smaller than the 31 percent estimate reported in Bayoumi and Masson (1995).

There could be two reasons for these large differences. First, this paper uses a more recent data set. Second, Bayoumi and Masson use a two-step estimation method, which reduces the sample to the number of states (48 in their study) and more importantly abstracts from changes in redistribution over time. The one-step procedure exploits both the cross-sectional and the time variation in the redistribution effect, which should yield more efficient estimates. The results also suggest that there was no substantial increase in redistribution over time (the coefficient of the trend variable is close to zero). Finally, the speed of adjustment coefficient is quite large, suggesting that about 70 percent of the deviation from the long-run equilibrium is corrected within one year.

Columns (3) and (4) report estimates for Canada. The magnitude of redistribution in Canada at 18–20 percent is larger than that in the U.S. This finding is consistent with the stronger redistribution mandate of the federal government in Canada, where the redistribution motive is enshrined in the constitution. Nevertheless, the redistributive effect is somewhat smaller than the average 36 percent obtained in the literature and the 31 percent obtained using the two-step methodology. Similar to the case of the U.S., the difference in estimates reflects both different estimation periods and different methodologies. The two-step pure cross-sectional method used in previous studies relies on only 10 observations in the case of Canada, a very small sample. Regarding risk-sharing, we find that fiscal transfers cushion only 4 percent of the initial regional income shock in Canada, even smaller than in the U.S. Bayoumi and Masson (1995) also obtained relatively modest risk-sharing effect in Canada. As in the case of the U.S., there is no evidence of a substantial increase in redistribution over time (the coefficient of the trend variable is close to zero). In addition, the speed of adjustment at 56–57 percent per year is also relatively large.

Columns (5) and (6) report estimates for Australia. The magnitude of redistribution in Australia, at 22–24 percent, is the largest among the three countries and comparable to the two-step estimate reported in the previous section. As in the case of Canada, the large magnitude of redistribution is consistent with the federal government's mandate to reduce income inequality following the establishment of the Commonwealth in 1933 (Koutsogeorgopoulou, 2007). The risk-sharing effect (4 percent) is modest and comparable to that in Canada.[14] However, the speed of adjustment coefficient is not as large as in the other two countries, suggesting that state-level incomes adjust more slowly to their long-run equilibrium level.[15]

VII. The role of individual components of net fiscal transfers in cushioning the impact of shocks

Weaknesses in the fiscal architecture of the euro area, as evidenced during the crisis, have provoked a discussion on options to strengthen fiscal insurance against macroeconomic shocks hitting individual member states. One approach that gained traction in recent policy debates is the creation of a rainy-day fund which would collect revenues from euro area members at all times and make transfers to countries when they experience negative macroeconomic shocks (see Chapter 5 for a fuller discussion).

Motivated by these discussions, this section explores the relative role of different components of net fiscal transfers in cushioning regional income shocks in federations. These can be decomposed into gross transfers to state budgets, gross transfers to individuals, and federal tax payments. We use the following empirical specification:

$$\left(\frac{T_{it}}{Ypot_{it}} * 100\right) = \alpha + \beta\left(\frac{Y_{it}}{\overline{Y_t}} * 100\right) + \gamma GAP_{it} + \mu_i + \lambda_t + \varepsilon_{it} \tag{2.2}$$

where i and t indices denote states and time, respectively. μ and λ are state and time fixed effects, respectively. The dependent variable is the ratio of various components of net fiscal transfers (T), including gross transfers to state budgets (TRANS), gross transfers to individuals (TRANSDIR), federal taxes (TAX), and net fiscal transfers (T = TRANS + TRANSDIR −TAX), over state potential GDP.[16] As transfers to state budgets are largely driven by predetermined formulas that do not account for regional cyclical fluctuations, while gross transfers to individuals and federal taxes are largely driven by automatic stabilizers and are more responsive to regional cycles, the comparison of results for each dependent variable would allow us to infer the relative importance of transfers to state budgets compared to taxes and gross transfers to individuals in cushioning regional income shocks.

There are two explanatory variables:

- The first explanatory variable measures the trend component of the relative income gap for each state (i.e., the trend component of the ratio of each state GDP over the national average GDP).[17] We use the trend component of this ratio to better capture the notion of *income convergence* since cyclical movements do not affect income convergence over the long term. A negative coefficient β (positive for the specification with federal taxes) would support the *redistribution* motive, suggesting that relatively poorer states receive more transfers and pay less in taxes than do richer states.
- The second explanatory variable is the state-specific output gap. Its coefficient γ captures the *risk-sharing* motive of fiscal transfers, after controlling for the *stabilization* motive through time fixed effects (λ). A negative

coefficient γ (positive for the specification with federal taxes) would indicate that fiscal transfers cushion the impact of idiosyncratic shocks hitting individual states, supporting the *risk-sharing* motive.

Intuitively, in the long-run, the output gap is averaging to zero (i.e., positive and negative cyclical effects cancel out) and the long-run relationship between transfers and relative income gap as measured by coefficient β captures the impact of fiscal transfers on income redistribution. Similarly, after controlling for the long-run component of fiscal transfers that contributes to redistribution, the remaining cyclical variation in fiscal transfers is associated with regional output gap through a measure of risk-sharing γ.

Our strategy is to estimate specification (2.2) without and with time fixed effects. In the former case, coefficient γ measures the impact of *risk-sharing* and *stabilization*, while in the latter case it measures the impact of *risk-sharing* only, as the impact of common shocks is controlled for through time fixed effects.[18]

Table 2.4 presents the estimates for Australia, Canada, and the U.S. Columns (1) to (4) display the results for the specification without time fixed effects, while columns (5) to (8) display the results for the specification with time fixed effects.

- **Transfers to state budgets:** Evidence is weak on the importance of transfers to state budgets in cushioning the impact of regional shocks. Only in Australia and Canada do transfers to state budgets have a significant albeit small (7–8 percent) impact on redistribution (*β*). This is consistent with the stronger redistribution mandate of the federal government in these countries relative to the U.S. There is largely no significant association between transfers to state budgets and regional cycles (*γ*), suggesting a limited role of these transfers for risk-sharing.
- **Gross transfers to individuals:** In contrast, evidence is strong in support of the hypothesis that gross transfers to individuals contribute to redistribution and risk-sharing. The impact on redistribution (12–16 percent) is much stronger than the impact on risk-sharing (7 percent). Moreover, the significant impact on gross transfers to individuals on risk-sharing vanishes when controlling for time fixed effects (common shocks), suggesting that these transfers serve an important stabilization role. Again, the limited evidence on risk-sharing is consistent with the more conventional approach used in the previous section.
- **Federal taxes.** Similar to gross transfers to individuals, federal taxes have significant impact on risk-sharing in the U.S. (21 percent) and Australia (17 percent), but do not significantly affect redistribution. The large size of the coefficients further confirms the important role played by these transfers for risk-sharing.
- **Net fiscal transfers.** When combining the net effect of all fiscal transfers into one variable, we find that in net terms fiscal transfers have significant impact on risk-sharing and redistribution in all three federations. However, when time fixed effects are included in the specification, columns (5)–(8),

Table 2.4 Estimates using an alternative specification to assess the impact of stabilization and risk-sharing

$$\left(\frac{T_{it}}{Ypot_{it}}*100\right) = \alpha + \beta\left(\frac{Y_{it}}{Y_t}*100\right) + \gamma GAP_{it} + \mu_i + \lambda_t + \varepsilon_{it}$$

	Without time fixed effects				With time fixed effects (controlling for stabilization)			
	Transfers to state budgets	Gross transfers to individuals	Federal taxes	Net federal transfers	Transfers to state budgets	Gross transfers to individuals	Federal taxes	Net federal transfers
	(1)	(2)	(3)	(4)	(5)	(6)	(7)	(8)
USA								
Relative real per capita income (β)	-0.01	-0.12**	0.01	-0.13**	-0.01	-0.12***	0.00	-0.13***
	[-0.63]	[-2.17]	[0.10]	[-2.11]	[-1.10]	[-7.19]	[0.15]	[-3.05]
State Output Gap (γ)	-0.01	-0.07***	0.21**	-0.28***	0.02**	0.01	0.15***	-0.12**
	[-1.33]	[-6.21]	[2.51]	[-3.13]	[2.20]	[0.95]	[3.11]	[-2.50]
Constant	4.50***	24.75***	15.07***	14.17***	4.55***	25.19***	17.09***	12.65***
	[3.11]	[4.46]	[3.08]	[2.22]	[5.83]	[14.98]	[5.19]	[2.88]
# of observations	672	672	672	672	672	672	672	672
# of states	48	48	48	48	48	48	48	48
R-squared	0.269	0.458	0.016	0.352	0.215	0.628	0.541	0.609
Canada								
Relative real per capita income (β)	-0.08***	-0.12*	-0.05	-0.15***	-0.08***	-0.12***	-0.05**	-0.15***
	[-6.58]	[-1.97]	[-0.76]	[-16.01]	[-6.57]	[-4.88]	[-2.60]	[-8.30]
State output gap (γ)	-0.02	-0.07***	0.05	-0.14*	0.00	-0.01	0.05	-0.05
	[-1.07]	[-3.25]	[1.43]	[-2.12]	[0.01]	[-0.65]	[1.39]	[-0.92]

(Continued)

Table 2.4 (Continued)

	Without time fixed effects				With time fixed effects (controlling for stabilization)			
	Transfers to state budgets	Gross transfers to individuals	Federal taxes	Net federal transfers	Transfers to state budgets	Gross transfers to individuals	Federal taxes	Net federal transfers
	(1)	(2)	(3)	(4)	(5)	(6)	(7)	(8)
Constant	15.12*** [11.82]	20.30*** [3.47]	20.06** [3.13]	15.36*** [16.20]	15.71*** [10.29]	19.07*** [8.06]	17.36*** [10.08]	17.43*** [8.84]
# of observations	180	180	180	180	180	180	180	180
# of states	10	10	10	10	10	10	10	10
R-squared	0.537	0.571	0.046	0.497	0.556	0.679	0.383	0.518
Australia								
Relative real per capita income (β)	-0.07*** [-3.75]	-0.16*** [-6.33]	-0.09* [-2.21]	-0.14** [-3.15]	-0.07*** [-7.59]	-0.16*** [-9.97]	-0.08** [-2.39]	-0.15*** [-4.16]
State output gap (γ)	-0.05* [-2.27]	-0.01 [-0.55]	0.17*** [3.66]	-0.23*** [-3.91]	-0.01 [-0.36]	-0.01 [-0.64]	0.02 [0.46]	-0.04 [-1.05]
Constant	15.47*** [8.23]	28.60*** [11.63]	28.28*** [6.93]	15.80*** [3.65]	15.68*** [15.79]	27.91*** [17.24]	26.24*** [7.81]	17.35*** [5.14]
# of observations	104	104	104	104	104	104	104	104
# of states	8	8	8	8	8	8	8	8
R-squared	0.001	0.819	0.108	0.104	0.003	0.846	0.244	0.157

Notes: The dependent variable is the ratio of the respective measure of fiscal transfers relative to state potential output. Y denotes the real per capita GDP, Ypot denotes potential output. GAP denotes output gap (measured for each state using a quadratic trend component of real per capita GDP). Estimations are performed using the fixed effects OLS estimator. Robust clustered standard errors are in brackets. Sample periods are: Australia (1998–2010), Canada (1992–2009), and USA (1998–2010). ***, **, and * denote significance at 1, 5, and 10 percent confidence level, respectively.

the coefficient on the output gap variable (γ) turns insignificant in Australia and Canada, and decreases in magnitude in the U.S.[19] This result indicates that the *stabilization* motive of net fiscal transfers plays an important role in all three countries. Thus, not controlling for it may provide a misleading picture of the impact of risk-sharing (in line with Von Hagen's criticism). The impact of net fiscal transfers on stabilization can be estimated as the difference between coefficients γ in columns (4) and (1).[20] The magnitude of stabilization in the U.S. (16 percent), Canada (14 percent), and Australia (23 percent) is quite sizeable and exceeds that of risk-sharing.

Overall, the analysis of individual components of net fiscal transfers suggests that transfers to state budgets play a limited role in cushioning the impact of regional shocks. The significant impact of net transfers comes mostly from gross transfers to individuals and federal taxes. Furthermore, the results suggest that federal governments' response to common shocks (stabilization) is stronger than their response to regional shocks (risk-sharing). In both cases, the response is driven largely by automatic stabilizers (gross transfers to individuals and federal taxes) rather than the relatively less cyclical component of net fiscal transfers (transfers to state budgets). However, the latter has a significant impact on redistribution in Canada and Australia.

VIII. Conclusions

All three methodologies used point to some common results:

• Net fiscal transfers have a larger impact on stabilization than on risk-sharing. The moderate impact on risk-sharing ranges between 4 percent in Australia and Canada and 11 percent in the U.S. Previous studies found similarly moderate estimates of risk-sharing. This could be due to the fairly synchronized business cycles and enhanced private risk-sharing facilitated by fiscal centralization. The impact of fiscal transfers on stabilization (that is, the response to common shocks) is larger. This suggests that net fiscal transfers have been more responsive to common shocks than to idiosyncratic shocks in the three federations under study. The responsiveness of net fiscal transfers to common shocks can benefit weaker economies more than stronger ones, as the latter have easier access to financial markets.
• The impact of fiscal transfers is mainly channeled through the establishment of cyclically-sensitive revenue and spending functions at the center. To the extent that these central revenue and spending functions are transferred from local governments, the overall countercyclical response of transfers (central plus local) will not change, and *ceteris paribus* the ability of states to cushion the impact of shocks will not improve greatly following centralization. This said, transferring to the center some cyclical spending and revenues can help if, for some reason, the local automatic stabilizers are not able to operate fully either because of local fiscal rules or because of financing

constraints. These two issues are discussed, respectively, in Chapter 3 and Chapter 5 of this book.

- Net fiscal transfers also have an impact on redistribution, ranging between 13 percent in the U.S. and 24 percent in Australia. Interestingly, the evidence on redistribution is found not only in Australia and Canada, where the constitution provides an explicit redistribution mandate to the federal government, but also in the U.S. This finding suggests that redistribution occur as a consequence of centralization of revenue and expenditure policies.[21]

What are the implications of these findings? The fact that net fiscal transfers from the center play a relatively modest role in offsetting common and (especially) idiosyncratic shocks in the three federations considered may be due to various reasons. It may suggest that the arguments in favor of risk-sharing are in practice outweighed by other considerations (as discussed in Section II). However, it may also imply that fiscal centralization in existing federations has facilitated the synchronization of business cycles and diminished the significance of regional shocks.

The case for enhancing fiscal risk-sharing would be stronger for currency unions like the euro zone, where economic cycles are less synchronized and where fiscal centralization can further enhance private risk-sharing mechanisms (through promotion of financial sector integration and creation of a central deposit insurance for example).

This could be achieved in various ways. One option is to set up an ad hoc rainy-day fund that transfers resources to states hit by shocks. An alternative, most commonly used in existing federations, is the centralization of some spending and revenue functions that are sensitive to the economic cycle (e.g., unemployment insurance and taxes). The common provision of public services can also prevent unduly pro-cyclical fiscal behavior in cases when the local automatic stabilizers cannot operate fully, either because of local fiscal rules or because of financing constraints. Over the long run, the establishment of a central budget would reduce the risk of idiosyncratic fiscal policies at the state level. The larger is the share of the spending responsibilities that are centralized, the lower is the likelihood that large fiscal imbalances will arise at the local level. Finally, centralization would allow for a much better coordination of fiscal policy in response to common shocks and, of course, for a larger countercyclical response at the central level (Cottarelli, 2013).

Appendix A.2.1

Empirical approaches used in existing literature to quantify the impact of fiscal transfers

This Appendix provides a brief overview of three main empirical approaches used in existing studies to quantify the impact of fiscal transfers by Sachs and Sala-i-Martin (1992), Von Hagen (1992), and Bayoumi and Masson (1995).

Sachs and Sala-i-Martin (1992) approach

One of the first empirical studies trying to quantify the impact of fiscal transfers is Sachs and Sala-i-Martin (1992).[22] The authors start from the definition of changes in the disposable income: $\Delta YD = \Delta Y - \Delta TX + \Delta TR$, where YD is the regional disposable income, Y is the regional GDP, TX denotes regional taxes paid to the federal budget, and TR denotes gross fiscal transfers from the federal government (all variables are expressed in real per capita terms). Further, they assume that changes in TX and TR are affected by changes in regional GDP through the working of automatic stabilizers. They define $\beta_{TX} = \dfrac{\Delta TX}{\Delta Y} \dfrac{Y}{TX}$ and $\beta_{TX} = \dfrac{\Delta TR}{\Delta Y} \dfrac{Y}{TR}$ as elasticities of taxes and fiscal transfers with respect to GDP and rewrite the disposable income identity as:

$$\Delta YD = \Delta Y - \beta_{TX}\frac{TX}{Y}\Delta Y + \beta_{TR}\frac{TR}{Y}\Delta Y = Y * \lambda \qquad (A.2.1)$$

where $\lambda = \left(1 - \beta_{TX}\dfrac{TX}{Y} + \beta_{TR}\dfrac{TR}{Y}\right)$ measures the effect of net fiscal transfers on the regional disposable income. To assess the magnitude of elasticities β, the authors run the following regressions:

$$log\left(\frac{TX_{it}}{\overline{TX}_t}\right) = \alpha_{TX} + \beta_{TX}log\left(\frac{Y_{it}}{\overline{Y}_t}\right) + \gamma_{TX}trend + \varepsilon_{it} \qquad (A.2.2)$$

$$log\left(\frac{TR_{it}}{\overline{TR}_t}\right) = \alpha_{TR} + \beta_{TR}log\left(\frac{Y_{it}}{\overline{Y}_t}\right) + \gamma_{TR}trend + u_{it} \qquad (A.2.3)$$

where i and t indices denote region and time, respectively, and $\overline{TX_t}$, $\overline{TX_t}$, and $\overline{Y_t}$ are national averages of respective variables in period t. The authors employ this methodology to quantify the impact of fiscal transfers in 9 U.S. regions for the period 1970–80.

Von Hagen (1992): Two-step approach

The main issue with the empirical approach of Sachs and Sala-i-Martin (1992) is that it only assesses the overall impact of fiscal transfers, but does not distinguish between redistribution and insurance motives. Von Hagen (1992) attempts to address this issue by using the following regressions:

$$\Delta log(TX_{it}) = \alpha_i + \theta_{TX}\Delta log(Y_{it}) + D_{oil} + \gamma_t + \varepsilon_{it} \qquad (A.2.4)$$

$$\Delta log(TR_{it}) = \alpha_i + \theta_{TR}\Delta log(Y_{it}) + D_{oil} + \gamma_t + \varepsilon_{it} \qquad (A.2.5)$$

where i and t indices denote region and time, respectively, D_{Oil} are dummies for three oil-producing states of the U.S. (Alaska, Oklahoma, Wyoming), αi are regional fixed effects to control for state-specific unobserved characteristics, and γ_t are time fixed effects to control for common shocks. Coefficients θ_{TX} and θ_{TR} are used to measure the risk-sharing effects of federal taxes and transfers, respectively. In Von Hagen's specification, the impact of aggregate shocks is controlled for by time fixed effects.[23] Von Hagen applies this methodology to study the impact of fiscal transfers on risk-sharing in 48 states in the U.S. over the period 1981–86. Von Hagen also conducts cross-sectional regression on regional average variables to assess the impact on redistribution.

Bayoumi and Masson (1995): Two-step approach

Unlike the previous two authors, Bayoumi and Masson (1995) do not distinguish between effects of federal taxes and transfers separately and assess their combined effect. Similar to Von Hagen (1992), they adopt a two-step approach for measuring redistribution and risk-sharing effects of fiscal transfers by running the following regressions:

$$\left(\frac{\overline{YD_i}}{\overline{\overline{YD}}}\right) = \alpha + \beta_{redist}\left(\frac{\overline{Y_i}}{\overline{\overline{Y}}}\right) + \varepsilon_i \qquad (A.2.6)$$

$$\Delta\left(\frac{YD_{it}}{\overline{YD_t}}\right) = \alpha_i + \beta_{risk-sharing}\Delta\left(\frac{Y_{it}}{Y_t}\right) + u_{it} \qquad (A.2.7)$$

where i and t indices denote region and time, respectively, $\overline{YD_i}$ and $\overline{Y_i}$ are state-specific averages of respective variables over the sample, YD_t and Y_t are national averages of respective variables in period t, and YD and Y are national averages of respective variables over the whole sample.

The slope coefficient from the first regression is used to measure the impact of redistribution ($1-\beta_{redist}$). It is obtained from a cross sectional relationship between state-specific mean values of regional incomes relative to the national average, which are free from short-term fluctuations driven by idiosyncratic shocks. The slope coefficient from the second regression is used to measure the impact of risk-sharing ($1-\beta_{risk-sharing}$). It is obtained from a panel regression of changes of state-specific regional incomes relative to the national average, which filters out the impact of long-term trends in both variables. It is important to note that unlike time fixed effects used in Von Hagen (1992), in this approach the impact of common shocks is controlled for by demeaning regional disposable income and GDP by their national averages (within transformation). The authors apply this methodology to study the impact of fiscal transfers on risk-sharing and redistribution in the states of the U.S. and Canadian provinces over the period 1969–1986.

The comparison of these three empirical approaches points to some pitfalls associated with each of them. The Sachs and Sala-i-Martin's approach can be used to evaluate the overall impact of fiscal transfers on redistribution and risk-sharing, but does not allow distinguishing between the two. The Von Hagen and Bayoumi and Masson approaches attempt to address this issue by running cross-sectional regressions on average variables (redistribution) and using time fixed effects and demeaning variables in panel regressions, respectively (risk-sharing). However, these approaches are inefficient as averaging substantially limits the degrees of freedom for statistical inference, especially in federations with small number of states (e.g., Canada). Therefore, in addition to the conventional two-step approach, we report results based on a one-step approach that addresses the efficiency issue and estimates the impact of fiscal transfers on redistribution and risk-sharing simultaneously.

Appendix A.2.2

Data description and sources

Macroeconomic variables

GDP

Australia – Australia Bureau of Statistics, from 1990 to 2011.
Canada – Department of Finance, from 1990 to 2010.
USA – U.S. Census Bureau, from 1997 to 2010.

CPI

Australia – Australia Bureau of Statistics, from 1990 to 2011, country-level.
Canada – Department of Finance, from 1990 to 2011, country-level.
USA – U.S. Census Bureau, from 1990 to 2010, country-level.

Population

Australia – Australia Bureau of Statistics, from 1990 to 2011.
Canada – Department of Finance, from 1990 to 2010.
USA – U.S. Census Bureau, from 1990 to 2010.

Fiscal variables

Gross transfers from central government to state budgets

Australia – Australia Bureau of Statistics, from 1999 to 2011.
Canada – Department of Finance, from 1990 to 2011.
USA – U.S. Census Bureau, from 1990 to 2010.

Gross transfers from central government to individuals

Australia – Australian Bureau of Statistics, Australian National Accounts table 5220.0, from 1998 to 2011.
Canada – Statistics Canada, Provincial and Territorial Economic Accounts, from 1990 to 2009.
USA – Bureau of Economic Analysis (BEA), from 1998 to 2010.

Taxes paid to central government

Australia – Australian Bureau of Statistics, Australian National Accounts table 5220.0, from 1998 to 2011.
Canada – Statistics Canada, Provincial and Territorial Economic Accounts, from 1990 to 2009.
USA – Internal Revenue Service (IRS), 1998 to 2010.

Notes

We would like to thank Celine Allard, Tamim Bayoumi, Helge Berger, John Bluedorn, Jorg Decressin, Davide Furceri, Emine Hanedar, Petya Koeva Brooks, and Todd Mattina for useful comments and suggestions. Malin Hu has provided excellent assistance.

1 Nevertheless, it is important to make a clear distinction between these roles, as terminology used in previous studies lacks consistency and contributes to some confusion (for instance, Bayoumi and Masson (1995) refer to the risk-sharing objective as "stabilization").
2 Restriction of the sample to these three federations is driven by data availability. For the purpose of this chapter, and unless otherwise specified, the term "net fiscal transfers" (or simply "fiscal transfers") refers to net fiscal flows between central and subnational governments. Specifically, net fiscal transfers are defined as the difference between gross transfers from the center to subnational governments (either to the subnational budget or to residents) and taxes paid by subnational government residents to the center. The term "subnational" refers to state/provincial governments. We do not consider lower level government such as local regions and municipalities.
3 In addition to the direct effect on risk-sharing, fiscal centralization can also contribute to enhancing risk-sharing through private markets. For instance, unified regulation and deposit insurance may reduce information asymmetries and encourage more diversified market portfolio holdings, thereby leading to greater risk-sharing via markets, an aspect that is not discussed in this chapter.
4 We disregard here the existence of transfers that take place purely to offset structural vertical imbalances that are the same across regions, as the focus here is on transfers that are different across regions, or that change over the cycle (see Chapter 1). We also do not analyze crisis episodes, when fiscal transfers from central government are used to bail out states under financial stress. A detailed discussion of subnational government crises is presented in Chapter 6.
5 The smaller redistribution effect may be due to differences in state coverage: Goodhart and Smith use data on 44 states only, excluding five oil-exporting states and Washington D.C. from the sample.
6 Since our objective is to distinguish between redistribution and insurance objectives, we do not consider the Sachs and Sala-i-Martin approach.
7 Similar to Bayoumi and Masson (1995), the demeaning of variables allows controlling for stabilization effects, but does not allow identifying their impact.
8 In technical terms, β represents the co-integration coefficient linking the long-run relationship between relative disposable income and relative income at the regional level.
9 Bayoumi and Masson (1995) acknowledge that a one-step co-integration approach akin to ours would be preferable compared to their two-step approach (footnote 6, p. 257). However, the one-step approach did not yield satisfactory results for the long-run coefficients in their sample, and therefore the authors decided to proceed with the two-step approach.
10 This is particularly relevant for the case of Canada, where the estimate of the redistribution effect is based on only ten observations (i.e., the number of states in Canada), as the two-step method relies on a purely cross-sectional regression where the number of observations is equal to the number of states.
11 To illustrate the intuition, recall that the PMG estimator constraints the long-run slope coefficients to be equal across all states. This is in contrast to the MG estimator, which does not impose the poolability constraints on the slopes. The pooling across countries yields efficient and consistent estimates when the restrictions are true. However, if the slope homogeneity assumption is false, the PMG estimates become inconsistent, while the MG estimates are consistent in either case. The Hausman test allows us to determine whether the homogeneity assumption is valid or not.

12 Discretionary changes in tax rates and exemptions may also affect tax revenues, but these changes are typically not as frequent as discretionary expenditure measures, making tax revenues more closely linked than expenditures to the cycles. In practice, it is common to assume zero elasticity for expenditures and unit elasticity for revenues when measuring cyclically adjusted fiscal balances (Bornhorst et al., 2011).

13 Extending the sample to earlier years was not possible due to unavailability of certain variables. For instance, the pre-1998 IRS data on federal taxes in the United States was not available at the state level.

14 For all three countries, we also tried adding lagged risk-sharing variable to the specification to account for possible additional dynamic effects on top of the error correction mechanism. The coefficients of lagged variables came out insignificant while the long-run slope (redistribution) was almost unaffected. In addition, standard information criteria (Akaike, Bayes-Schwartz) provide support to a more parsimonious specification (1).

15 The smaller speed of adjustment coefficients for Australia and Canada compared to those of the United States may reflect the relative longevity of business cycles, as the latter are expected to be lengthier in commodity exporting countries.

16 State potential GDP is estimated using linear and quadratic trends, which is an equivalent of the HP filter with the smoothing parameter of 100.

17 Measured as the real GDP per capita trend in each state divided by its country-wide average in each period. The trend component is estimated using a quadratic trend.

18 As a robustness check, we replaced time fixed effects with national output gaps to control for common shocks in specification (2). The results on the sizeable effect of stabilization are qualitatively similar and are available from the authors upon request.

19 A separate analysis of the relative importance of common and idiosyncratic shocks suggests that regional cycles are more synchronized in Australia and Canada than in the United States. The greater synchronization of regional cycles in Australia and Canada could explain the insignificant impact of automatic stabilizers when common shocks are controlled for.

20 In this calculation, the coefficients that are not statistically significant are set equal to zero.

21 To avoid persistent transfers that are redistributive, the transfer system should offset only transitory shocks. The problem is that policymakers do not know whether a shock is transitory or persistent in real time and hence it is difficult to design a transfer scheme targeted to only transitory shocks. Furthermore, it can be shown that schemes that do not take into account the risk profile of countries – for example one where all countries contribute the same share of their GDP – generally lead to permanent transfers.

22 The role of fiscal transfers in offsetting long-run regional income differentials and cushioning regional shocks was recognized earlier in the MacDougall Report (Commission of the European Communities, 1977). However, the discussion in this report was largely qualitative rather than quantitative.

23 The literature does not quantify the impact of fiscal transfers on stabilization. Instead, it controls for the stabilization effect by using either time effects (e.g., Von Hagen, 1992) or by demeaning variables used in the regressions (e.g., Bayoumi and Masson, 1995) and assesses the impact of fiscal transfers on redistribution and risk-sharing.

References

Andersson, L., 2004, "Regional Risk-Sharing Provided by the Fiscal System: Empirical Evidence from Sweden," *Regional Studies*, 38 (3): pp. 269–80.

Bayoumi, T., and Masson, P., 1995, "Fiscal Flows in the United States and Canada: Lessons from Monetary Union in Europe," *European Economic Review*, 39: pp. 253–74.

————, 1998, "Liability-Creating versus Non-Liability-Creating Fiscal Stabilization Policies: Ricardian Equivalence, Fiscal Stabilization, and EMU," *Economic Journal*, 108: pp. 1026–45.

Beetsma, R. and Debrun, X., 2004, "The Interaction between Monetary and Fiscal Policies in a Monetary Union: A Review of Recent Literature," in *Monetary Policy, Fiscal Policies, and Labor Markets: Macroeconomic Policymaking in the EMU*, edited by Roel Beetsma (Cambridge: Cambridge University Press).

Beetsma, R., and Giuliodori, M., 2010, "The Macroeconomic Costs and Benefits of the EMU and Other Monetary Unions: An Overview of Recent Research," *Journal of Economic Literature*, 48: pp. 603–641.

Bornhorst, F., Dobrescu, G., Fedelino, A., Gottschalk, J., and Nakata, T., 2011, "When and How to Adjust Beyond the Business Cycle? A Guide to Structural Fiscal Balances," Technical Guidance Note, Fiscal Affairs Department (Washington: International Monetary Fund).

Cottarelli, C., 2013, "European Fiscal Union: A Vision for the Long Run," *Swiss Journal of Economics and Statistics*, 149 (2): pp. 167–174.

Decressin, J., 2002, "Regional Income Redistribution and Risk-Sharing: How Does Italy Compare in Europe?" *Journal of Public Economics*, 86: pp. 287–306.

European Commission, 1977, "Report of the Study Group on the Role of Public Finances in European Integration," MacDougall Report (Brussels: European Commission).

Friedman, M., 1957, *A Theory of the Consumption Function* (Princeton: Princeton University Press).

Goodhart, C., and Smith, S., 1993, "Stabilization," in *The Economics of Community Public Finance, European Economy Reports and Studies*, 5: pp. 417–55 (Brussels: European Commission).

Hamada, K., 1985, *The Political Economy of International Monetary Interdependence* (Cambridge: MIT Press).

Koutsogeorgopoulou, V., 2007, "Fiscal Relations across Levels of Government in Australia," OECD Economics Department Working Paper No. 541 (Paris: OECD).

Masson, P., and Taylor, M., 1993, "Fiscal Policy within Common Currency Areas," *Journal of Common Market Studies*, 31 (1): pp. 29–44.

Melitz, J., and Zumer, F., 2002, "Regional Redistribution and Stabilization by the Centre in Canada, France, the U.K. and the U.S.: A Reassessment and New Tests," *Journal of Public Economics*, 86 (2): pp. 263–84.

Obstfeld, M., and Peri, G., 1998, "Regional Non-Adjustment and Fiscal Policy," *Economic Policy*, 26: pp. 205–69.

Pesaran, H., Shin, Y., and Smith, R., 1999, "Pooled Mean Group Estimation of Dynamic Heterogeneous Panels," *Journal of the American Statistical Association*, 94: pp. 621–34.

Sachs, J., and Sala-i-Martin, X., 1992, "Fiscal Federalism and Optimum Currency Areas: Evidence for Europe from the United States," in *Establishing a Central Bank: Issues in Europe and Lessons from the U.S.*, edited by Matthew Canzoneri, Vittorio Grilli, and Paul Masson (Cambridge: Cambridge University Press).

Von Hagen, J., 1992, "Fiscal Arrangements in a Monetary Union: Evidence from the US," in *Fiscal Policy, Taxes, and the Financial System in an Increasingly Integrated Europe*, edited by Don Fair and Christian de Boissieux (London: Kluwer).

3 Constraints on subnational fiscal policy

Luc Eyraud and Raquel Gomez Sirera

I. Introduction

In federations, the fiscal position of the general government as a whole is often highly dependent on the behavior of local and regional entities. As seen in Chapter 1, federal countries tend to be highly decentralized countries, with larger and more autonomous subnational governments than in unitary countries. Therefore, maintaining fiscal discipline cannot be achieved without the full participation of sub-central authorities.

This participation cannot be taken for granted. Subnational finances are often difficult to control, in part because the vertical structure of the government creates moral hazard problems and bailout expectations. As a result, federations resort to a wide range of arrangements in order to enforce fiscal discipline at the subnational level and ensure that fiscal policies of the different government levels are mutually consistent.

This chapter assesses the design and effectiveness of such constraints on subnational fiscal policy. Broadly speaking, they can be divided into two categories. The first type bears on *fiscal targets* and is the main focus of this chapter.[1] For instance, spending caps limit the amount of subnational expenditure that can be authorized within a year. The second type of constraints is imposed on *procedures* governing the budget process. Subnational governments may, for instance, be required to commit to a multi-year fiscal strategy and publish fiscal outcomes on a regular and timely basis. These "procedural constraints," aimed at improving fiscal management, are analyzed in Chapter 4 of this book.

This chapter centers on *ex ante* constraints in a decentralized fiscal framework, also called "early warning systems." It does not consider *ex post* measures dealing with the consequences of protracted fiscal indiscipline, such as debt restructuring, or mergers of subnational entities, which are discussed in Chapter 6.

The chapter is organized as follows. Section II analyzes the motivations for restricting the fiscal authority of subnational governments. Section III proposes a typology of subnational constraints and reviews present arrangements based on this classification. Section IV analyzes some key features of current control mechanisms. Section V compares the EU supranational governance framework to the constraints existing in federal countries. Section VI draws some lessons from federations' experiences, and Section VII concludes.

II. Why do federations constrain the fiscal discretion of subnational governments?

As discussed in Chapter 1, fiscal decentralization may generate efficiency gains. However, the vertical structure of the government has also some drawbacks highlighted by the more recent empirical and theoretical literature (Oates, 2006):

- **Deficit bias:** Fiscal decentralization may undermine fiscal discipline. Subnational governments do not fully internalize the cost of public expenditure and thus have an incentive to undertax and overspend. For instance, local authorities may expect bailouts from the center ("soft budget constraint"[2]) and/or partly finance their marginal expenditure with central transfers that are paid by taxpayers in other jurisdictions ("common pool problem"). In addition, the lack of discipline of an individual subnational entity may have spillover effects on the general government's fiscal position (Box 3.1).
- **Coordination failure:** In a decentralized system, subnational and national governments' policies are not necessarily consistent, even when local authorities are fiscally responsible. It is not uncommon that subnational authorities steer fiscal

---

Box 3.1 Vertical and horizontal externalities in federations

Vertical spillovers. The central government's position may be affected by fiscal problems originating at the subnational level (IMF, 2009a). Subnational governments that have borrowed too much and accumulate arrears may receive bailout transfers from the center. Vertical spillovers can also take more subtle forms, for instance, when high subnational borrowing or difficulties in implementing consolidation plans in a decentralized framework result in higher risk premia on sovereign issuances.

Horizontal spillovers. If an individual entity is fiscally irresponsible, its behavior may negatively affect the fiscal position of other subnational governments for several reasons (Inman, 1996; Landon, 2003): (i) An implicit or explicit guarantee by the other members of the federation could directly raise their credit risk premium; (ii) An implicit or explicit guarantee by the central government may also negatively affect other subnational entities, through the higher risk of inflation (if the guaranteed debt is monetized), or through tax increases borne by the whole federation; (iii) The investors' perception of similarities among subnational governments may be sufficient to trigger spillover effects, for instance when problems in a particular state signal that similar problems are more likely in other states; (iv) Real linkages (regional trade) or financial linkages (solvency of the financial sector) may also transmit the externality.

policy in the opposite direction of the center. Analyzing seven federations, Rodden and Wibbels (2010) show that subnational governments generally pursue pro-cyclical policies, which undermine the stabilization efforts of the center.

The deficit bias and lack of coordination are, to different degrees, present in all decentralized systems. The second problem is however more acute in federations than in unitary countries, as states enjoy more autonomy and account for a larger share of the general government (both in terms of revenue and expenditure). Subnational autonomy is indeed at the very heart of federal systems, because the constituent units had generally some influence in the formulation of the original constitutional contract and the "bottom-up" delegation of fiscal responsibilities to the center (Rodden, 2002). For instance, the U.S. Constitution assigns to the states all "residual powers" – that is, all responsibilities not explicitly vested with the federation. In unitary countries, it is often the opposite: reforms proceed by assigning new responsibilities to lower levels of government. This "top-down" decentralization model is de facto associated with lower subnational autonomy.

Whether the deficit bias is more prevalent in federations is an open question. As states generally enjoy higher fiscal autonomy, the tax-benefit link is tighter in federations. This may enhance fiscal responsibility and accountability. On the other hand, the risk of moral hazard is also higher. The econometric literature does not provide evidence of a systematic relationship between the governmental structure (federal versus unitary states) and the fiscal position of subnational governments, other factors being equal (see for instance, Rodden 2002).

In Europe, deficit bias and coordination issues between member states have also been prevalent. First, some European governments did not face hard budget constraints in the 2000s, because market discipline was undermined by the lack of credibility of the "no bailout clause" enshrined in the Treaty on the Functioning of the European Union.[3] Anticipating that fiscally imprudent countries would receive financial assistance from the rest of the union, financial markets did not discriminate between individual sovereign risks, and borrowing costs did not show significant cross-country dispersion in the Euro Area during most of the first decade of the new millennium.[4] A second issue is the common pool problem, which is amplified in Europe by a number of factors, including the large number of constituencies and decision makers, cultural cleavages, and the lack of transparency and democratic control (Von Hagen, 2012). Finally, coordination failures and fiscal spillovers are also present, not so much between member states and the (small) central budget, but between the fiscal policies of individual member states.

In order to address the deficit bias and coordination problems, federations resort to institutional arrangements whose aim is to reduce the fiscal discretion of subnational governments with two main objectives: enforce and signal fiscal discipline, and strengthen coordination across levels of government.[5] Constraints may be self-imposed by subnational governments with the purpose of signaling rather than eliciting fiscal discipline: fiscally-responsible subnational governments may find it in their own interest to reveal their creditworthiness to investors through the imposition of rules that less prudent authorities cannot credibly replicate (Inman, 1996).

Box 3.2 Brazil's fiscal responsibility law

The fiscal responsibility law (FRL), adopted in 2000, is considered a milestone in Brazilian fiscal governance reforms. The FRL imposes constraints on spending and budget balances (such as ceilings on wage expenditure and indebtedness of the federal, state, and municipal governments) and establishes harmonized rules for budget formulation and fiscal reporting. It also introduces penalties on managers and political authorities who do not comply with its requirements. The FRL assigns to the central government the responsibility of setting an annual primary balance target for the non-financial public sector as a whole. Sub-targets then are identified for each level of government (central, states, and municipalities), and the central government is in charge of monitoring compliance and implementing sanctions in case of breach.

The constraints are often formalized in the legal framework – either through an overarching fiscal responsibility law (see Box 3.2 for the case of Brazil), or in subnational law. Many federations have also established fiscal policy coordination bodies grouping representatives of the central and subnational governments.[6] In Europe the need for more coordination is the main rationale behind the "preventive arm" of the Stability and Growth Pact, which coordinates fiscal policies *ex ante* through a peer review of stability and convergence programs (European Commission, 2013).

III. Which subnational constraints are most prevalent in federations?

A. Typology of constraints

Constraints can be classified according to the degree of "fiscal autonomy" (FA) they leave to subnational governments.[7] In the literature, FA is a broad concept referring to the authority for decision-making and management, in all areas of the budget – expenditure, revenue, and financing. In this chapter, we adopt a more narrow definition and refer to FA as the capacity of subnational governments to set their own fiscal targets.

Figure 3.1 depicts the FA axis, ranking arrangements according to the autonomy allowed to subnational governments. On the left, direct (administrative) controls by the central government are associated with the lowest degree of FA. For instance, central government may set and revise every year's ceilings on subnational debt or regulate the type of borrowing allowed. Fiscal rules (including explicit numerical targets) come next.[8] Although rules impose stringent restrictions on fiscal discretion, they are less binding than direct controls, because rules preclude the central government from micromanaging subnational fiscal policy, and because their design often preserves some policy flexibility (for instance, deficit ceilings constitute an asymmetric constraint). In addition, subnational

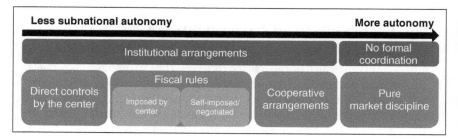

Figure 3.1 Arrangements to constrain subnational fiscal policy

Source: IMF staff.

governments generally have margins to comply with rules. Rules themselves can be ranked, depending on whether they are imposed by the center[9] or self-imposed (or negotiated). Cooperative approaches ensure the highest degree of subnational FA among institutional arrangements. Unlike fiscal rules, they allow subnational governments to renegotiate their fiscal targets on a regular basis. Finally, constraints may be imposed by investors, enforcing market discipline. In this case, subnational governments are free to set their own targets, as long as their fiscal policy does not impair market confidence.

This typology is not without its shortcomings. There is no clear-cut separation between different arrangements. In particular, fiscal rules are not always distinguishable from direct controls and cooperative approaches (Appendix A.3.1). In addition, federations resort to multiple arrangements. In particular, state and local governments are often constrained by distinct mechanisms. Finally, as discussed below, in several respects, market discipline is qualitatively different from institutional constraints.

B. Institutional arrangements prevalent in federations

Appendix Table A.3.2 provides details about the constraints imposed on subnational fiscal policy in the sample of the federations chosen for this book – including self-imposed constraints and some state controls on local entities. Fiscal rules are by far the most common form of institutional constraint in the sample, accounting for almost 90 percent of the constraints; the rest is somewhat evenly distributed between cooperative approach and direct controls (Table 3.1). On average, subnational governments are subject to 3 different constraints (2 if the analysis is limited to the subset of constraints imposed by the federal level).

Fiscal rules are present in all the federations surveyed. Some countries, such as Spain, have a larger number of subnational constraints, covering all the main fiscal aggregates, including the debt stock, debt service, expenditure, and fiscal balance. In our sample, it seems that fiscal rules and cooperative approaches are substitutes, in the sense that the number of rules is, on average, smaller in countries with a tradition of negotiation. Interestingly, about half of the subnational rules in federations tend to be self-imposed or negotiated, rather than imposed

Table 3.1 Institutional constraints on subnational governments: Types and number[1]

	Fiscal rule	*Direct control*	*Cooperative approach*
Argentina[2]	3	...	...
Australia	3	...	1
Austria	1	...	1
Belgium	1	...	1
Brazil	3	...	...
Canada	3	1	...
Germany	3	...	...
India	4	1	...
Mexico	2	...	...
South Africa	2	...	...
Spain	6	...	...
Switzerland	5	...	...
United States	5	...	...

Source: IMF staff.

[1]Self-imposed constraints and state controls on local entities are included. Market discipline is not considered. The classification is based on the information collected in Appendix Table A.3.2, with one line representing one constraint.
[2]In Argentina, fiscal rules have been suspended since 2009.

by the central government (Figure 3.2). For instance, in Canada and the United States, provinces and states set their own balanced budget rules and other types of fiscal rules. In Australia, rules are also self-imposed and differ from state to state. The same occurs at the canton level in Switzerland. This differentiates federations

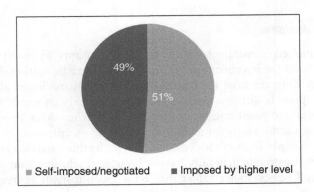

49%

51%

■ Self-imposed/negotiated   ■ Imposed by higher level

Figure 3.2 Origin of fiscal rules on subnational governments

Source: IMF staff.

Note: The shares are based on the rules reported in Appendix Table A.3.2. Rules on Argentinian provinces are also included.

from unitary countries, where most rules are imposed by the center (Joumard and Kongsrud, 2003; Sutherland et al., 2005).

Cooperative approaches exist in some countries. For example, in Austria, annual fiscal targets are negotiated by federal, regional, and local governments via the Austrian Stability Program. A similar negotiation process occurs in Belgium through cooperation between the federal and regional levels and the High Finance Council, a supervisory authority that proposes annual ceilings on borrowing requirements consistent with EU commitments. In Australia, cooperation occurs via the Loan Council, a federal-state body which coordinates the financial borrowing arrangements of the federal and regional governments. Although it is difficult to draw general lessons from a small sample of countries, anecdotal evidence suggests that cooperative approaches are progressively abandoned in favor of fiscal rules. For instance, Germany has had a tradition of coordination and negotiation of fiscal targets, with the Financial Planning Council monitoring fiscal developments and making recommendations on the budgetary plans of the Federation and the Länder (Joumard and Kongsrud, 2003; Lübke, 2005).[10] In 2009, a new rule-based approach was introduced, which will submit the federal and the Länders' budgets to structural balance targets after a transition period.

Direct controls from the central government are rare in federations, in contrast with unitary countries (Ter-Minassian and Craig, 1997).[11] They generally appear in the form of borrowing restrictions at the regional and local government levels. In India, states must request permission to raise loans if they are indebted to the central government or have taken guarantees from it. The center must assess the debt sustainability of the state and its ability to repay. In Canada, municipalities need authorization from provinces to borrow on the domestic market. Although direct controls are rare in normal times, they are still commonly used in case of breach of fiscal targets, as discussed below.

C. Market discipline

Financial markets constrain subnational fiscal authority by imposing higher borrowing costs for imprudent policy. In several respects, market discipline is qualitatively different from the institutional constraints reviewed above. First, market discipline is difficult to quantify. It does not rely on explicit numerical targets, contrary to fiscal rules or cooperative approaches. Also, its strength and effectiveness cannot easily be measured outside crisis episodes. In contrast, it is relatively simple to monitor compliance with institutional constraints. Second, market constraints generally have a broader reach, imposing restrictions on the overall policy stance rather than on a specific fiscal aggregate. Third, market discipline comes on top of existing institutional mechanisms. As soon as subnational governments have market access, some degree of market discipline exists. By contrast, institutional arrangements are often substitutes. For instance, the overall balance cannot be, at the same time, negotiated and subject to direct controls.

No country relies on pure market discipline; institutional arrangements are present in all the federations reviewed in this chapter. Interestingly, the countries where the market discipline is the strongest, such as Australia, Canada, and the United States, are those where subnational rules are self-imposed. As discussed in Section VI, one reason could be that subnational governments establish these rules to signal to the market their commitment to fiscal discipline.

Purely market-based discipline remains atypical because conditions for its effectiveness are seldom met (Ter-Minassian and Craig, 1997; Ter-Minassian, 2007). First, subnational authorities should not have privileged access to borrowing. For instance, loans should not be obtained from publicly owned credit institutions with administratively-decided interest rates and should not be guaranteed by higher levels of government. Second, adequate information on the borrower's existing liabilities and repayment capacity should be readily available, so that potential lenders can correctly discriminate between borrowers. Third, the borrower should have the capacity and willingness to respond to market signals. This may not be the case if electoral cycles foster a short-sighted conduct of fiscal policy, or if subnational authorities have little authority over their revenue and expenditure.

The coexistence of market discipline and institutional controls is becoming more widespread and is not limited to advanced economies. In Mexico, the new regulatory framework for domestic borrowing introduced in 2000 stipulates that the federal government does not guarantee subnational debt and relinquishes some of its power over discretionary transfers (to avoid possible bailouts). Subnational debt is subject to normal credit exposure ceilings, and bank's capital risk weighting of subnational loans is based on international credit ratings (Braun and Tommasi, 2002; Webb, 2004). In 2003, South Africa also introduced a regulatory framework for municipal borrowing in order to fill the regulatory gap that emerged from the elimination of the central underwriting and guarantee of municipal debt. Article 139 stipulates that in case of financial difficulties the provincial government has to seek "solutions to resolve the financial problem in a way that would be sustainable and would build the municipality's capacity to manage its own financial affairs."

IV. What are the main features of subnational constraints in federations?

A. Fiscal aggregate

In the sample of federations, constraints are primarily imposed on the fiscal balance of subnational governments. Borrowing constraints and debt rules are also widespread, followed by expenditure rules.[12] Revenue rules are rare at the subnational level (Table 3.2). The prevalence of fiscal balance constraints and borrowing restrictions is not specific to federations; Sutherland et al. (2005) find the same result for subnational governments in unitary countries.

Two evolutions have been particularly noticeable in recent years. First, the use of balanced budget rules seems to have gained momentum with the recent crisis.

Table 3.2 Fiscal indicator targeted by the institutional constraint[1]

	Fiscal Balance			Borrowing[2]	Debt		Expenditure		Revenue
	Overall balance	Golden rule	Structural balance		Debt stock	Debt service	Aggregate	Subcomponent	Tax ceiling
Argentina[3]		x				x	x		
Australia	x						x		
Austria	▲	x		▲	x	x			
Belgium	▲/x								
Brazil				x	x			x	
Canada	x			o	x		x		
Germany[4]	x		x	x					
India	x		x	o	x	x			
Mexico	x			x					
South Africa	x			x					
Spain	x		x		x	x	x		
Switzerland	x	x	x				x		
United States	x	x		x	x	x	x		x

Source: IMF staff.

[1] All the fiscal aggregates pertain to subnational governments. x denotes a fiscal rule, o denotes a direct control from a higher government level, and ▲ denotes a cooperative arrangement.
[2] India and Mexico have distinct restrictions on domestic and foreign borrowing.
[3] In Argentina, fiscal rules have been suspended since 2009.
[4] In Germany, the Länder have the option to follow an overall balance rule (instead of a structural balance rule), although the debt brake targets are set in structural terms. At the time of the drafting of this chapter, most Länder were still in the process of designing their rules.

Using data from the European Commission Fiscal Rules database, we see that the share of balanced budget rules has increased significantly in the subset of European federations between 2005 and 2011 (Figure 3.3), and this increase has been more pronounced than in unitary countries. In the context of the crisis, budget balance rules may have been perceived by federations as critical to supporting the credibility of fiscal consolidation plans.

Second, a few countries have adopted cyclically-adjusted balance rules at the subnational level, providing some flexibility to accommodate for output shocks. These rules take different forms. In Germany, the Länder budgets must be balanced in structural terms as of 2020. Implementation at state level is the sole responsibility of the Länder, which are free to specify the legal basis and implementation provisions,[13] including whether to apply this objective via a nominal or structural rule, the methodology for cyclical adjustment, and whether to use a control account.[14] In Spain, the regions' annual fiscal balance target depends on the cyclical position, net of exceptional and temporary measures. In Switzerland, cantons set their own balanced budget rules; for instance, in Graubünden, Lucerne, and Valais, the government's deficit must be balanced over the business cycle (Stalder and Röhrs, 2005). Nonetheless, cyclically-adjusted rules remain uncommon at the subnational level, in part because local GDP indicators are either nonexistent for small entities or not reported on a timely basis.

Another way to introduce flexibility is through the creation of "rainy day funds" (RDFs), whose purpose is to smooth public spending. RDFs are budget stabilization funds consisting of resources that are set aside during good years to be used by subnational governments when the deterioration in economic conditions

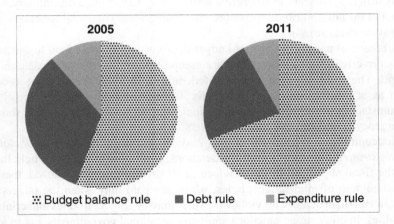

Figure 3.3 Distribution of subnational fiscal rules in EU federations

Source: European Commission Fiscal Rules Database (2011); IMF staff estimates.

Note: 2005 is the first year available in the EC Fiscal Rule Database with sufficient rules to make a relevant comparison. Federal countries include Austria, Belgium, Germany, and Spain. There was no revenue rule in 2005 and 2011 in the sample of federations.

produces an unexpected drop in revenue or an increase in expenditure. In the absence of RDFs, states, which are often compelled to run balanced budgets, would have to conduct pro-cyclical fiscal policies (Balassone et al., 2007; Ter-Minassian, 2007).[15] Empirical evidence on the United States shows that RDFs have been effective in cushioning the impact of the recent crisis on states' expenditures (McNichol and Boadi, 2011).

In the United States, RDFs were introduced in the aftermath of the recession of the early 1980s. Today, almost all U.S. States have RDFs, although their sizes differ significantly. Prior to the crisis, some states had very small amounts set aside (for example, Wisconsin and Michigan), while mineral-rich states (such as Wyoming and Alaska) had reserves equivalent to more than one third of their annual expenditure. Outside of the United States, RDFs are not common.

B. Sanctions and corrective actions

Institutional constraints generally include a number of provisions to deal with non-compliance and strengthen enforcement. In particular, subnational governments failing to abide by the rules may be subject to sanctions and/or corrective actions. Appendix Table A.3.3 gives a non-exhaustive overview of some of the measures provided for by national and subnational legislations.[16]

From the start, it should be noted that the distinction between sanction and corrective actions is not always clear-cut. In this chapter, we define corrective actions as a set of measures intended to put local finances back on a sound footing and which entail some temporary loss of autonomy for subnational entities. Sanctions are financial and administrative penalties imposed on the subnational government or its officials; contrary to corrective actions, they have only a disciplinary function and do not contribute to restore fiscal soundness (financial sanctions may aggravate fiscal stress).

A breach of a subnational fiscal target does not immediately lead to sanctions and corrective actions when there are escape clauses in case of predetermined events. These clauses exist in several federations, although they are not as common as at the national level (Appendix Table A.3.3). The list of exceptional circumstances seems quite standard, including large macroeconomic shocks, emergency situations, and natural disasters.

Noncompliance with fiscal targets may occasionally result in *financial or administrative sanctions*. In some federations, individual officials are held liable for the fiscal slippages. In the province of British Columbia in Canada, there is a withholding of ministerial salaries, which are paid only when the targets are met. In Brazil, officials who violate the rules may be subject to fines and criminal penalties. In other cases, sanctions apply to subnational governments, not to individuals. In Germany, consolidation payments may be suspended if Länders under consolidation programs miss their targets. In Austria, interest-bearing deposits are converted into fines in case of noncompliance with the domestic stability pact targets. In Spain, regions may incur fines if they cause the country to breach EU rules. Interestingly, financial sanctions are quite widespread despite their pre-sumed lack of credibility.[17]

Corrective actions can be ranked according to the loss of autonomy they impose on subnational governments. A minimal requirement is for officials to justify the breach of the target, as in Australia. They may also have to produce a plan for rectifying the situation. Corrective actions are more demanding when the center imposes direct controls on subnational policies in cases of breach. These controls range from borrowing restrictions (in Argentina, India, and Belgium), to a mandatory agreement on rebalancing plans (Germany) and a temporary loss of authority on fiscal matters (Switzerland). Spain combines several layers of cor-rection mechanisms. Regions having missed their budget balance target, public debt objective, or expenditure rule are required to present an annual rebalancing plan, with quarterly monitoring by the central government. They are also subject to borrowing restrictions. In case of noncompliance with the plans, regions lose some fiscal autonomy (capacity to set taxes, spending authorization reduction) and may, as a last resort, be placed under central administration.

V. A comparative perspective on the European Union supranational rule framework

Constraints on fiscal targets are the area where parallels can be more explicitly drawn between the European Union and fiscal federations.[18] This is because the adoption of a common currency and common monetary policy without a match-ing fiscal union raised meaningful risks that justified the establishment of a bind-ing and extensive set of constraints on the fiscal policies of EU members.

The comparison clearly has its limits. The EU is not a federation, and the links between the "center" (EU institutions) and the member states are looser and at times ambiguous. Thus, some design features of the EU rules may in fact com-pensate for the weaker enforcement capacity of the center and greater reliance on peer pressure. Similarly, the absence of a fiscal union in the EU may require a larger number of constraints with a view to ensuring enforcement for a wide range of circumstances.

A. Number and type of constraints

The EU fiscal governance framework has four main supranational rules – the 3 percent deficit rule, the 60 percent debt rule, an expenditure benchmark, and medium-term budgetary objectives (MTO) defined in structural terms. It also requires countries to enshrine a structural balance rule in national legislation.[19] Appendix A.3.2 provides detailed information on those five requirements. There is also a cycle of economic policy coordination at the EU level.

Compared to the European Union, most federations tend to impose a smaller set of constraints on subnational governments, except Spain which adopted an extensive fiscal rule framework during the crisis. On average, the federal level imposes about two constraints (Figure 3.4). Canada, Switzerland and the United States have no federal restriction on subnational fiscal targets.[20]

Several factors may explain the higher number of supranational rules in the EU. First, the Maastricht Treaty initially included only three supranational rules, of which only one was really binding.[21] Later, the fiscal crisis and the unsuccessful experience with a small set of constraints prompted the adoption of additional rules. Although rules are mutually consistent and tied by well-defined relationships, successive legislative changes make their monitoring, communication, and fiscal planning complex, as countries need to ensure that they comply with the most stringent of all requirements. Second, the growing complexity of the EU system also reflects the relative paucity and lack of confidence in self-imposed national rules, particularly in the initial years.[22] By contrast, in federations, about half of constraints on subnational governments are self-imposed. Third, the large number of constraints ensures enforcement for a wide range of circumstances – a necessity given the limited size of the EU budget, the decentralization of almost all spending and taxation decisions and, more generally, the absence of a full-fledged fiscal union in the EU. For instance, structural balance rules and expenditure benchmarks are used to prevent lax policies in good times.

The EU fiscal governance framework rests almost exclusively on fiscal rules. As explained above, institutional constraints can take three different forms: fiscal rules, direct controls, and cooperative arrangements. Although some policy

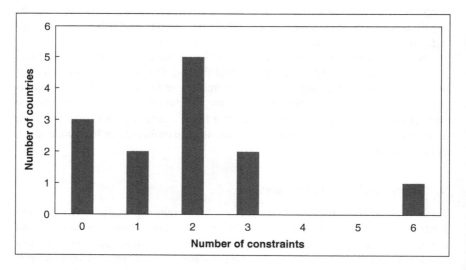

Figure 3.4 Number of countries with federal constraints on subnational governments

Source: IMF staff estimates.

Note: The sample includes the 13 federations surveyed in the book. The constraints in the chart include negotiated and imposed fiscal rules, direct controls by the center, and cooperative arrangements. Constraints that are self-imposed by subnational governments are, by definition, not included, which explains the difference with Table 3.1.

coordination exists among European countries (in particular through the European Semester), this exercise cannot be described as a full-fledged cooperative approach, primarily because fiscal plans are examined rather than negotiated between European (supranational) institutions and member states.[23] The EU framework does not resort either to direct controls from the center.[24] The predominance of fiscal rules is not EU-specific. In the sample of federations, rules are also the most common type of constraint, although as mentioned above, cooperative approaches prevail in Australia, Austria, and Belgium.

Some differences also exist regarding fiscal targets. Compared to existing federations, borrowing controls are absent from the EU fiscal framework.[25] Another difference is that budget balance rules are relatively strong requirements in the EU (at least "on paper"), while they seem less stringent in the sample of federations, where they are often negotiated rather than imposed by the center.

B. Design features

Three features distinguish EU rules from usual federal constraints. First, most EU rules include restrictions on both the level and the first difference of fiscal targets, the second restriction being conditioned on the breach of the first one. Fiscal rules are, thus, implemented in stages (Figure 3.5). For instance, when countries do not comply with the 60 percent debt ceiling, a constraint on debt changes – the 1/20th rule – applies. Similarly, if a member state's structural deficit is higher than its MTO, it has to improve its fiscal position by at least 0.5 percent of GDP per year in structural terms. Corrective actions and sanctions are also progressive, becoming more stringent when the target in level is breached *and* efforts to correct the imbalance are deemed insufficient. This multi-step approach is probably motivated by the relative weakness of enforcement tools and the desire to make peer pressure more effective.

Another (recent) peculiarity of the EU fiscal framework is that it requires supranational requirements to be enshrined in national legislation in order to strengthen enforcement. In particular, the adoption of national structural balance rules should ensure that MTOs are achieved. This may create inconsistencies if a specific fiscal target is constrained by both national and supranational rules with slightly different definitions. To our knowledge, there is no similar case of duplication in federations.[26]

Third, in accordance with the "subsidiarity principle," EU rules apply to the general government, with countries being responsible to distribute the target internally among government units. By contrast, in federations, central constraints generally apply separately to different government levels, and states/regions are not held responsible for the achievement of lower–tier targets. For instance, there are distinct rules for Länder and local governments in Germany. In Belgium, regions and communities' fiscal balance targets are negotiated, while local governments are subject to a budget balance rule. The fact that the EU governance framework remains silent on the internal working of supranational objectives has led several European countries to adopt domestic stability pacts, whose purpose is to coordinate fiscal outcomes and ensure that all governments levels are involved in the

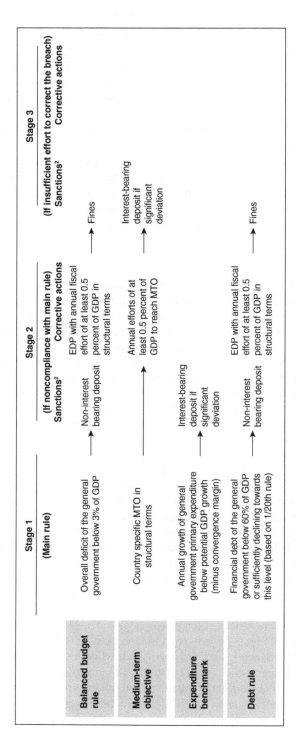

Figure 3.5 Multi-step approach with EU fiscal rules[1]

Source: EC, and IMF staff.

[1]The figure provides a *simplified* overview of EU fiscal rules. Detailed information can be found on the European Commission website and publications (European Commission, 2013).

[2]Sanctions (deposits and fines) apply only to euro area countries. Countries benefiting from structural funds may face a suspension of commitments when insufficient action is taken under the EDP.

achievement of supranational targets. The performance of these internal pacts is nonetheless mixed (Sutherland et al., 2005; Ambrosanio and Bordignon, 2007).

C. Enforcement

Enforcement mechanisms are notoriously weak in some federations, but the EU framework is particularly hampered in this area, for three main reasons (Appendix Table A.3.3). First, sanctions apply only to euro area member states. For instance, countries under the excessive deficit procedure (EDP) that are not part of the euro area are neither required to hold a deposit at the EU, nor liable to a fine in case of insufficient progress. By contrast, in federations, central constraints usually bear on *all* subnational governments in a nondiscriminatory way.

Second, sanctions are relatively mild in the EU. They usually consist in opportunity costs from financial deposits. The conditions to convert these deposits into outright fines are very strict and have, so far, never been applied. In addition, the EU framework does not provide for administrative sanctions, while, as mentioned above, they exist and are applied in several federations.

Third, corrective actions required in case of noncompliance are also relatively weak, in part because the European authorities do not have the ability to impose direct controls on national budgets. For instance, borrowing restrictions imposed by the federal level do not exist in the EU, while they exist in some federations. More generally, decisions on sanctions and corrective actions are taken by the center in federations, while they are adopted by the European Council in the EU; that is, by representatives of national ("sub-central") authorities. This may undermine the capacity to enforce European rules.

Recent reforms of the EU fiscal governance have strengthened enforcement mechanisms. The Treaty on Stability, Coordination, and Governance (TSCG), signed in 2012 by 25 EU member states, requires countries to introduce structural balance rules in national legislation (preferably in the constitution); these rules should be monitored by independent institutions and incorporate correction mechanisms in case of deviations. In addition, sanctions for euro area countries have become more automatic, as they are now adopted by the "reverse qualified majority" procedure. This new voting system gives more power to European institutions by ensuring that a recommendation or a proposal of the Commission is approved by the Council unless a qualified majority of member states votes against it. The six-pack regulations, which entered into force in 2001, introduced reverse qualified majority voting for most sanctions, while the TSCG extended it to earlier stages of the EDP.

VI. Five lessons on the effectiveness of subnational fiscal constraints

The experience of federations with subnational control mechanisms suggests five lessons regarding their possible role in enhancing fiscal responsibility and sustainability at the subnational level.

Lesson 1: Institutional constraints on subnational fiscal targets do have a disciplinary effect

While standard public finance theory holds fiscal institutions as simple veils, the empirical literature shows that they can affect the behavior of subnational governments (Poterba, 1996; Strauch and Von Hagen, 2001). Existing studies have examined the effects of subnational constraints on a wide range of fiscal outcomes, including subnational deficits, debt, tax, and expenditure.

Evidence from the U.S. States

Most of the empirical papers on subnational fiscal institutions focus on the U.S. States.[27] Von Hagen (1991) provides evidence that debt limits and budget balance rules reduce per capita state debt and state debt-income ratios. According to Poterba (1994), a $100 state deficit overrun leads, on average, to a $17 expenditure cut in states with weak budget balance rules, while the cut is much larger ($44) in states with strict anti-deficit rules.[28] Also, states with tax limitation rules enact smaller tax increases in response to unexpected deficits than do states without such limits. Rueben (1995) shows that tax and expenditure limits lower state spending. Bohn and Inman (1996) find that budget balance rules that restrict end-year budget deficits reduce state deficits. Clemens and Miran (2010) and Lutz and Follette (2012) extend Poterba's results to the most recent period and confirm that strong-rule states adjust spending more significantly than states with weaker rules following an unexpected deficit.

These studies also suggest that not only the choice but also the design of constraints matter (Inman, 1996; and Bohn and Inman, 1996). First, the stringency of state rules affects their disciplinary effect. Although most U.S. States have budget balance rules, these differ in terms of strictness (Figure 3.6). Budget balance rules with a no-carryover provision requiring an *ex post*, end-of-the-year balanced position are found to reduce state deficits. By contrast, *ex ante* rules requiring only a beginning-of-the-year balanced budget are not effective. Second, enforcement mechanisms are also important. Constitutionally-based state rules requiring two thirds of the citizens to overturn are found to be more effective than statutorily-based rules needing only a simple majority of the legislature to suspend or overrule.[29] Finally, the independence of the monitoring entity matters. Rules which are enforced by directly elected, and presumably more independent, supreme courts are more effective than rules which are enforced by politically appointed courts (either by the governor or the legislature). This result is consistent with recent evidence showing that fiscal rules and fiscal councils often coexist and complement each other (IMF, 2013).[30]

Overall, available evidence suggests that constraints on U.S. States have been effective. It is not clear whether these results are entirely relevant for other federations, as the effect of institutional constraints is probably reinforced by market discipline in the United States (see Lesson 4).[31]

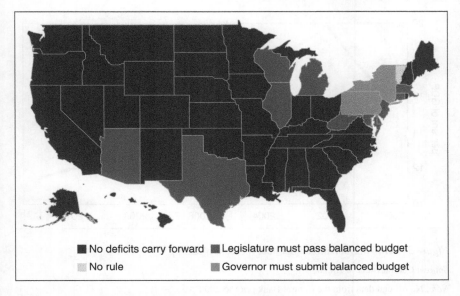

Figure 3.6 United States: Strictness of balanced budget requirements

Source: National Conference of State Legislatures (2010).

Evidence from other federations[32]

Outside of the United States, the empirical evidence of the effect of subnational constraints is more limited. Brazil has had considerable success with fiscal rules in the last decade (Figure 3.7), although it is difficult to disentangle the effect of the new fiscal framework, including, as mentioned earlier, the adoption of an overarching fiscal responsibility law, from that of debt restructuring arrangements (Webb, 2004; Liu and Webb, 2011). India is also an example of country where the introduction of FRLs at the state level has catalyzed fiscal consolidation by bringing elements of discipline into the state budgeting process (Kishore and Prasad, 2007). The effectiveness of the fiscal rule framework also partly explains the high degree of subnational fiscal discipline in Switzerland (IMF, 2012). Most cantons have fiscal rules, which vary with respect to their target, operational implementation, exemption clauses, and sanction mechanisms. In Spain, Cabasés et al. (2007) shows that municipal borrowing restrictions had a significant effect on the indebtedness of local governments during the 1990s.

***Lesson 2: Subnational constraints cannot substitute for a properly
designed system of intergovernmental fiscal relations***

While subnational constraints may instill some fiscal discipline, they are not a panacea. They can improve fiscal outcomes where there are coordination failures

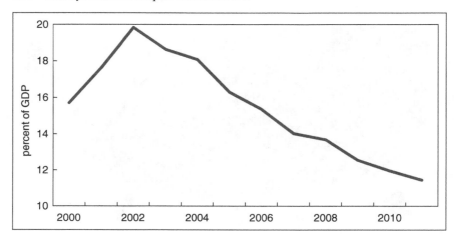

Figure 3.7 Brazil: Subnational net debt (percent of GDP)

Source: Central Bank of Brazil

Note: No official data from the Central Bank prior to 2000.

or a lack of fiscal discipline. They are less effective if the mismanagement of sub-national fiscal accounts is due to flaws inherent in the decentralization framework (e.g., ill-designed transfer system, unclear expenditure assignments, mismatch between revenue and spending responsibilities) or to central government policies (e.g., unfunded mandates, pork-barrel politics, pro-cyclical provision of transfers).

Spain provides an example of how efforts to tighten the rules could not overcome underlying flaws. The 2001 Budget Stability Law distributed the general government deficit target between different levels. The law was amended in 2006 to take into account the pro-cyclical nature of the rule and to target a fiscal balance over the cycle. To further strengthen the control of the regions, additional conditions were introduced to obtain debt authorization and to increase transparency by providing the information in a timelier manner. These new rules did not prevent the buildup of fiscal imbalances in the run-up to the crisis. Despite a favorable macroeconomic outlook until 2007, the regions' fiscal deficit was almost systematically higher than initially budgeted (Figure 3.8). In part, this reflected a widening gap between their spending responsibilities and revenue raising powers. This mismatch intensified during the crisis. The regions' revenues became more uncertain, reflecting a significant erosion in the tax base (housing market) and higher unemployment. In contrast, their expenditure was of a structural nature (health and education), with pressures arising from population aging (IMF, 2010).

Argentina is another example. The Fiscal Solvency Law approved in 1999 did not include provisions for subnational governments but invited the provinces to pass similar laws, which several did. These laws differed across provinces,

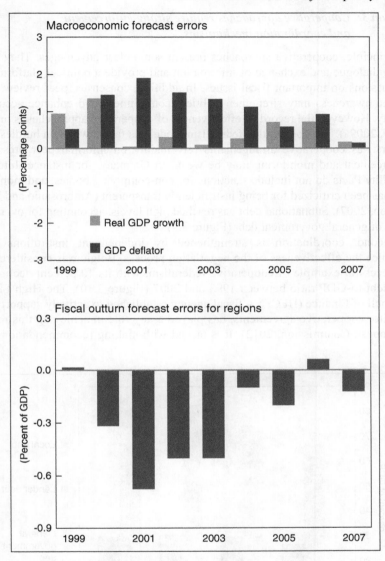

Figure 3.8 Spain: Pre-crisis forecast errors, 1999–2007

Source: IMF (2010).

although most deficit and debt limits. However, in 2001, it was the incapacity of the federal government to meet its legally-binding spending obligations, most notably intergovernmental transfers, that pushed the provinces into a fiscal crisis. Even with strong enforcement procedures, the FRLs could not have addressed this problem (Webb, 2004).

Lesson 3:   *Cooperative approaches require strong enforcement and coordination mechanisms*

In principle, cooperative approaches present some clear advantages. They promote dialogue and exchange of information and provide a political platform for discussions on important fiscal issues. In addition, consensus, peer review, and public awareness may strengthen political commitment and enhance accountability. However, the record of effectiveness of cooperative approaches is mixed (IMF, 2009a). The cooperative federalism model has faced two main hurdles.[33]

First, as cooperative arrangements rely mainly on informal peer pressure, enforcement and monitoring may be weak. In Germany, for instance, Internal Stability Pacts do not include sanctions for non-complying bodies, and monitoring has been criticized for being insufficiently transparent (Ambrosanio and Bordignon, 2007). Subnational debt has reached high levels, accounting for over one third of general government debt (Figure 3.9).

Second, coordination is strengthened by independent institutions that enhance the effectiveness of the negotiation process. Belgium is considered as a successful example of cooperative federalism, with its 40 percent decline in the debt-to-GDP ratio between 1993 and 2007 (Figure 3.10). The High Fiscal Council of Finance (HFCF), a fiscal agency established to actively support and monitor cooperative agreements, has played a key role in achieving this result (European Commission, 2012). It is tasked with making recommendations on

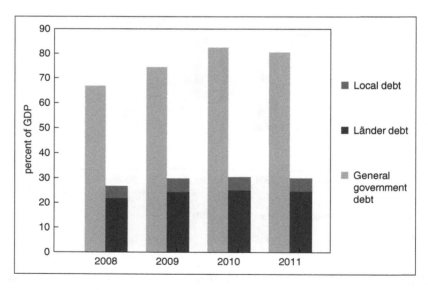

Figure 3.9 Germany: Public debt (percent of GDP)

Source: Eurostat.

Note: Local and state debts are not consolidated.

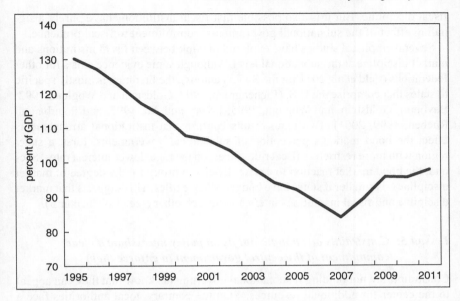

Figure 3.10 Belgium: General government debt (percent of GDP)

Source: Eurostat.

the fiscal targets of each government level. The HFCF also monitors the fiscal outcomes of subnational governments and evaluates the implementation of stability programs.

Lesson 4: Well-designed fiscal constraints may improve the market's perception of subnational fiscal policy

In federations where market discipline plays an important role, as in Canada and the United States, states have voluntarily adopted fiscal rules. U.S. States impose budget balance rules in different forms. For instance, 41 of the 50 U.S. States require the legislature to enact a balanced budget; and 38 states cannot carry forward a deficit into the next fiscal period (National Conference of State Legislatures, 2010). Switzerland is another example of successful combination of effective fiscal rules and market discipline (IMF, 2012). As mentioned earlier, other federations, such as Mexico and South Africa, have also tried to combine both approaches.

Fiscal institutions are used by subnational governments to improve their credit rating and reduce borrowing costs (Joumard and Kongsrud, 2003). Financial market participants, who monitor and assess states' fiscal performance, seem to consider their presence as relevant elements to evaluate fiscal positions. This may reflect the perception that these institutions are effective mechanisms to enforce fiscal discipline. But it is also possible that fiscal institutions have purely a signaling effect of the subnational governments' commitment to fiscal prudence.

Several empirical studies have explored the link between fiscal institutions and market discipline at the subnational level. Although some evidence exists for other federations (Feld et al., 2011 for the Swiss cantons), the literature is mostly specific to states that comprise the U.S. (Eichengreen, 1992; Goldstein and Woglom, 1992; Bayoumi, Goldstein, and Woglom, 1995; Lowry and Alt, 1997; and Poterba and Rueben, 1999, 2001). Two main results confirm that institutional arrangements affect the bond market's perception of subnational governments. First, a state/region with more restrictive fiscal rules faces, on average, lower interest rates. Second, the bond market reaction to a state deficit – a proxy for the degree of market discipline – is smaller if states have budget balance rules. This suggests that market discipline and fiscal institutions interact with each other (see also Chapter 5).

Lesson 5: *Constraints on subnational fiscal policy necessitate a clear commitment of the central government to enforce them*

Constraints are not binding if subnational governments know that they can appeal to the center for additional resources.[34] On the contrary, local authorities face a hard budget constraint when the central government can commit to a no bailout policy. Somewhat paradoxically, subnational constraints are thus more stringent and credible if the central government's discretion is also restricted.

A strong central government's commitment is key to ensuring that institutional arrangements such as fiscal rules are enforced. Such a commitment is also necessary to preserve the effectiveness of market mechanisms. If lenders believe that the center provides an implicit guarantee to subnational governments, the disciplinary effect of markets is undermined. As discussed in Chapter 6, stemming bailout expectations is however no easy task. A sustained history of no bailouts may be a necessary condition to build the central government's credibility. Rodden et al. (2003) argue that subnational fiscal rules and market oversight have been broadly effective in the United States, partly because the discretionary use of federal powers is limited by the American Constitution, but also because the federal government has consistently resisted pressures to provide financial assistance to subnational governments under financial stress since the 19th century.[35] Bailout expectations were contained in Switzerland when the Swiss Supreme Court decided in 2003 that that the canton Valais was not responsible for the liabilities of a highly indebted municipality (Feld et al., 2011). In contrast, the lack of fiscal discipline of the German Länder is often attributed to the bailout expectations created by the implicit federal guarantee of subnational debts in the German equalization system and confirmed by the federal bailouts of Bremen and Saarland in the early 1990s.[36]

VII. Conclusions

Although subnational governments have generally more fiscal authority in federations than in unitary countries, their fiscal powers are constrained by a broad range of arrangements, whose purpose is to contain the deficit bias and strengthen fiscal coordination. This review identified the following main features:

• Constraints on subnational governments are frequent and broad in their scope in federations. The most prevalent form of constraint is fiscal rules, which are often self-imposed by subnational governments. Cooperative arrangements are less widespread, and direct controls rare. But there is a growing interest in using market signals to keep fiscal policy in check, mostly as a complement to institutional arrangements.

• Empirical evidence shows that constraints do have a disciplinary effect on the behavior of sub-central authorities, and they affect financial markets' reactions. However, they cannot substitute for a properly designed system of intergovernmental fiscal relations, and they necessitate a clear commitment of the central government to enforce them.

• Like most federations, the EU fiscal governance framework relies primarily on fiscal rules. The various forms of coordination in Europe, including the European Semester, fall short of a full-fledged cooperative approach. The EU framework does not resort to direct controls from the center either, despite proposals in that direction for countries in breach of the rules. In addition, and possibly because of weaker enforcement mechanisms, supranational rules in the EU tend to be more numerous and extensive in scope than those used in federations.

Appendix A.3.1
Methodology underlying the typology of constraints

In order to categorize subnational constraints, three main criteria are taken into account: whether the constraint is (i) institutional or market-based, (ii) permanent or ad hoc (frequently revised,) and (iii) negotiated or imposed. The combination of these three criteria results in six types of arrangements, presented in the following tree (Figure A.3.1).

In some cases, it may be difficult to distinguish between fiscal rules and other institutional arrangements:

- **Fiscal rule imposed by the center vs. direct control:** As pointed out by Joumard and Kongsrud (2003), there is no clear separation between fiscal rules imposed by the center and direct controls. The main difference is that fiscal rules are "permanent" constraints, whereas direct controls are imposed on an ad hoc basis. More generally, fiscal rules leave more autonomy to subnational governments for four main reasons: (i) rules preclude the micro-management of subnational budgets by the center; (ii) direct controls entail more frequent interventions of the center, while rules are a more permanent and stable form of constraint; (iii) rules are generally less prescriptive as to how the constraint should be met, leaving subnational governments some margins to achieve the objective as they see fit (for instance, expenditure cuts or revenue increases to comply with a budget balance rule); and (iv) targets may be relaxed under specific pre-determined circumstances (escape clauses).
- **Negotiated fiscal rule versus cooperative approach:** Subnational fiscal rules may be self-imposed, imposed by the center, or negotiated (Sutherland et al., 2005). Drawing a clear line between negotiated rules and cooperative arrangements may be difficult. In this chapter, the criterion to distinguish between them is that targets set by cooperative approach are revised on a regular basis (at each renegotiation), while fiscal rule targets are not, or are revised less frequently (Table A.3.1). As argued by Balassone et al. (2002), rules can also be the outcome of negotiations, but once defined they avoid the need for consensus.

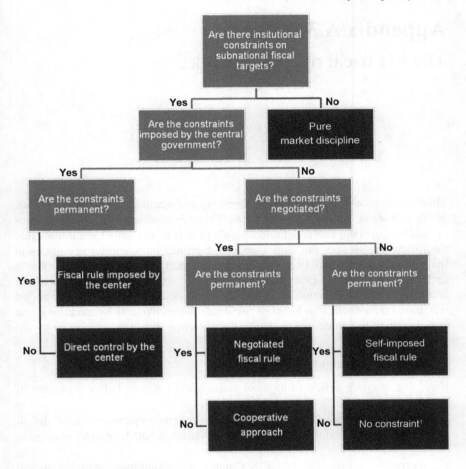

Figure A.3.1 Types of subnational constraints

Source: IMF staff.

[1]Restrictions imposed by subnational governments upon themselves on an ad-hoc basis are not treated as constraints.

Appendix Table A.3.1 Institutional arrangement

	Negotiated	*Not negotiated*
Permanent	Negotiated rule	Rule imposed by the center or self-imposed
Revised regularly	Cooperative approach	Direct control from the center

Source: IMF staff.

Appendix A.3.2
The EU fiscal rule framework[37]

There is a degree of judgment in the inventory and numbering of EU fiscal rules. Some may argue, for instance, that the MTO and expenditure benchmark are conceptually equivalent and constitute a single rule. It is also important to note that the following rules are not simultaneously binding; some apply to countries in the preventive arm of the Pact, while others are in effect when a member state is under Excessive Deficit Procedure (EDP). Finally, European procedures are long and complex, entailing multiple steps; they are presented below in a simplified way based on a distinction between fiscal rule, corrective actions, sanctions, and stepping up of the procedure in case of insufficient effort.

Three percent budget balance rule

Rule. The nominal deficit of member states should remain below 3 percent of GDP.

Corrective action and sanctions. An EDP is generally opened when the deficit exceeds 3 percent of GDP, except when the deviation is both temporary and small:

- Corrective action: The ECOFIN Council sets a timeframe with the annual fiscal effort to be at least 0.5 percent of GDP in structural terms. Deadlines for the correction of the excessive deficit can be extended in case of adverse economic developments. The Council monitors implementation of its recommendations and abrogates the EDP when the excessive deficit is corrected.
- Sanctions resulting from the EDP apply only to euro area members.[38] They are imposed in a gradual way. The initial sanction is a non-interest-bearing deposit of 0.2 percent of GDP with the EU.

Insufficient effort. For euro area members, lack of effective action can lead to closer surveillance and fines. Failure to comply with the Council recommendations to correct the excessive deficit results in a fine of 0.2 percent of GDP. The fine can rise up to 0.5 percent of GDP per year depending on the persistence of the violation.

Sixty percent debt rule

Rule. General government debt should remain below 60 percent of GDP or, if above 60 percent, should diminish sufficiently towards this level. With the November 2011 governance reform, a required annual pace of debt reduction was introduced, based on a benchmark of 1/20th of the distance between the actual debt ratio and the 60 percent threshold. The 1/20th rule is complex and takes into account the cyclical position, as well as the debt prospects two years ahead.

Corrective action and sanctions. If progress in debt reduction is insufficient, an EDP can be opened, and a 0.2 percent of GDP non-interest-bearing deposit may be imposed (for euro area members).

Insufficient effort. The stepping up of the procedure is identical to that following a breach of the 3 percent deficit. Fines can be imposed to euro area countries, ranging from 0.2 to 0.5 percent of GDP.

Medium-term objectives (MTO) in structural terms

Rule. MTOs are fiscal balance targets in structural terms. MTOs are country-specific, but should be set below 0.5 percent of GDP (1 percent for countries with a debt ratio significantly below 60 percent of GDP). The MTO rule is part of the "preventive arm" of the governance framework and applies only to countries outside the EDP. Its main purpose is to ensure that fiscal policy of member states is sustainable, while allowing the operation of automatic stabilizers.

Corrective action. Member states that are not at their MTO should follow an "appropriate" path towards the MTO, which corresponds, in general, to annual efforts of at least 0.5 percent of GDP in structural terms.

Insufficient effort. Lack of action to correct a significant deviation from the MTO or the path towards it (corresponding to at least 0.5 percent of GDP in one year or 0.25 percent on average per year in two consecutive years) can lead to the imposition of an interest-bearing deposit of 0.2 percent of GDP for euro area member states. Assessment is partly based on the expenditure benchmark (see below).

Expenditure benchmark

Rule. For member states at their MTO, the annual growth of primary expenditure – excluding unemployment benefits and subtracting revenue discretionary increases – should not exceed potential nominal GDP growth. For member states not at their MTO, the rule is stricter: the annual growth of primary expenditure should not exceed potential growth minus a "convergence margin," which should ensure sufficient improvement of the structural position to eventually converge towards the MTO.

Corrective action and sanctions. No EDP can be opened when the rule is violated but sanctions can be applied to euro area member states. In particular, in case of significant deviation from the MTO or the path towards it, a 0.2 percent of GDP interest-bearing deposit may be imposed.

Structural balance rule (national rule but supranational requirement)

Rule. The Fiscal Compact requires member states to enshrine the country-specific MTOs in national binding laws by 2014. The structural balance rule is thus a national rule imposed by supranational legislation. It does not supersede the MTO; in fact the MTO and the structural balance rule can have slightly different definitions. More specifically, the Fiscal Compact requires that (i) the structural budget rule be implemented through provisions of "binding force and permanent character, preferably constitutional"; (ii) correction mechanisms (such as debt break) be established to ensure that appropriate action is taken in case of deviation from the structural target or the adjustment path towards it, with escape clauses for exceptional circumstances; (iii) and compliance be monitored by independent institutions.

Corrective action and sanctions. Compliance and enforcement should be carried out at the national level.

Appendix Table A.3.2 Institutional Constraints on Subnational Governments (2012)[1]

Country	Type of constraint	Sector	Enforcement	Fiscal aggregate	Description
Argentina	FR	RG	Negotiated	Expenditure growth	**This rule was suspended by Congress in 2009.** Rules are imposed in states' FRLs which were negotiated with the center. Nominal growth rate of primary spending must be lower than GDP growth; in provinces with debt below 15 percent of current revenue, the restriction applies only to current spending.
Argentina	FR	RG	Negotiated	Debt service	**This rule was suspended by Congress in 2009.** Rules are imposed in states' FRLs which were negotiated with the center. Regions must keep their debt service below 15 percent of current revenue (net of transfers to municipalities).
Argentina	FR	RG	Negotiated	Golden rule	**This rule was suspended by Congress in 2009.** Rules are imposed in states' FRLs which were negotiated with the center. Balanced budget is net of capital expenditure, interests on debt and spending on loans from international organizations.
Australia	FR	RG	Self-imposed	Debt stock	New South Wales and Queensland have a debt rule.
Australia	FR	RG	Self-imposed	Nominal fiscal balance	Queensland has a balanced budget rule.
Australia	FR	RG	Self-imposed	Expenditure	Queensland has an expenditure rule.
Australia	CA	RG	Negotiated	Domestic and foreign borrowing	The Loan Council, composed of the Prime Minister, each State Premier and the Commonwealth Treasurer, is in charge of analyzing and approving financing requirements of each state and the Commonwealth as a whole, as well as monitoring the execution of the decisions.
Austria	CA	RG, LG	Negotiated	Nominal fiscal balance	The Austrian Stability Programme allocates annual deficit/surplus targets to the federal, regional and local governments.
Austria	FR	LG	Imposed	Borrowing	As a general rule, municipalities are only allowed to take loans in order to cover extraordinary expenditure. Each Land has a different set of criteria for debt requiring higher-level approval, and different borrowing limits.

Source: IMF staff.

[1]Acronyms stand for: FR: fiscal rule; CA: cooperative approach; DC: direct control; RG: regional level; LG: local level.

(*Continued*)

Appendix Table A.3.2 (Continued)[1]

Country	Type of constraint	Sector	Enforcement	Fiscal aggregate	Description
Belgium	CA	RG	Negotiated	Nominal fiscal balance	The High Finance Council sets yearly guidelines for the deficit level of federal government, regions, and communities.
Belgium	FR	LG	Imposed	Nominal fiscal balance	Obligation for local governments to balance their budget.
Brazil	FR	RG, LG	Imposed	Wages	In states and municipalities, wage and salary cost may not exceed 60 percent of current revenue.
Brazil	FR	RG, LG	Imposed	Borrowing	Authorization required from the federal government for subnational access to credit. FRL also prohibits governors and mayors from contracting obligations to pay within the last 6 months of their administrations, unless these can be paid off in the reminder of their term in office.
Brazil	FR	RG, LG	Imposed	Debt stock	The Federal Senate sets overall limits for the debt of each level of government (in percent of revenue).
Canada	FR	RG	Self-imposed	Nominal fiscal balance	The four biggest provinces require balanced budget on annual basis.
Canada	FR	RG	Self-imposed	Debt stock	In New Brunswick. Debt ratio to GDP at end year should be lower than at the end of the previous year.
Canada	FR	RG	Self-imposed	Expenditure	Many provinces have expenditure rules.
Canada	DC	LG	Imposed	Domestic borrowing	Strict limits on local borrowing, including prior approval by the provincial government or restrictions to specific purposes, like capital spending.
Germany	FR	RG	Imposed	Structural fiscal balance	Transition toward the debt break rule by 2020, implemented either via structural or nominal budget balance rule.
Germany	FR	LG	Imposed	Nominal fiscal balance	Municipal budget law obliges municipalities to balance their administrative account budget unless they have a deficit in their capital account and/or must make redemption payments. In the latter case, the budget of the administrative account has to be in surplus by this amount.
Germany	FR	RG	Self-imposed	Borrowing	Some Lander have self-imposed borrowing constraints.

Source: IMF staff.

[1]Acronyms stand for: FR: fiscal rule; CA: cooperative approach; DC: direct control; RG: regional level; LG: local level.

Appendix Table A.3.2 (Continued)[1]

Country	Type of constraint	Sector	Enforcement	Fiscal aggregate	Description
India	FR	RG	Imposed	Foreign borrowing	Indian constitution prohibits states from borrowing abroad.
India	DC	RG	Imposed	Domestic borrowing	Indian constitution requires states to obtain central permission for domestic borrowing if they are indebted to the central government or have taken guarantees from the Center. However, there is no limitation regarding borrowing from private entities.
India	FR	RG	Self-imposed	Nominal fiscal balance	Rules are self-imposed and vary by state, but national FRL recommends adoption of state FRLs. In general, states have a fiscal deficit target below 3 percent of gross subnational domestic product.
India	FR	RG	Self-imposed	Debt service	Rules are self-imposed and vary by state, but national FRL recommends adoption of state FRLs. Some states have debt service rules.
India	FR	RG	Self-imposed	Debt stock	Rules are self-imposed and vary by state, but national FRL recommends adoption of state FRLs. Some states have debt stock rules.
Mexico	FR	RG	Imposed	Domestic borrowing	The constitution prohibits domestic borrowing, except for the construction of works intended to produce directly an increase in their revenues.
Mexico	FR	RG	Imposed	Foreign borrowing	Borrowing overseas is not allowed by constitutional amendment.
South Africa	FR	RG	Imposed	Nominal fiscal balance	Balanced budget rule.
South Africa	FR	LG	Imposed	Borrowing	The South African constitution prohibits borrowing for consumption expenditure.
Spain	FR	RG	Imposed	Structural fiscal balance	The annual fiscal balance target depends on cyclical position.

Source: IMF staff

[1] Acronyms stand for: FR: fiscal rule; CA: cooperative approach; DC: direct control; RG: regional level; LG: local level.

(Continued)

Appendix Table A.3.2 (Concluded)[1]

Country	Type of constraint	Sector	Enforcement	Fiscal aggregate	Description
Spain	FR	RG, LG	Imposed	Debt stock	Debt ceiling in percent of GDP. (13 percent of own GDP for regions, 3 percent of own GDP for local governments).
Spain	FR	RG, LG	Imposed	Debt service	Debt service rule.
Spain	FR	RG, LG	Imposed	Expenditure level	Expenditure ceiling.
Spain	FR	RG, LG	Imposed	Expenditure growth	The annual growth of the eligible expenditure cannot exceed the average medium-term growth rate of GDP, in nominal terms.
Spain	FR	LG	Imposed	Nominal fiscal balance	Balanced budget.
Switzerland	FR	RG	Self-imposed	Structural fiscal balance	Most cantons have self-imposed budget balance rules, for instance, on the over-the-cycle balance.
Switzerland	FR	RG	Self-imposed	Nominal fiscal balance	Most cantons have self-imposed budget balance rules, for instance, on the annual overall balance (golden rule in some cases).
Switzerland	FR	LG	Imposed	Nominal fiscal balance	Some cantons can set fiscal rules to control the communes.
Switzerland	FR	RG	Self-imposed	Expenditure level	Fiscal referendum: If the outlays for some project exceed a certain limit, the citizens are asked whether they agree on the spending project.
Switzerland	FR	RG	Self-imposed	Expenditure growth	Expenditure growth below economic growth in some cantons.
United States	FR	RG, LG	Self-imposed	Nominal fiscal balance	In many states, golden rule.
United States	FR	RG, LG	Self-imposed	Expenditure growth	In many states, expenditure growth cap.
United States	FR	RG, LG	Self-imposed	Tax growth	In many states, tax growth cap.
United States	FR	RG, LG	Self-imposed	Debt service and stock	Debt and debt service limits in some states.
United States	FR	RG, LG	Self-imposed	Borrowing	Debt issuance restrictions in some states.

Source: IMF staff.

[1]Acronyms stand for: FR: fiscal rule; CA: cooperative approach; DC: direct control; RG: regional level; LG: local level.

Appendix Table A.3.3 Non-Exhaustive Overview of Measures in Case of Breach (2012)

Country	Type of constraint	Sector	Fiscal aggregate	Breach	Description
Argentina[2]	FR	RG	Debt service, Expenditure growth, golden rule.	Conditions for breach	Non-compliance with any of the three rules.
				Escape clause	
				Sanction	Limits to guarantees and transfers provided by the central government.
				Corrective actions	Regions cannot do new borrowing. Provincial governments must put money into stabilization funds.
Australia	CA	RG	Domestic and foreign borrowing	Conditions for breach	If non-financial operating receipts exceed by more than 2 percent in either direction.
				Escape clause	
				Sanction	
				Corrective actions	States are obliged to provide an explanation to the Loan Council, which will be made public.
Austria	CA	RG, LG	Nominal fiscal balance	Conditions for breach	Non-compliance with targets.
				Escape clause	In case of exceptional burden (serverere economic downturn), revised deficit targets can be negotiated among the government levels.
				Sanction	Once the domestic stability pact is ratified, it fixes the amount of the financial sanctions, which take the form of an interest-bearing deposit. If, in the following year, the respective target is not reached, the deposit is supposed to be transferred to those governments that are in compliance. However, if the target is achieved, the deposit is reimbursed.
				Corrective actions	
Belgium	CA	RG	Nominal fiscal balance	Conditions for breach	Non-compliance with targets.
				Escape clause	
				Sanction	
				Corrective actions	Federal level can impose borrowing limits.

Source: IMF staff.

[1] Acronyms stand for: FR: fiscal rule; CA: cooperative approach; DC: direct control; RG: regional level; LG: local level.

(Continued)

Appendix Table A.3.3 (Continued)[1]

Country	Type of constraint	Sector	Fiscal aggregate	Breach	Description
Belgium	FR	LG	Nominal fiscal balance	Conditions for breach	Non-compliance with targets.
				Escape clause	
				Sanction	
				Corrective actions	Regions are automatically responsible for correcting any slippage. The regional level is responsible for monitoring municipalities and can enforce expenditure cuts or tax increases if necessary.
Brazil	FR	RG, LG	Public wages	Conditions for breach	When total personnel expenditures exceed 95% of the ceiling.
				Escape clause	Public calamities including state of defense, and low growth rate.
				Sanction	Officials who violate the rules may be subject to criminal penalties and fines.
				Corrective actions	New hiring, wage increases and contracting overtime work are suspended.
Brazil	FR	RG, LG	Borrowing	Conditions for breach	Non-compliance with rule.
				Escape clause	Public calamities including state of defense, and low growth rate.
				Sanction	Officials who violate the rules may be subject to criminal penalties, and fines.
				Corrective actions	Any borrowing that has taken place above the threshold ceilings established by the senate is required to be repaid in full, not including interest, which is a penalty to lenders as well as borrowers. In the interim, governments are ineligible for discretionary transfers or federal guarantees and are prohibited from contracting new debt.
Brazil	FR	RG, LG	Debt stock	Conditions for breach	Non-compliance with rule.
				Escape clause	Debt limits are established by the federal senate, though they may be revised in the context of the annual budget and adjusted to macroeconomic conditions.
				Sanction	Officials who violate the rules may be subject to criminal penalties and fines.
				Corrective actions	

Source: IMF staff.

[1] Acronyms stand for: FR: fiscal rule; CA: cooperative approach; DC: direct control; RG: regional level; LG: local level.

Appendix Table A.3.3 (Continued)[1]

Country	Type of constraint	Sector	Fiscal aggregate	Breach	Description
Canada	FR	RG	Nominal fiscal balance	Conditions for breach	Non-compliance with targets.
				Escape clause	In many provinces, legislation builds in exemptions for special events, such as natural disasters, unusual weather conditions, war, or revenue shortfalls.
				Sanction	In four provinces, executive council members and ministries are subject to potential cuts in wages. For example, In British Columbia, withholding of 20 per cent of ministerial salaries, is only paid when certain targets are met (British Columbia, Manitoba, Ontario).
				Corrective actions	
Germany	FR	RG	Structural fiscal balance	Conditions for breach	Non-compliance with rule.
				Escape clause	Natural disasters and emergency situations outside of government control.
				Sanction	Suspension of consolidation payments for those states under consolidation assistance program.
				Corrective actions	If risk for budgetary crisis is established, the Stability Council agrees a consolidation program with the state.
Germany	FR	LG	Nominal fiscal balance	Conditions for breach	Non-compliance with rule.
				Escape clause	
				Sanction	
				Corrective actions	The communal supervisory agencies of the Lander can refuse to authorize the communal budgets. Communes with financial difficulties can be obliged to implement consolidation programs. In some cases, the supervisory agencies can also temporarily take over the administration of the commune.

(Continued)

Source: IMF staff.

[1] Acronyms stand for: FR: fiscal rule; CA: cooperative approach; DC: direct control; RG: regional level; LG: local level.

Appendix Table A.3.3 (Continued)[1]

Country	Type of constraint	Sector	Fiscal aggregate	Breach	Description
India	DC	RG	Domestic borrowing	Conditions for breach	Debt service ratio exceeding 20 percent.
				Escape clause	Exceptional cirumstances (natural disaster, national security) specified by state.
				Sanction	
				Corrective actions	Central government's close monitoring of new borrowing by the state.
Spain	FR	RG, LG	Structural fiscal balance, debt stock, nominal fiscal balance, debt service, expenditure ceiling, and expenditure rule.	Conditions for breach	When debt is above 95 percent of the established limits and/or non-compliance with any of the 6 rules.
				Escape clause	
				Sanction	A failure to present or get approval of a rebalancing plan can lead to fines. In extreme cases, officials may incur penalties if responsible for Spain not achieving European objectives.
				Corrective actions	Breaches must be justified. The first layer in the corrective action mechanism is to require central authorization for long-term borrowing and limit transfers. Regions in non-compliance have to provide annual rebalancing plans and will undergo quarterly monitoring by the central government. In some severe ocassions of disregard for corrective action mechanism, there is a possibility to take region into central administration,
Switzerland	FR	RG	Structural fiscal balance	Conditions for breach	Non-compliance with targets.
				Escape clause	Several cantons define escape clauses, for instance in case of economic slump, or natural catastrophe.
				Sanction	
				Corrective actions	In some cantons, automatic adjustment of cantonal tax rates, or automatic spending cuts.

(Continued)

Source: IMF staff.
[1] Acronyms stand for: FR: fiscal rule; CA: cooperative approach; DC: direct control; RG: regional level; LG: local level.

Appendix Table A.3.3 (Concluded)[1]

Country	Type of constraint	Sector	Fiscal aggregate	Breach	Description
Switzerland	FR	LG	Nominal fiscal balance	Conditions for breach	Non-compliance with targets.
				Escape clause	
				Sanction	
				Corrective actions	In some communes, cantonal supervisory body controls compliance with targets and if the commune does not comply, the canton can take decisions on its behalf.
United States	FR	RG	Debt service and stock	Conditions for breach	Non-compliance with rules.
				Escape clause	
				Sanction	
				Corrective actions	Constitutional amendments or other special votes may be needed to issue new debt.

Source: IMF staff.

[1]Acronyms stand for: FR: fiscal rule; CA: cooperative approach; DC: direct control; RG: regional level; LG: local level.

Notes

1 "Fiscal targets" refer to quantitative targets on revenue, expenditure, and financing aggregates that capture a large share of public finances. Governments control and adjust fiscal targets with a view to meeting "final objectives" of fiscal policy, such as fiscal sustainability or allocative efficiency (Sutherland et al., 2005). For instance, subnational governments can revise legal appropriations mid-year (procedure) in order to contain capital expenditure (fiscal target), as part of the fiscal consolidation effort (final objective).
2 The term "soft budget constraint" describes a situation in which subnational governments do not face a fixed envelope of resources.
3 Article 125 of this Treaty stipulates that: "The Union shall not be liable for or assume the commitments of central governments, regional, local or other public authorities, other bodies governed by public law, or public undertakings of any Member State, without prejudice to mutual financial guarantees for the joint execution of a specific project. A Member State shall not be liable for or assume the commitments of central governments, regional, local or other public authorities, other bodies governed by public law, or public undertakings of another Member State, without prejudice to mutual financial guarantees for the joint execution of a specific project."
4 The gaps that led to the euro crisis are discussed in detail in Chapter 7 of this book as well as in Allard et al., 2013.
5 Other motivations include reducing inter-jurisdiction competition, preventing tax exporting, and limiting distortions in allocation decisions (Carlsen, 1998; Sutherland et al., 2005).
6 These bodies often have multiple functions, including the coordination of fiscal policy targets, the harmonization of budget processes, definition of common standards, monitoring of fiscal outcomes, and at times revenue assignment and sharing.
7 This typology draws on and extends the classification proposed by Ter-Minassian and Craig (1997) in the context of subnational borrowing controls.
8 Fiscal rules are defined as constraints that cannot be frequently changed (IMF, 2009b; Schaechter et al., 2012). The "permanent" nature of fiscal rules is what distinguishes them from annual budget targets and from multiyear targets subject to regular revisions such as medium-term budget frameworks (Debrun et al., 2008).
9 Constraints mandated by federal legislation are also recorded as "imposed by the center."
10 The golden rule in effect until 2009 was not enforced.
11 The secondary role of direct controls reflects the balance of powers between the central government and subnational entities in federal systems. Direct controls may also be less warranted in federations than in unitary countries, because subnational governments are less likely to expect bailouts from the center (Von Hagen and Eichengreen, 1996). This is because states have sufficient own resources and tax authority to cope with unexpected shocks that affect their economy. By contrast, subnational governments in unitary countries are generally more dependent on transfers and may enter into a fiscal crisis when faced with even small adverse shocks.
12 Borrowing constraints apply to gross borrowing flows. Hence, they differ from debt ceilings (stock concept), and fiscal balance targets (net concept).
13 At the time of the drafting of this chapter, most Länder were still in the process of designing their rules, although the debt brake principle has been in the Constitution since 2009.
14 A *control account* is one in which deviations from a structural budget balance target are stored. When the accumulated deviation exceeds a threshold, improvements in the structural balance are required within a pre-defined time frame to undo these deviations.
15 Balanced budget rules are exclusive of accumulation or withdrawals from the RDFs.

16 This section focuses on controls introduced in case of breach. Chapter 6 discusses ad hoc controls related to the resolution of subnational fiscal crises.
17 Subnational governments in difficult situations are more likely to receive additional support than to pay fines (Joumard and Kongsrud, 2003).
18 This section compares the European supranational rules with the constraints imposed by the federal level on subnational entities. The comparison does not extend to self-imposed subnational constraints (whose equivalent, for Europe, would be the national rules) or constraints imposed by the states/regions on local governments.
19 Although the MTO and the structural balance rule are closely related, they constitute distinct constraints.
20 Admittedly, such restrictions are less needed in the federations where constraints are self-imposed by subnational governments.
21 The initial rules were the 60 percent debt cap, the three percent deficit ceiling, and the requirement that medium-term budget positions should be "close to balance or in surplus."
22 In the mid-1990s, there was, on average, one national rule per country in the European Community.
23 During the "European semester" in the spring, EU countries receive feedback from other member states on their medium-term fiscal plans (peer review). The Commission assesses stability programs and proposes country-specific recommendations in July. In October, euro area member states also must submit draft budgets to the Commission, which analyzes their consistency with the Stability and Growth Pact requirements and with the European Semester recommendations.
24 Even when EU rules are breached and corrective actions/sanctions are triggered, no European institution gets direct authority over a member state's budget.
25 Subnational borrowing is indirectly constrained by budget balance rules.
26 In India, the national FRL recommends that states adopt their own FRLs with self-imposed rules, but the national FRL does not impose subnational constraints.
27 The U.S. federation presents three characteristics that facilitate the econometric analysis: constraints vary across states; many rules have been in effect for a long period of time; and control variables are available (Inman, 1996).
28 Poterba (1994) uses the strength indicator developed by the Advisory Commission on Intergovernmental Relations (1987), which catalogs state balanced-budget provisions and assigns a score between one and ten to the stringency of these rules.
29 In the United States, each state has its own constitution.
30 Fiscal councils are independent public institutions aimed at promoting sustainable public finances through various functions, including public assessments of fiscal plans and performance and the evaluation or provision of macroeconomic and budgetary forecasts.
31 In addition, the correlation between fiscal institutions and fiscal outcomes is difficult to interpret. It is possible that this correlation reflects the effect of an omitted third variable; that is, the voters' preference for fiscal restraint.
32 The cross-country empirical literature is less conclusive, as well as less relevant to, our analysis, as existing studies do not specifically consider the sub-sample of federations and generally limit their analysis to borrowing constraints.
33 Other problems include: the excessive bargaining power of large states/regions in federations with regional disparities; inconsistencies and loopholes resulting from political compromises; the lack of stability, transparency, and predictability of the fiscal framework; unclear and overlapping assignments; and the greater scope for free riding.
34 This may happen in several contexts. Local authorities may receive bailout transfers from the center; get subsidized loans from public banks or state-owned enterprises; run arrears to their suppliers or creditors; or underfund public sector pensions.
35 Other factors can contribute to harden the subnational budget constraint: the political system should not over-represent local interests in the central legislature; spending and revenue assignments should be clearly defined and duplication minimized; transfer

dependency should be reduced to give local governments more autonomy in the face of economic shocks; and some key sensitive expenditure responsibilities should remain central government responsibility, especially in the presence of mandates and standards.

36 See Chapter 6 for details. The German Constitutional Court subsequently rejected a similar request by Berlin, arguing that it did not qualify for such transfers as it was still able to reduce spending and increase revenues without federal support.

37 This Appendix proposes a simplified overview of the EU fiscal governance framework. More detailed information can be found on the European Commission website and publications (European Commission, 2013).

38 EU Member States that are not part of the euro area do not face sanctions in the form of a financial deposit or a fine. But for the beneficiaries of structural funds (some of which are non-euro area countries), failure to comply may lead to the suspension of commitments.

References

Advisory Commission for Intergovernmental Relations (ACIR), 1987, "Fiscal Discipline in the Federal System: Experience of the States," (Washington: U.S. Government Printing Office).

Allard, C., P. Koeva Brooks, J. C. Bluedorn, F. Bornhorst, K. Christopherson, F. Ohnsorge, and T. Poghosyan, 2013, "Toward a Fiscal Union for the Euro Area," IMF Staff Discussion Note SDN/13/09.

Ambrosanio M. F., and M. Bordignon, 2007, "Internal Stability Pacts: The European Experience," European Economic Governance Monitor, Papers.

Balassone, F., D. Franco, and S. Zotteri, 2002, "Fiscal Rules for Subnational Governments: What Lessons from EMU Countries?" prepared for conference on Rule-based macroeconomic policies in emerging market economies, IMF and World Bank, Oaxaca-Mexico.

———, 2007, "Rainy day funds: Can they make a difference in Europe?" Occasional paper No. 11, Bank of Italy.

Bayoumi, T., M. Goldstein, and G. Woglom, 1995, "Do credit markets discipline sovereign Borrowers: Evidence from U.S. States," *Journal of Money Credit and Banking*, Vol. 27, pp.1046–1059.

Bohn H., and R. P. Inman, 1996, "Balanced Budget Rules and Public Deficits: Evidence from the U.S. States," NBER Working Paper No. 5533.

Braun, M., and M. Tommasi, 2002, "Fiscal Rules for Subnational Governments. Some Organizing Principles and Latin American Experiences," Working Papers 44, Universidad de San Andres, Departamento de Economia.

Cabasés, F., P. Pascual Arzoz, and J. Vallés-Giménez, 2007, "The effectiveness of institutional borrowing restrictions: Empirical evidence from Spanish municipalities," *Public Choice*, Vol. 131, No. 3, pp. 293–313.

Carlsen, F., 1998, "Central Regulation of Local Authorities," Public Finance Review, Vol. 26, No.4, pp. 304–326.

Clemens, J., and S. Miran, 2010, "The Effects of State Budget Cuts on Employment and Income," Working Paper, Harvard University. Available at http://www.people.fas.harvard.edu/~miran/statecuts.pdf

Debrun, X., L. Moulin, A. Turri ni, J. Ayuso-i-Casals, and M. Kumar, 2008, "Tied to the Mast? National Fiscal Rules in the European Union," *Economic Policy*, Vol. 23, No. 54, pp. 297–362.

Eichengreen, B., 1992, *Should the Maastricht Treaty Be Saved? (Princeton Studies in International Finance)*(Princeton: Princeton University).

European Commission, 2012, "Fiscal frameworks across Member States: Commission services country fiches," from the 2011 EPC peer review," Occasional Paper N.91.

———, 2013, "Vade Mecum on the Stability and Growth Pact," Occasional Papers 151.

Feld, L., A. Kalb, and M.D. Moessinger, and S. Osterloh, 2011, "Sovereign Bond Market Reactions to Fiscal Rules and No-Bailout Clauses – The Swiss Experience," Discussion Paper No. 13-034, Centre for European Economic Research, available at http://ftp.zew.de/pub/zew-docs/dp/dp13034.pdf.

Goldstein, M., and G. Woglom, 1992, "Market-based fiscal discipline in monetary unions: Evidence from the U.S. municipal bond market" in *Establishing a Central Bank: Issues in Europe and Lessons from the United States*, edited by Canzoneri, V. Grilli, and P. Masson (Cambridge UK: Cambridge University Press).

IMF (International Monetary Fund), 2009a, "Macro Policy Lessons for a Sound Design of Fiscal Decentralization," IMF Board Paper SM/09/208. (Washington: International Monetary Fund).

———, 2009b, "Fiscal Rules: Anchoring Expectations for Sustainable Public Finances," IMF Board Paper SM/09/274. (Washington: International Monetary Fund).

———, 2010, "Spain: 2010 Article IV Consultation Staff Report," (Washington: International Monetary Fund).

———, 2012, "Switzerland: 2012 Article IV Consultation Staff Report," (Washington: International Monetary Fund).

———, 2013, "The Functions and Impact of Fiscal Councils," IMF Policy Paper. (Washington: International Monetary Fund).

Inman, R.P., 1996, "Do Balanced Budget Rules Work? U.S. Experience and Possible Lessons for the EMU," NBER Working Paper No.5838.

Joumard, I., and P.M. Kongsrud, 2003, "Fiscal Relations across Government Levels," OECD Economics Department Working Papers 375 (Paris: Organization for Economic Cooperation and Development).

Kishore, A., and A. Prasad, 2007, "Indian Subnational Finances: Recent Performance," IMF Working Paper 07/205 (Washington: International Monetary Fund).

Landon, S., 2003, "Sub-National Government Borrowing in Federal Systems: Evidence from Argentina and Mexico," in *Fiscal Relations in Federal Countries: Four Essays*, edited by P. Boothe (Ottawa: The Forum of Federations), pp. 53–68.

Liu, L., and S.B. Webb, 2011, "Laws for fiscal responsibility for subnational discipline: International experience," World Bank Policy Research Working Paper No. 5587 (Washington: The World Bank).

Lowry, R., and J. Alt, 1997, "A Visible Hand? Bond Markets, Political Parties, Balanced Budget Laws, and State Government Debt," Economics & Politics, Vol. 13, Issue 1: pp. 49–72.

Lübke, A., 2005, "Fiscal Discipline between Levels of Government in Germany," OECD *Journal on Budgeting*, Vol. 5, No. 2.

Lutz, B., and G. Follette, 2012, "Fiscal Rules, What Does the American Experience Tell Us?" *Finance and Economics Discussion Series 2012–38*, Board of Governors of the Federal Reserve System (U.S.).

McNichol, E., and K. Boadi, 2011, "Why and How States Should Strengthen Their Rainy Day Funds: Recession Highlighted Importance of Funds and Need for Improvements," Center on Budget and Policy Priorities.

National Conference of State Legislatures, 2010, "NCSL Fiscal Brief: State Balanced Budget Provisions."

Oates, W.E., 2006, "On Theory and Practice of Fiscal Decentralization," IFIR Working Paper Series, 2006–05 (Lexington: Institute for Federalism & Intergovernmental Relations).

Poterba, J., 1994, "State Responses to Fiscal Crises: The Effects of Budgetary Institutions and Politics," *Journal of Political Economy*, Vol. 102, pp. 799–821.

———, 1996, "Do Budget Rules Work?" NBER Working Paper No. 5550.

———, and K. Rueben, 1999, "State Fiscal Institutions and the U.S. Municipal Bond Market," in *Fiscal Institutions and Fiscal Performance*, edited by J. Poterba and J. von Hagen (Chicago: University of Chicago Press).

———, and K. Rueben, 2001, "Fiscal News, State Budget Rules, and Tax-Exempt Bond Yields," *Journal of Urban Economics*, Vol. 50, pp. 537–562.

Rodden, J., 2002, "The Dilemma of Fiscal Federalism: Grant and Fiscal Performance around the World," *American Journal of Political Science*, Vol. 46, pp. 670–687.

———, G. S. Eskeland, and J. Litvack, 2003, *Fiscal Decentralization and the Challenge of Hard Budget Constraint* (Cambridge: The MIT Press).

———, and E. Wibbels, 2010, "Fiscal Decentralization and the Business Cycle: An Empirical Study of Seven Federations," *Economics and Politics*, Vol. 22, No. 1.

Rueben, K., 1995, "Tax Limitation and Government Growth: The Effect of State Tax and Expenditure Limits on State and Local Government." Mimeo, Department of Economics, MIT.

Schaechter, A., T. Kinda, N. Budina, and A. Weber, 2012, "Fiscal Rules in Response to the Crisis – Toward the 'Next-Generation' Rules: A New Dataset," IMF Working Paper 12/187 (Washington: International Monetary Fund). Available at http://ww.imf.org/external/pubs/ft/ wp/2012/wp12187.pdf

Stalder, K., and S. Röhrs, 2005, "Answers to OECD Questionnaire: Fiscal rules for cantons and communes" (St. Gallen: Universität St. Gallen Insitut für Finanzwissenschaft und Finanzrecht).

Strauch, R. R., and J. Von Hagen, 2001, "Formal Fiscal Restraints and Budget Processes as Solutions to a Deficit and Spending Bias in Public Finances: U.S. Experience and Possible Lessons for EMU," ZEI Working Papers B 14, ZEI (Center for European Integration Studies, University of Bonn).

Sutherland, D., I. Joumard, and R. Price, 2005, "Sub-Central Government Fiscal Rules," *OECD Economic Studies*, No. 41 (Paris: Organization for Economic Cooperation and Development).

Ter-Minassian, T., 2007, "Fiscal Rules for Subnational Governments: Can They Promote Fiscal Discipline?" *OECD Journal on Budgeting*, Vol. 6, No. 3, pp. 1–11.

———, and J. Craig, 1997, "Control of Subnational Government Borrowing," in *Fiscal Federalism in Theory and Practice*, edited by T. Ter-Minassian (Washington: International Monetary Fund).

Von Hagen, J., 1991, "A Note on the Empirical Effectiveness of Formal Fiscal Restraints," *Journal of Public Economics*, Vol. 44, pp. 199–211.

———, 2012, "European Common Pool Pools and Their Governance, A Politico-Economic Perspective of the European Public Debt Crisis." Available at *http://www.hazine.gov.tr/File/?path=ROOT%2FDocuments%2FGenel+%C4%B0%C3%A7erik%2FvonHAGEN.pdf*

———, and B. Eichengreen, 1996, "Federalism, Fiscal Restraints, and European Monetary Union," *The American Economic Review*, Vol. 86 (2), Papers and Proceedings of the Hundredth and Eighth Annual Meeting of the American Economic Association San Francisco, pp. 134–138.

Webb, S. B., 2004. "Fiscal Responsibility Laws for Subnational Discipline: The Latin American Experience" World Bank Policy Research Working Paper No. 3309 (Washington: The World Bank).

4 Budgeting, accounting, and reporting

Israel Fainboim, Almudena Fernandez,
Manal Fouad, Duncan Last, Mario Pessoa,
and Sami Ylaoutinen, with inputs from
Ralph Schmitt-Nilson

I. Introduction

As discussed in Chapter 3, institutional constraints imposed on the design of sub-national fiscal policies, such as fiscal rules, play an important role in ensuring prudent fiscal management at all government levels. To be successful they need to be underpinned by robust public financial management (PFM) systems that ensure that subnational governments (SNGs) follow sound budgeting practices both "upstream" (with reliance on a shared and realistic macroeconomic outlook) and "downstream" (timely reporting and monitoring, disclosed according to har-monized and transparent standards, and subject to independent audits to confirm that accounts are reliable and fairly reflect the financial situation).

This chapter maps the role played by the central government and coordinating institutions in the formulation, execution, and accountability of subnational bud-gets in selected federal states.[1] Section II presents the elements of a framework for sound public financial management across government levels. Sections III to V draw on country experiences to analyze the various components of the bud-get cycle, from formulation to execution and compliance processes. Section VI examines the role of two cross-cutting institutions in these processes: intergovern-mental coordination bodies, and accounting standards and budget classification. Section VII looks at European Union (EU) practices, and Section VIII concludes.

II. A framework for sound fiscal management across government levels

Various institutions affect the soundness of fiscal management across government levels in federations. They range from the adoption of consistent macro-fiscal assumptions and indicators for medium-term projections to the harmonization of accounting standards for reporting. Most federations have launched initiatives to harmonize standards and consolidate information – to avoid unanticipated demand for resources or the emergence of unidentified contingent liabilities. For federa-tions to function sustainably, a sound budget cycle must be in place at all govern-ment levels, supported by an effective oversight at the central level. A framework of relevant components is presented in Figure 4.1.

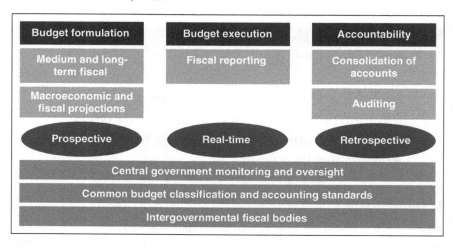

Figure 4.1 Features of sound fiscal and budgetary management and oversight in federations

A sound budget system comprises common prospective, real-time, and retrospective features that should be applied at all levels of government:

- Shared medium- and long-term fiscal objectives that guide budget formulation and help prioritize budgetary choices.
- Shared macroeconomic assumptions to ensure consistent budgetary projections across all levels of government.
- Timely and frequent in-year fiscal reports at each level to monitor fiscal developments, including emerging fiscal risks.
- Timely production of annual accounts and financial statements at each government level and their auditing by an independent external auditor, to underpin accountability and governance standards throughout the federation.
- Consolidated in-year fiscal reports and annual accounts, and financial statements for at least the general government sector and preferably the public sector, with clearly assigned responsibility for performing this task, to provide timely and comprehensive federation-wide fiscal information for decision-makers.

These features should be underpinned by institutional arrangements and common standards, notably:

- Central government monitoring of SNGs' budgets and borrowing at different stages of the process provides early warning of risks as well as possible financial distress in a particular SNG, allowing timely action to maintain aggregate general government fiscal stability.

- Intergovernmental coordination bodies, a common feature in most federations, articulate and coordinate fiscal targets, revenue sharing arrangements, and accounting standards.[2]
- Legal and institutional arrangements for harmonizing budget classification and accounting standards to facilitate the preparation of consistent fiscal information.

Table 4.1 summarizes the situation in the 13 federations of our sample and the EU along four dimensions. It shows that few federations in the sample have homogenous budget processes across levels of government. At the budget formulation stage, the use of consultative or formalized arrangements between the central government (CG) and SNGs is relatively common for medium- and long-term fiscal objectives, but less common when it comes to macroeconomic indicators and fiscal

Table 4.1 Summary of selected PFM practices across federations

	Coordination of medium-term and long-term objectives?	Who defines macroeconomic indicators and macro-fiscal projections?	What is the mandate of the CG's supreme audit institution?	Who sets accounting rules and standards?
Argentina	Limited medium-term at SNG level	SNG	Transfers to SNG	Law
Australia	Consultative	SNG	Only CG	Standards Board
Austria	Consultative	SNG	Covers SNGs	SNG
Belgium	Consultative	Coordinated	Covers SNGs	SNG
Brazil	Formalized	Coordinated	Transfers to SNG	Law
Canada	Independent	SNG	Only CG	SNG/ Standards Board
Germany	Consultative	Coordinated	Transfers to SNG	SNG
India	Formalized	Coordinated	Covers SNGs	CG
Mexico	Limited medium-term at SNG level	SNG	Transfers to SNG	Law
South Africa	Formalized	CG	Covers SNGs	CG
Spain	Formalized	CG	Covers SNGs	SNG
Switzerland	Voluntary	SNG	Only CG	SNG
United States	Independent	SNG	Only CG	SNG/ Standards Board
EU requirements	Formalized	Member states	EU budget and structural funds	Member states and Eurostat

projections: in South Africa and Spain (Spain, 2012), the definition of these indicators is actually made by the central government. There is somewhat more homogeneity "downstream": in the majority of countries in the sample, the supreme audit institutions cover the central government as well as SNGs, or at least the resources transferred by the central government to SNGs, and accounting rules and standards are defined by a national law, a national accounting standard board, or the central government itself. In contrast, harmonization of budget processes in the EU is largely limited to common medium- and long-term objectives and fiscal reporting requirements (European Parliament and European Council 2011a, 2011b, 2011c, 2011d, 2011e, 2013a, 2013b). However, efforts are underway to increase the comparability and coverage of fiscal data across member states.

Some countries have formalized the above practices and arrangements in their legal frameworks – either in an overarching fiscal responsibility law or in their local government law (Brazil, 2000; Argentina, 2004).[3] Others such as Mexico (Mexico, 2006) and Spain (Spain, 2003a), where SNGs autonomy is more deep-seated and historical, continue to manage their SNGs budget process through a more fragmented regulatory process, while a few (e.g., Switzerland) retain an essential informal process.

Sections III–VI detail the country practices for each of these features.

III. Budget formulation

Coordination between the central government and SNGs during budget formulation can take many forms. At one end of the spectrum is information exchange: from the central government – the projected revenue pool to be shared, any equalization resources, and any tied or earmarked grants; and from the SNGs – their expenditure plans and own-revenue projections. At the other end of the spectrum, the central government may issue stringent instructions to SNGs on how to formulate their budgets. Requiring all levels of government to set out their medium- and long-term fiscal objectives can help in understanding policy priorities beyond the usual annual budget horizon. The central government can also play an active role in disseminating information, communicating the country's strategic priorities, and ensuring that the general government's fiscal strategy and targets are understood by SNGs.

A. Coordination of medium- and long-term fiscal objectives

Medium- and long-term fiscal objectives should set out general government policy priorities and provide corresponding medium- to long-term projections of revenues and expenditures. For federations, shared medium- and long-term fiscal objectives can be an effective tool for coordinating the budget dialogue between central and subnational governments. The fiscal objectives define a common vision about the future fiscal direction of the country as a whole, given the main fiscal challenges and areas of priority. The associated budget frameworks should establish common targets for macroeconomic and social indicators at both subnational and national levels – GDP growth, demographics, energy generation and consumption, provision of infrastructure, education, health, and other public policies.

The approach to intergovernmental coordination of medium-term fiscal frameworks, investment planning strategies, and the annual budget varies widely across the sample of federations under consideration in this book. The coordination practices broadly fall into three groups: formal coordination, whereby the central government or intergovernmental council discusses with SNGs the main medium- and long-term fiscal objectives; independent arrangements, where SNGs can decide these objectives independently; and less formal consultative mechanisms, falling in between the two. Table 4.1 shows that in our sample, coordination is either formalized or consultative, with only a few federations having full SNGs independence.

South Africa is a good example of the use of formal provisions to ensure coordination. The National Treasury must ensure that the provincial budgets follow the form and timing prescribed by national legislation (notably the Public Finance Management Act, PFM Act – South Africa, 1999) and show the sources of revenue and the way the proposed expenditure will comply with national legislation, as outlined by the constitution. The PFM Act prescribes a more detailed set of responsibilities for provincial treasuries, including the obligation to prepare detailed, multi-year revenue and expenditure projections each year. These projections – the Medium Term Financial Framework – must be tabled in the National Assembly and in provincial legislatures. At least quarterly, the provincial treasury must submit to the National Treasury a statement of revenue and expenditure with regard to the provincial revenue fund.

In Mexico (Mexico, 1978), a significant portion of SNGs' resources comes in the form of sector specific transfers from the central government, which, together with tight central government control over borrowing, curtails the SNGs' ability to formulate their own independent medium- to long-term fiscal strategies. In practice, medium-term frameworks are not well developed at the SNGs level.

In Brazil (Brazil, 2000), coordination relies on a mix of formal requirements on SNGs and incentives/sanctions to ensure respect of fiscal targets: the states are obliged to prepare a fixed four-year program-based plan, the same length as the mandate of state governors, and therefore strongly linked to political responsibility – effective coordination of these plans is particularly critical where projects are co-financed by the federal and state budgets. However, if the states fail to achieve their aggregate fiscal targets, the central government must adjust its own target by cutting the central government budget. Monthly monitoring of the fiscal targets is essential to allow the central government to adjust its own targets as needed.

Other federations rely more on consultative or collaborative mechanisms.[4]

In Australia, collaboration on policy development and service delivery as well as the implementation of economic and social reforms in areas of national importance is governed by the Intergovernmental Agreement on Federal Financial Relations (Australia, 2008), which sets out various levels of institutional coordination across governments, the results of which are set out in the National Budget documents.

In Belgium, despite being an advisory body by law, the High Council of Finance has, over time, become *the* institution which sets budgetary objectives due to the quality of its work and its politically balanced composition. The Council monitors fiscal policy of the regional governments and recommends, each year, a coordinated fiscal plan for the various SNGs (Belgium, 2006; Bogaert et al., 2006).

In Germany, while each level of government is expected to prepare its own five-year plan (Knörzer, 2008), the legal framework provides for a coordination mechanism – the Stability Council, which replaced the older Financial Planning Council in 2009 (Germany, 1949; Lübke, 2008; Zipfel, 2011b). It sets broad macro-fiscal targets for the medium term and acts as a surveillance body. The Council projects the development of public debt for the Bund (federal government) and the Länder. Länder have to provide the Council with a "standard projection" for the seven years ahead and a set of indicators about the future development of their public finances. These indicators are used to identify fiscal problems at an early stage.

Switzerland relies on a voluntary approach – state and local governments are informed about the central government's fiscal policy and macroeconomic assumptions and, although there is no formal obligation to use them or to provide medium-term frameworks, all state and large local governments (mainly cities) prepare detailed four-year medium-term expenditure and revenue frameworks.

In contrast, Canada and the United States have generally avoided any form of joint multiyear planning across jurisdictions.

B. Macroeconomic and fiscal projections

Credible and timely macroeconomic and fiscal projections are key to ensuring that budget decisions at all levels are well informed. Using the same or consistent assumptions for macro-fiscal projections at all levels of government should enhance consistency and uniformity and facilitate the production of a national macro-fiscal framework.

Preparation of the macroeconomic assumptions. Macroeconomic indicators of common interest across all levels of government include: GDP growth data and forecasts – national GDP data should suffice except where regional size or activity is significant and SNGs have significant own-revenue generating powers, in which case regional GDP data is desirable to cater for regional variations; inflation; interest rates; and exchange rates. Responsibility for the production and dissemination of these data at the national level varies from the national ministry of finance to an intergovernmental body (where one has been established) to an independent institution. However, the degree to which SNGs have to adhere to a "nationally" defined set of macroeconomic indicators varies considerably across jurisdictions – from mandatory use (in the case of South Africa, 2009), to consensus-based use (often the case where an intergovernmental fiscal or budgetary council has been established), to independent setting (as in the case of the United States and Canada). With the exception of South Africa, coordination in the use of macroeconomic assumptions does not rely much on formal provisions, although in most cases SNGs tend to follow nationally produced macroeconomic projections, augmented, where capacity exists, by regional projections of key indicators such as GDP.

Preparation of the fiscal projections. Fiscal projections rely on readily available macroeconomic data. The two aggregate fiscal indicators of particular relevance to federations are the aggregate revenue base to be used for sharing between central and subnational governments, and the deficit target. Chapter 3 of this book discusses institutional constraints on SNGs deficits and borrowing capacity. As discussed in Chapter 1, revenue sharing is usually prescribed in a law (or sometimes even the Constitution) which defines the base (or individual taxes) to be shared and how the sharing formula is to be established.[5] Projecting the aggregate revenue base for revenue sharing can be a sensitive issue in federations, which is why in many federations an independent body – a local government finance or grants commission – has been set up to vet projections and establish equitable sharing, both vertical – between central government and SNGs – and horizontal – among SNGs. This independent body is also frequently entrusted with reviewing and adjusting the formula at given intervals (most often every five to seven years). In Argentina, which does not have such an independent body, it is noteworthy that revenue sharing among SNGs is highly discretionary and influenced by political considerations.

The macroeconomic assumptions and fiscal projections generated by the central government can be useful for SNGs as they can utilize this information in their own budget planning. However, generally speaking, they are under no obligation to do so. Table 4.1 shows, for the countries in our sample, the degree to which the central government determines the macroeconomic assumptions and fiscal projections used by SNGs – this ranges from "mandatory" use of central government projections, to agreeing projections through a "coordinated" approach, to each SNG having "independent" authority to choose its own projections. South Africa imposes mandatory use of central government macroeconomic and fiscal indicators; its National Treasury develops a Medium Term Fiscal Framework and uses it to issue Guidelines to Provinces which include, among other things, three-year projections for macroeconomic variables and fiscal projections that the Provinces are obliged to use in planning their own budgets (South Africa, 2009). As EU members, Austria, Belgium, Germany, and Spain must submit their Stability Program each year, by the end of April, which specifies the macroeconomic and fiscal projections of general government as a whole (Austria, 2012; Belgium, 2013; Germany, 2013; Spain, 2014). Therefore, in these countries, SNGs cannot adopt a fiscal scenario that contradicts the Stability Program – although there is evidence that compliance has not been fully observed. In other countries, the ability of any SNG to prepare its own macroeconomic projections is directly linked to capacities at that level – there is a clear tendency to use central government projections where capacity is weaker.

In order to be effective, macroeconomic assumptions and fiscal projections – in particular SNG revenue projections – should ideally be communicated by the central government to SNGs in the early stages of budget preparation according to a timetable set out in the budget calendar.

IV. Budget execution: Fiscal reporting

Once SNGs start executing their budgets, the central government's influence is generally substantially curtailed. However, the importance of timely in-year and annual monitoring of fiscal developments at the general government level is increasingly recognized in federations, with the possible exception of the United States. The adoption of fiscal rules and the impact of the global financial crisis on SNGs have also raised the profile of timely monitoring reports providing early warning of deviations from fiscal rules or of local finances coming under stress.[6] Monitoring reports are also becoming more frequent (i.e., they occur at more stages of budget execution) and more comprehensive, driven by the need to monitor and contain the evolution of SNG debt and contingent liabilities, and to monitor expenditure arrears where control has traditionally been more elusive.

Monitoring practices, however, vary widely in our sample. The effectiveness of monitoring arrangements, whether by units at the federal level or by coordinating councils, depends on their capacity (both in terms of analytical skills and of overall staffing levels) to analyze reports and raise red flags, the availability of SNGs fiscal data, and the political willingness to address any emerging problem in a timely manner.

In addition, external pressures to establish comparability and to enhance the transparency of government operations have led federations to adopt common reporting standards and formats, based on similar budget and accounting classifications across all levels of governments. This strengthens the central government's ability to oversee and monitor SNGs budget execution. In many federations, this has been achieved through the adoption of Fiscal Responsibility Laws (FRLs) or stability pacts (Box 4.1). Some federations have bucked the

---

Box 4.1   Trends in fiscal reporting obligations under Fiscal Responsibility Laws (FRLs) and stability pacts

In *Australia*, the 1998 Charter of Budget Honesty prescribes mid-year economic and fiscal outlook reports covering the general government. The implementation of this law was facilitated by earlier work on harmonizing general government reporting requirements to the GFS standard.

In *Brazil*, the 2000 FRL requires that each level of government prepares and publishes bi-monthly, quarterly, and annual fiscal reports within 30 days after end of period. Publication of fiscal information for central and SNGs is now well established and routine. Under the FRL states and municipalities that fail to publish their fiscal reports are not allowed to receive voluntary, non-obligatory transfers from the central government or to access banking credit, and the SNG head may be sanctioned and barred from elections.

In *Mexico*, the 2006 Budget and Fiscal Responsibility Law, the 2007 Integral Fiscal Reform, and the 2008 Government Accounting Law increased the volume of information to be published by all levels of government:

quarterly reports, not later than one month after the end of the period. The states should provide almost the same extensive information as the federal government (including financial statements, information on contingent liabilities, overall debt and debt service, detailed budget information, and performance indicators).

In *Spain*, the 2012 Organic Law on budget stability and financial sustainability introduced monthly reporting requirements for budget execution for regions, and quarterly reporting for municipalities. The accounting and budgeting information should contain sufficient information to verify the financial situation and the compliance with the fiscal goals and to facilitate the link between the budget information and the national accounts in line with ESA 95.

Other European federations (*Austria, Belgium,* and *Germany*) have also recently introduced country-level stability pacts or laws that bind SNGs to share responsibility for Maastricht obligations. These pacts or laws prescribe reporting obligations that facilitate monitoring, although the reports are generally more aggregated than those prescribed in FRLs. More substantive fiscal reporting is mostly produced by independent statistical offices but with a significant delay.

In *Argentina* the FRL defines the content and timeliness to publish fiscal reports by SNGs, including budget execution, debt, number of civil servants, and relevant financial indicators.

---

trend, most notably the United States, where many states consider any imposition of common reporting standards as incompatible with their constitutionally derived autonomy. Canada, on the other hand, is able to routinely collect and report both disaggregated and consolidated government finance statistics without recourse to a legal requirement (Statistics Canada, 2014). At the other end of the spectrum, South Africa's and India's approaches are closer to those of unitary governments, in that the central government has a prescriptive role (India, 2003; South Africa, 1997).

V. Accountability

Two components have been emblematic of the efforts to build up better accountability processes in federations: the consolidation of accounts across government levels (whose objective is to gather fiscal information at a level that allows comparability with macroeconomic and fiscal objectives and projections) and external independent auditing systems (whose role is to ensure that fiscal information is reliable).

A. Consolidation of accounts across government levels

Many federations prepare consolidated annual financial statements, but these may take many months to become available, and they are rarely prepared with fiscal accountability in mind (Box 4.2). They are rather produced for statistical purposes (Brazil, Switzerland, and the United States) and inter-governmental monitoring (Australia).[7] All EU members (including all four in the sample of federations covered in this book) are required to submit general government financial statistics to Eurostat on an annual basis using the European System of National and Regional Accounts standard (ESA95) methodology (see Box 4.2).[8] It is generally not mandatory for the supreme audit institution to produce an audit report on the general government consolidated accounts. In the United States, there is no mandatory consolidation, but the Economic Report of the President produces general government tables based on the National Income and Product Accounts (United States, 2014), and the Federal Reserve produces general government borrowing and debt tables (Federal Reserve, 2014).

A recurrent issue is the unwillingness of reporting entities to release pre-audited financial statements for consolidation, in the event that adjustments would have to be made as a result of the audit (in some countries sanctions may be imposed if released accounts are later found to be incorrect). This can lead to long delays, and countries often rely on more expedient statistical aggregates to meet annual reporting requirements. However, while countries such as Australia do this quite efficiently, others take much longer to consolidate their government finance statistics – Germany, for example, takes nearly one year to release consolidated general government financial statistics. In addition, purely statistical consolidation is generally not sufficient for fiscal monitoring, particularly if consolidated accounting data are needed for revenue sharing.[9]

B. Auditing

Auditing by the Supreme Audit Institution (SAI)[10] and the follow up of its recommendations increase transparency and accountability and improve financial

---

Box 4.2　Consolidation of accounts in some federations

In *India* the central government publishes an annual report of the consolidated position of the central and state government finance statistics covering revenues, expenditures, deficit, financing, and debt.

In *Brazil*, the Treasury is responsible for consolidating general government accounts. The information available in the financial statements includes assets and liabilities, and revenues and expenditures (with analytical information by economic, geographic, and functional classification). Brazil takes eight months to produce a general government financial report encompassing the accounts of the central government, 26 states, the Federal District, and the majority of the 5,500 municipalities.

In *Austria*, consolidated general government reports are only produced for statistical purposes once a year to meet the Eurostat obligation and to report Maastricht deficit and debt.

management, which in turn can facilitate the task of consolidating general government accounts.

The SAI arrangement varies significantly across federations. In most federations, SNGs have their own SAIs. Exceptions are South Africa, where only one SAI is responsible for overseeing the audit of all levels of government, and India, where the national SAI, the Comptroller and Auditor General, is also the auditor for the states.

Relations between national and subnational SAIs also vary, along three basic models (Table 4.1):

- *The national SAI audits only the central government budget.* In Australia, Canada, Switzerland, and the United States, the national SAI has no jurisdiction over SNG SAIs, and its remit at the SNG level is limited to special federal programs executed by SNGs (Government of South Australia, 1987; Switzerland, 2014).
- *The national SAI audits central government entities plus transfers to SNGs.* In Brazil (Brazil, 1992) and Mexico (Mexico, 2009), the national SAI audits the central government transfers to SNGs as well as programs where there is "federal participation" (as above). The SNG audits are usually performed in coordination with the local SAIs. Argentina is an exception, where the federal SAI is responsible for the audit of the autonomous city of Buenos Aires.
- *The national SAI audits both central government and SNGs.* In Austria, Belgium, and Spain (Spain, 2003b) the national SAI has authority to audit SNGs, often (but not always) in collaboration with the SNG SAI. In Spain, the Autonomous Communities are also allowed to create their own SAIs, but the national SAI (*Tribunal de Cuentas*) has supremacy over them (Spain, 2003b). The national SAI can also delegate its functions to the SNG SAIs and request that the SNG SAI audit any specific local entities; at the same time, all the individual audit reports done by the SNG SAIs should be submitted to the national SAI. In Germany, the audit bodies of the Länder liaise and work on equal terms with the Federal SAI in areas where there is dual responsibility for the provision and delivery of public services. Where the Federal SAI works with one or more of the Länder SAIs, they perform joint audits or agree to divide audit responsibilities between their respective organizations.

VI. Coordination and common standards

While the preceding sections focused mainly on specific processes, this section looks at the institutional and regulatory arrangements that underpin effective and coherent budgeting in federations. Coordination across levels of government can be entrusted to specific coordinating bodies, although in a few cases it is also a responsibility of the central government. In addition, there is a growing trend towards adoption of common classifications and common accounting rules and standards across levels of government. These arrangements are cross-cutting in nature, as they often apply to all three phases of the budget process: formulation, execution, and accountability.

A. Institutional arrangements for coordination

Federal governments do not generally have the authority to oversee budget execution at SNGs level, as the latter typically operate with a high degree of autonomy. In most cases in our sample (including Austria, Australia, Canada, Germany, Switzerland, and the United States), SNGs rely on their own institutions – their own ministry of finance, legislature, and SAI – to oversee budget execution. However, fiscal responsibility legislation has enhanced the central government's coordination and monitoring role in some federations (Australia, Brazil, and Mexico). And most federal governments do nevertheless get involved in monitoring spending programs with joint responsibility as well as federally-funded SNG programs in which the federal government has a legitimate interest – federally-funded SNG programs can be quite substantial (education or health), for example, in the case of Mexico.

A few federations do give a much stronger oversight role to the central government – this is generally associated with a clear lack of capacity at the subnational level to adequately monitor fiscal developments, or when self-imposed mechanisms have failed – as discussed in more detail in Chapter 6:

- In Brazil, stronger oversight by the federal ministry of finance followed the resolution of the debt crisis in the 1990s.[11]
- Similarly in Mexico, the oversight role of the federal ministry of finance has been progressively strengthened as SNGs became more dependent on federal transfers.
- India's central oversight role stems from the Constitution, which vests significant PFM oversight responsibility in the central government exercised partly through a constitutional body, the Finance Commission, which monitors SNGs and advises the government on a range of fiscal issues related to the finances of states (India, 1949).
- South Africa also has a well-established and influential Intergovernmental Fiscal Relations Department within the National Treasury that oversees SNGs fiscal developments and enforces discipline through the PFM Act (for provincial governments) and the Municipalities Act.

Where harmonized budget execution is anticipated in the Constitution (e.g., India) or prescribed in the underlying regulatory framework (South Africa, Belgium, Germany, Brazil), the federal government may have authority to prescribe some or all of the rules for SNG budget execution processes and expenditure controls, as well as requiring the establishment of common support functions, such as internal audit or minimum qualifications for key staff involved in financial management (India and South Africa). These measures give some fiduciary assurance to federal governments, but do not guarantee it. Enforcement and follow up of external audit findings are usually left to the SNGs.

In most federations, however, intergovernmental arrangements have been established to ensure appropriate coordination across government levels. These institutional arrangements vary quite significantly. They have traditionally taken the form of political and technical meetings between ministers and staff of finance ministries, although more recently there has been a trend in some federations to formalize this coordination within a more institutionalized setting established by law.

• South Africa follows a traditional approach whereby finance ministers from central and provincial governments meet up to four times a year to discuss issues of common interest. Two of these meetings are centered on the budget process and provide the mechanism for agreeing to policy priorities and fiscal targets between the two layers of government.

• In Brazil the ministry of finance created a unit in the Treasury to oversee SNGs' fiscal situations. Every year a team of treasury officials visits each state to discuss the fiscal situation and propose measures to assure that the fiscal targets are observed. In the case of the states that renegotiated the debt with the federal government in the 1990s, the Treasury can be more directive and stringent regarding the definition of the fiscal targets.

In some federations, the coordination role falls on intergovernmental entities established for this purpose. They often play many roles, including the setting of SNG fiscal targets (as discussed in Chapter 3) and the provision of advice on the vertical and horizontal division of revenue (as discussed in Chapter 1). More broadly, they provide a mechanism for coordinating fiscal and budgetary policy across jurisdictions:

• In Spain, two intergovernmental institutions are charged with reviewing the horizontal distribution of the deficit target among government units. First, the Autonomous Communities' Council of Fiscal and Financial Policy (Consejo de Política Fiscal y Financiera) works as a consultative body (Spain, 1980). Its members include the Minister of Finance of the CG and the Finance Counselors of the Autonomous Communities. Second, the National Commission of Local Administration represents all provincial and local governments and leads the negotiations with the national government (Spain, 1985).

• In Belgium, the High Council of Finance set up in 1989 comprises two sections, one looking into public sector borrowing requirements, the other into taxation and social security contributions. Furthermore, the High Council has set up a study group on ageing. Although it has an advisory role, its politically balanced membership and the high quality of its work has given it an important role in the Belgian political sphere. The High Council carries out both backward and forward looking budgetary analysis, usually looking forward over three years. As discussed in Chapter 3, it coordinates a top-down approach to setting budgetary targets for each participating government which are then formalized in an inter-governmental agreement.

• In Germany, while the recommendations of the Stability Council are not binding, their effectiveness is enhanced by two features of the German Federation, namely the "solidarity" principle which results in the redistribution of wealth from richer to poorer Länder as well as shared financial responsibility for external debt or supranational obligations (i.e., the European Union), and the expansion over the years of areas of joint responsibility subject to federal laws. Furthermore, since the bulk of Länder resources comes from revenue sharing rather than tax assignment, the importance of the coordination mechanism is significantly enhanced (Zipfel, 2011a).

- Austria amended its Stability Pact in 2012 with a focus on the implementation of fiscal rules and their division between the levels of government as well as transparency and procedural rules (Austria, 2012). This Pact is the main regulatory mechanism for general government fiscal policy coordination and establishes reporting procedures to monitor fiscal results. The Pact foresees sanctions: Statistics Austria calculates fiscal numbers for the SNGs, and the Court of Audit states the violation of a rule, which then is discussed in a dispute resolution committee.

- In Argentina, the Federal Council of Fiscal Responsibility comprises the central government, and 21 out of 23 provinces. The Council is responsible for ensuring that the federal government and each of the member provinces observe the fiscal rules defined in the 2004 fiscal responsibility law No. 25917, particularly regarding transparency of fiscal reports. However, the Council has no power to sanction non-compliers.

- In Mexico, the Fiscal Coordination Law (Mexico, 1978), reformed several times, created several intergovernmental councils, including: (i) the National System of Fiscal Coordination, to which the SNGs must adhere in order to receive the whole transfers from the federal government. A precondition for accepting adherence is to renounce to the application of some fees and other non-tax revenues and to apply a few other taxes according to rules established by the federal government; (ii) the National Meeting of Fiscal Officials; (iii) the Permanent Commission of Fiscal Officials; and (iv) the Fiscal Coordination Board. The Government Accounting Law of 2008 created a National Council of Accounting Harmonization and a Consultative Committee on accounting matters (Mexico, 2008).

- Fiscal coordination in Australia has evolved considerably from a much weaker and informal arrangement in the past to the formalized and more effective arrangement in place today. In 2008, the Council of Australian Governments agreed to a significant reform of Australia's federal relations. The *Intergovernmental Agreement on Federal Financial Relations* created a Ministerial Council for Federal Financial Relations which has responsibility for the general oversight of the operation of the Intergovernmental Agreement and the on-going monitoring and maintenance of reforms, including ensuring that National Agreements and National Partnerships are aligned with the design principles of the Intergovernmental Agreement (Australia, 2008). The Intergovernmental Agreement provides (a) clarity and assurance of funding for the states' service delivery efforts, (b) rationalization in the

number of special purpose federal transfers, (c) greater flexibility in states' service delivery, (d) clearer roles and responsibilities for each jurisdiction, and (e) centralized payments arrangements.
• In the United States, institutions such as National Conference of State legislatures and the National Association of State Budget Officers play the role of intergovernmental councils although they have no enforcement powers.

In addition, quite a few federations have formal institutions – usually a Council or a Commission of experts – that advise the government and/or the legislature on the division of revenues between jurisdictions. These bodies are generally independent and often established either in the Constitution or by a special law. Their role is to advise on both the vertical and horizontal division of revenues, taking into account expenditure needs at each level. The vertical division of revenues concerns nationally raised taxes and is applied variously to individual taxes, such as VAT, or total revenue collected at the national level. This division is generally set as a percentage of revenues and is reflected in the federal annual budget framework. The horizontal division, where the revenue pool for SNGs is divided up between the various SNGs, is most often done by formula, which is revised periodically – typically every five to seven years.

Prominent examples of intergovernmental fiscal bodies with an advisory role in revenue sharing include:

• The Finance Commission of India, an independent advisory council with a mandate of five years first established in 1951 under Article 280 of the Constitution (India, 1949). Its stated role is to review the financial relations between the central and state governments, including the rules and percentage of revenue transfers from the central government to the states, and to make recommendations on changes to the President. While the Finance Commission's role is purely advisory, its constitutional status and reputation is such that it is highly unusual and potentially controversial for the central government to ignore the recommendations.
• The Australian Commonwealth Grants Commission, established in 1973, recommends how the revenues raised from the Goods and Services Tax should be distributed to the States and Territories to achieve horizontal fiscal equalization (Australia, 1973; Australia, 2012; Bhajan, 2012). It is an independent statutory body that responds to requests sent to it by the Commonwealth Treasurer. It makes its recommendations in consultation with the States and Territories and based on data provided by them and independent statistical sources.
• The South African Financial and Fiscal Commission (South Africa, 1997) is an independent constitutional advisory institution established in 1995. It advises and makes recommendations to Parliament, provincial legislatures, organized local government, and other organs of State on financial and fiscal matters. Its primary role is to ensure the creation and maintenance of an

effective, equitable, and sustainable system of intergovernmental fiscal relations in South Africa.

B. Common budget classifications, accounting rules, and accounting standards

Use of common budget classifications and standards across government, whether in budgets or in financial statements, is critical for accountability and transparency. It facilitates comparison, peer review, and monitoring by the central government, and the consolidation of general government fiscal information. The ability to consolidate fiscal information across all layers of government is particularly important for overall fiscal management in federations, a function normally assigned to federal ministries of finance. Given this need, the federal government is often the main driver in efforts to harmonize classifications and to establish common accounting and reporting standards.[12]

In practice, however, many countries have different standards for the central government and SNGs, and some even have different standards between local governments. In the absence of common standards, fiscal reports consolidated by the general government tend to be statistical compilations rather than consolidated accounting reports.

Budgetary classifications and charts of accounts are generally not specified in detail in accounting standards. They are usually country specific.

The benefits of accrual accounting and annual balance sheets are widely recognized today, especially in federations with fiscally distressed SNGs. Countries which in the past have contented themselves with cash based accounting modified with a few statements of stocks such as debt and guarantees, are now actively engaged in accrual accounting reforms. Statistical reports are clearly no longer sufficient to determine the level of fiduciary risk, as these are traditionally compiled on the basis of estimated rather than hard data. Furthermore, unlike statistical reports, accrual accounts and balance sheets are audited, which provide a much higher level of assurance on the quality and coverage of the data provided. For federations, the move to accrual accounting as a standard for government accounts at all levels is particularly urgent given the autonomous nature of SNGs, as evidenced by the number of federations in the sample under consideration which have initiated significant accounting reforms in recent years.

In only three countries in our sample (Brazil, India, and South Africa) is the central government vested with powers to define accounting rules and may even sanction SNGs that do not observe them.[13] In addition, in Argentina, Brazil, and Mexico, specific laws on government accounting apply to all government entities. For example, Mexico adopted a Government Accounting Law in 2008 (Mexico, 2008) which introduced an obligation to harmonize the accounting systems of central, state, and municipal governments and to shift to accrual-based accounting and financial reporting by 2012.[14] Responsibility for drawing up standards under Mexico's Accounting Law has been assigned to a National Council of Accounting Harmonization (CONAC).

Three federations in our sample (Australia, Canada, and the United States) have autonomous accounting standard boards. In Australia and Canada, accounting standards are set for all government levels. The Australia's Commonwealth and State and Territory Governments were among the first to introduce the IMF's Government Finance Statistics (GFSM, 2001) standard across governments. This has facilitated the regular consolidation of reliable in-year and annual consolidated general government budgets, reports, and accounts. In Canada, where the change is most recent, a detailed accrual accounting handbook has now been issued to guide SNG accounting procedures and rules, and SNG auditors are auditing to the new standards. In the United States, the Government Accounting Standards Board (GASB), an independent body established in 1984 by agreement of the Financial Accounting Foundation (FAF), a private sector not-for-profit entity, produces Generally Accepted Accounting Principles (GAAP) for use by states and local governments. Compliance is purely voluntary (the GASB does not have enforcement authority), but GAAP standards are prescribed in the regulatory frameworks of over two thirds of U.S. States, and at least half of the remaining states report adherence to the same standards. Furthermore, state-level external auditors routinely render opinions on the conformity of the state's comprehensive annual financial reports with GAAP standards.

In Switzerland, the central government introduced the International Public Sector Accounting Standards (IPSAS) and full accrual accounting and budgeting in 2007, quickly adopted by some cantons. The current national recommendations for Swiss public sector financial reporting also lean towards IPSAS standards, but leave open the option to differ from the recommended valuation basis for assets which are considered as administrative assets – assets needed by the governments to fulfill their service commitments. To promote the harmonization of the accounting and financial reporting rules, the Swiss Public Sector Financial Reporting Advisory Committee was established in 2008. The committee publishes recommendations but has no responsibility to ensure that rules and standards are followed. Among the recommendations issued are: the use of harmonized classifications by nature and function for the budget as well as reporting at all levels of government, and to allow mapping, to the greatest possible extent, of the national classifications to ESA 95 or to GFSM 2001.

In the remainder of the sample of federations, rules and standards are left to the individual SNGs, which can either set its own standards or adopt standards similar to those at the federal level. In line with the progressive acceptance of international accounting standards, notably IPSAS, some countries have tried to encourage harmonization across SNGs. Germany and Belgium are two examples of this trend (Austria has also achieved some harmonization).

In Germany, accounting practices and charts of accounts were historically left up to the individual Länder to develop. However, recent amendments to the Law on Budgetary Principles now require that the Federation and the Länder set up a joint committee for the standardization of government accounting. The work of this committee, which reports to the Stability Council, has progressed, although consensus has not yet been reached on moving to accrual accounting. The same law also establishes the requirement for all governments to produce financial statistics for inclusion in the national accounts and for reporting to Eurostat.

In Belgium, two federal laws were adopted in 2003 to upgrade budget and accounting rules and procedures, including classifications and chart of accounts, one applied to the central government, the other to all SNGs (Belgium, 2003a; Belgium, 2003b). The Ministry of Interior at the level of each region is responsible for the accounting regulations of each three regions: Flanders, Wallonia, and Brussels Capital (Khrouz and Brusca, 2007). The new accounting standards follow IPSAS. Implementation however has been considerably delayed across all jurisdictions. One ensuing complication is that within one country, SNGs end up with different accounting bases – the more advanced SNGs will use accrual basis while the less advanced will use cash basis.

Less progress has been made in harmonizing the presentation of budgets. In addition to Australia, India, and South Africa (mentioned above), the German Law on Budgetary Principles of 1969 (Germany, 1969) established a range of standardized budgetary practices for all levels of government to follow, including a common system of classifications by object and by function. In Austria, regulation on budgets and reports of local and regional levels includes a classification which is closely harmonized with the federal level with some minor differences (Austria, 1997).

VII. European Union practices

As discussed in Chapter 3, in the wake of the crisis, the EU has made attempts to strengthen economic policy coordination. While the bulk of these efforts have to do with strengthening numerical fiscal rules in member states, some important efforts are being taken also in the area of budget execution and accountability. In particular, the Council Directive 2011/85/EU of November 8, 2011 on requirements for budgetary frameworks of the member states (part of the "six pack") introduces a set of demands to member states related to, inter alia, accounting and statistical standards (European Parliament and European Council, 2011f). The member states were required to modify their national laws to comply with the directive by December 31, 2013.

EU practices foster harmonization of budget processes in the following two areas:

- **Medium- and long-term fiscal objectives:** Each year EU member states are required to submit their Stability Program (for Euro zone members) or their Convergence Program within the Stability and Growth Pact. Programs are submitted in April allowing the Commission and the Council to assess whether member states have reached their medium-term budgetary objectives or are on an appropriate adjustment path towards them. The Commission also checks the consistency of member state plans with policy guidelines adopted at the European level. These assessments, returned in June, are then to be used to guide member state budget formulation (European Council, 2012).

- **Fiscal reporting:** EU member states submit quarterly fiscal statistics based on ESA 95. These statistical reports have recently been extended to cover issues that can impact on the fiscal position of member states, such as public-private partnerships.

There is little harmonization, however, in most of other areas of public financial management:

- **Macroeconomic and fiscal projections:** In the context of the annual Stability and Convergence Programs, euro area member states and member states participating in the Exchange Rate Mechanism II should use common external assumptions on the main extra-EU variables used by the European Commission in its forecast. Otherwise, other than commenting on the Programs and the consistency of the plans, the EU does not attempt to harmonize macroeconomic and fiscal projections across member states.
- **Annual accounts and financial statements:** The accounting basis and standards for the preparation of annual accounts and financial statements and the choice of external audit arrangements are left entirely up to member states to determine. Nevertheless, the EU Directive of 2011 is intended to bring about changes to member state practices that enhance data comparability. It is worth noting that the EU's own budget, including any structural funds executed within member states, is subject to accounting rules and standards set by the Commission, and its accounts and financial statements are externally audited by the European Court of Auditors.
- **Consolidation of fiscal reports and annual accounts:** There is no EU-wide consolidation of in-year fiscal reports or of member states' annual accounts and financial statements. Such a consolidation would in any case pose a challenge, since there is no harmonization of charts of accounts across the EU member states. However, Eurostat does publish some EU-wide indicators on government finance statistics.
- **Intergovernmental coordination bodies:** The EU does not have any revenue sharing authority, although some of its structural fund programs do target less-developed regions or social groups. The Economic and Financial Affairs Council (ECOFIN), which consists of the ministers of finance from all member states, is primarily a consultative body on fiscal policy matters, a process which has occasionally resulted in policy coordination.

Looking forward, further harmonization of fiscal reporting can be expected. Already the 2011 Directive requires member states to start generating both cash-based fiscal data and the information needed to prepare accrual data according to the ESA 95 standard to facilitate the reporting of verifiable government finance statistics. According to the Directive, member states must ensure timely and regular public availability of fiscal data for all sub-sectors of general government by publishing:

- Cash-based fiscal data (or the equivalent figure from public accounting if cash-based data are not available).[15]
- A detailed reconciliation table showing the methodology of transition between cash-based data and data based on the ESA 95 standard.

The Directive states that those public accounting systems shall be subject to internal control and independent audits, but it does not prescribe the accounting standard to be used.

The Directive also demands member states to identify and present all general government bodies and funds which do not form part of the regular budgets at sub-sector level, together with other relevant information. The combined impact on general government balances and debts of those general government bodies and funds should be presented in the framework of the annual budgetary processes and the medium-term budgetary plans.

Finally, to increase the transparency of general government finances, EU member states will be required to publish relevant information on contingent liabilities with potentially large impacts on public budgets, including government guarantees, non-performing loans, and liabilities stemming from the operation of public corporations. Member states will also be required to publish information on the participation of general government in the capital of private and public corporations in respect of economically significant amounts.

VIII. Conclusions

As this chapter has shown, very few federal countries have common or homogeneous guidelines for budget formulation, reporting, and auditing at the central and SNG level. This is in large part due to the very essence of the federalist approach which grants autonomy to lower levels of governments to enhance the efficiency of spending and the welfare of local populations. However, insufficient harmonization and coordination between the center and SNGs hampers the maintenance of macroeconomic stability and fiscal discipline (Fedelino and Ter-Minassian, 2009). Increased coordination is needed (i) at the budget formulation level, to ensure that budgets are realistic and prepared within a setting that is consistent with the central government framework, particularly regarding consistency of macro-fiscal projections; (ii) at the budget execution level to ensure monitoring and transparency of fiscal developments at the SNG level; and (iii) *ex post*, to have an accurate picture of the general government fiscal stance. All these components require homogeneous, clear, and transparent statistical reporting and accounting standards, as well as accountability mechanisms such as audit to ensure the accuracy and legitimacy of budget execution.

It is interesting to note that there is less resistance from SNGs to implement harmonized guidelines that are related to standardization of chart of accounts and provision of *ex post* information (for example, end of the year financial statements and definition of budget and accounting classification), while there is more resistance regarding *ex ante* fiscal projections and budget preparation. This is mainly because *ex ante* measures are considered more intrusive and carry a risk of compromising the autonomy of the SNGs. Recent federal legislations tend to have more provisions for coordination at the budget preparation level, reflecting lessons from SNG debt crises (e.g., South Africa, Brazil, India, and, recently, Spain). However, in many other countries, more could be done to enhance coordination and oversight at the *ex ante* stage, without undermining the principles of autonomy.

The harmonization of budget processes is also limited in the EU to some alignment of medium and long-term objectives and common fiscal reporting requirements, and no common PFM standards. However, efforts are underway to increase the comparability and coverage of fiscal data across member states.

Notes

1 For the definition of the sample, and general terminology, see "Introduction and Overview."
2 See Chapter 3 for a discussion on subnational fiscal policy constraints.
3 See Chapter 3 for a discussion of fiscal responsibility laws.
4 As discussed in Chapter 3, Austria, Australia, and Belgium also rely on cooperative approaches in the setting of the fiscal targets.
5 In addition to formula based shared revenues, many central governments provide earmarked transfers to SNGs. These range from specialized transfers – for infrastructure projects, for example – to sector specific grants for the provision of major services, such as education and health in the case of Mexico. Such earmarked transfers are usually not fungible and are often subject to audit by the central government, and therefore cannot be redeployed by the SNG where they are in excess of requirement.
6 Monitoring reports differ from (consolidated) annual financial statements which are often available only after a significant time lag – anywhere up to a year – as their release is linked to the completion of external audits (see Section V).
7 Under the Charter of Budget Honesty, Australia (Australia, 1998) also produces an annual budget outcome report covering general government.
8 Although these are statistical reports, the ESA 95 methodology ensures that they are compiled from underlying accounting reports.
9 Statistical consolidations often involve interpretation or extrapolation of data, which may involve estimations based on past trends or on a sample. Accounting consolidations are based on accounting statements which have generally been audited and are compiled using clearly defined netting out rules and rarely any interpretation of data. Accounting statements provide a degree of assurance that the data has been through a rigorous and readily traceable process, which may not always be the case with statistical data.
10 SAIs are a key institution in the independent oversight arrangements found today in most countries. Their auditors provide an independent expert view of accounts and financial statements produced by public sector entities – government as well as publicly-owned enterprises – generally reporting directly to the Legislature and informing it of any issue to take up with the executive over the collection and use of public resources. The International Organization of Supreme Audit Institutions (INTOSAI) recommends a cycle of nine months from annual closure of accounts to review by Parliament.
11 See Chapter 6 for a detailed discussion.
12 When establishing their own accounting and reporting standards, most countries draw from one of two internationally recognized standards – either the International Public Sector Accounting Standards (IPSAS) or the International Financial Reporting Standard (IFRS). These adaptations usually seek to address various accounting

shortcomings, and, as a result, national standards may at times lack comprehensiveness. For statistical reports, many countries follow the IMF's Government Finance Statistics standard (GFSM, 2001), although European countries also follow the European System of National and Regional Accounts standard (ESA, 95).

13 In Brazil, PFM principles and accounting standards are established by law and apply to all levels of government; in India, the Constitution assigns responsibility for setting accounting rules and standards to the union government; and in South Africa, the one PFM Act applies to both central and provincial governments while a common municipal finance management Act applies to all municipalities and covers PFM requirements at that level. Under these legislations, the National Treasury has developed common classifications, charts of accounts, and financial statements and reporting formats for all levels of government.

14 The deadline was extended to 2014 for the federal and state governments and to 2015 for municipalities.

15 Monthly for central government, state government, and social security sub-sectors, and quarterly for the local governments.

References

Argentina, 2004, Regimen Federal de Responsibilidad Fiscal, Law 25917 (Buenos Aires), available at http://infoleg.mecon.gov.ar/infolegInternet/anexos/95000–99999/97698/norma.htm

———, 2005, Federal Council of Fiscal Responsibility, *Internal Resolution No 1/ 2005* (Buenos Aires).

Australia, 1973, Office of Legislative, Drafting, and Publishing, Attorney General's Department, *Commonwealth Grants Commission Act* (Canberra).

———, 1998, Office of Legislative, Drafting, and Publishing, Attorney General's Department, *ComLaw Authoritative Act – Charter of Budget Honesty Act 1998 – Act No. 22* (Canberra).

———, 2008, Council of Australian Governments, Intergovernmental Agreement on Federal Financial Relations (Canberra), available at http://www.federalfinancialrelations.gov.au/content/inter_agreement_and_schedules/IGA_federal_financial_relations_aug11.pdf

———, 2012, Australian Government Commonwealth Grants Commission, *Report on GST Revenue Sharing Relativities* (Canberra).

Austria, 2012, 1997, "Regulation on budgets and reports of local and regional level (Voranschlags- und Rechnungsabschlussverordnung)" (Vienna), available at http://www.ris.bka.gv.at/GeltendeFassung.wxe?Abfrage=Bundesnormen&Gesetzesnummer=10005022

———, "Austrian Stability Pact (Österreichischer Stabilitätspakt)" (Vienna: Federal Ministry of Finance), available at https://english.bmf.gv.at/ministry/press/pressreleases2012/april/stabilitypact.html

Belgium, 2006, *Royal Decree of 3 April 2006 on the High Council of Finance* (Brussels), available at http://docufin.fgov.be/intersalgen/hrfcsf/onzedienst/Onzedienst.htm

———, 2013, "Belgium Stability Programme 2013–2016" (Brussels: Federal Public Service Finance), available at http://stabiliteitsprogramma.be/en/Stabilityprogramme.htm

Bhajan, Grewal S., 2012, *Tax Sharing and Fiscal Equalisation in Australia* (Melbourne: Victoria University).

Bogaert, H., L. Dobbelaere, B. Hertveldt, and I. Lebrun, 2006, *Fiscal Councils, Independent Forecasts and the Budgetary Process: Lessons from the Belgium Case* (Brussels: Federal Planning Bureau).

Brazil, 1992, *Lei Organica do Tribunal de Contas da Uniao* (Brasília), available at http://www.planalto.gov.br/ccivil_03/Leis/L8443.htm

——, 2000, *Fiscal Responsibility Law* (Brasília), available at https://www.tesouro.fazenda.gov.br/pt/responsabilidade-fiscal/lei-de-responsabilidade-fiscal

European Commission, 1996, "European System of Account 1995, ESA 95" (Luxembourg: European Coal and Steel Community, European Community, and European Atomic Energy Community), available at http://bookshop.europa.eu/en/european-system-of-accounts.-esa-1995-pbCA1596001/downloads/CA-15–96–001-EN-C/CA1596001ENC_001.pdf?FileName=CA1596001ENC_001.pdf&SKU=CA1596001ENC_PDF&CatalogueNumber=CA-15–96–001-EN-C

European Council, 2012, *Treaty on Stability, Coordination, and Governance in the Economic and Monetary Union* (Strasbourg), available at http://european-council.europa.eu/home-page/highlights/treaty-on-stability,-coordination-and-governance-signed

European Parliament and European Council, 2011a, Regulation (EU) No 1173/2011 "on the effective enforcement of budgetary surveillance in the euro area" (Strasbourg), available at http://eur-lex.europa.eu/legal-content/EN/ALL/?uri=CELEX:32011R1173

——, 2011b, Regulation (EU) No 1174/2011 "on enforcement measures to correct excessive macroeconomic imbalances in the euro are" a (Strasbourg), available at Internet: http://eur-lex.europa.eu/LexUriServ/LexUriServ.do?uri=OJ:L:2011:306:0008:0011:EN:PDF

——, 2011c, Regulation (EU) No 1175/2011 "amending Council Regulation (EC) No. 1466/97 on the strengthening of the surveillance of budgetary positions and the surveillance and coordination of economic policies" (Strasbourg).

——, 2011d, Regulation (EU) No 1176/2011 "on the prevention and correction of macroeconomic imbalances" (Strasbourg).

——, 2011e, Council Regulation (EU) No 1177/2011 "amending Regulation (EC) No. 1467/97 on speeding up and clarifying the implementation of the excessive deficit procedure" (Strasbourg).

——, 2011f, Council Directive 2011/85/EU "on requirements for budgetary frameworks of the Member States" (Strasbourg).

——, 2013a, Regulation (EU) No 472/2013 "on the strengthening of economic and budgetary surveillance of Member States in the euro area experiencing or threatened with serious difficulties with respect to their financial stability" (Strasbourg).

——, 2013b, Regulation (EU) No 473/2013 "on common provisions for monitoring and assessing draft budgetary plans and ensuring the correction of excessive deficit of the Member States in the euro area" (Strasbourg). Available at http://eur-lex.europa.eu/LexUriServ/LexUriServ.do?uri=OJ:L:2013:140:0011:0023:EN:PDF

Fedelino, A., and T. Ter-Minassian, 2009, *Macro Policy Lessons for a Sound Design of Fiscal Decentralization* (Washington: International Monetary Fund).

Federal Reserve, 2014, *Financial Accounts of the United States: Flow of Funds, Balance Sheets, and Integrated Macroeconomic Accounts*, (Washington: Federal Reserve Statistics Release March 2014). Available at http://www.federalreserve.gov/releases/z1/Current/

Germany, 1949, Basic Law (*Constitution*) (Bonn). Available at http://www.bundesregierung.de/Content/EN/StatischeSeiten/breg/basic-law-content-list.html?nn=709674

——, 1969, *Budgetary Principles Act* (Bonn). Available at http://www.bundesrechnungshof.de/en/bundesrechnungshof/rechtsgrundlagen/budgetary-principles-act

——, 2013, *German Stability Programme 2013 Update* (Berlin: Federal Ministry of Finance).

GFSM, 2001, *Government Finance Statistics Manual 2001* (Washington: International Monetary Fund), available at http://www.imf.org/external/pubs/ft/gfs/manual/pdf/all.pdf

Government of South Australia, 1987, *Public Finance and Audit Act of 1987* (Adelaide). Available at http://www.legislation.sa.gov.au/LZ/C/A/Public%20Finance%20and%20 Audit%20Act%201987.aspx

India, 1949, *Article 280 of the Constitution of India That Creates the Finance Commission* (New Delhi). Available at http://fincomindia.nic.in/

―――, 2003, *The Fiscal Responsibility and Budget Management Act No. 39* (New Delhi). Available at http://finmin.nic.in/law/frbmact2003.pdf

Khrouz, F., and I. Brusca, 2007, *Accounting Rules and Practice at Local Level*, Council of Europe (Strasbourg).

Knörzer, Thomas, 2008, *The Budget System of the Federal Republic of Germany* (Berlin: Bundesministerium der Finanzen).

Lübke, Astrid, 2008, "Medium-Term Financial Planning in the Federal Republic of Germany," *Journal on Presupuesto y Gasto Publico*, Vol. 51 (2008), pp. 133-144 (Madrid: Instituto de Estudios Fiscales).

Mexico, 1978, *Ley de Coordinacion Fiscal* (Mexico City), available at http://www. funcionpublica.gob.mx/scagp/dgorcs/reglas/2002/r33_aportafederales/completos/ LEY_COORD_FISCAL_2002.htm

―――, 2006, *Ley Federal de Presupuesto y Reponsabilidad Hacendaria de 2006* (Mexico City), available at http://www.conaculta.gob.mx/donativos/donativos2013/ley_federal_ presupuesto_y_responsabilidad_hacendaria.pdf

―――, 2008, *Ley General de Contabilidad Gubernamental* (Mexico City), available at http://www.uv.mx/contraloria/files/2013/02/2.-Ley-General-Contabilidad-Gubernamental.pdf

―――, 2009, *Ley de Fiscalizacion y Rendicion de Cuentas de la Federacion* (Mexico City), available at http://www.uv.mx/contraloria/files/2013/02/1.-Ley-Federal-de-Fiscalizacion-Superior-de-la-Federacion.pdf

South Africa, 1997, *Intergovernmental Fiscal Relations Act No 97* (Cape Town), available at http://www.ffc.co.za/index.php/mandate

―――, 1999, *Public Finance Management Act* (Cape Town), available at http://www. treasury.gov.za/legislation/pfma/default.aspx

―――, 2009, Accounting Officers and Heads of Provincial Treasurers, *Guidelines and Manuals for the Members of the Executive Council (MECs)* (Cape Town), available at http://www.treasury.gov.za/publications/guidelines/induction/

Spain, 1980, *Ley Organica 8/1980 de Financiacion de las Comunidades Autonomas, LOFCA* (Madrid), available at http://www.minhap.gob.es/Documentacion/Publico/Normativa Doctrina/FinanciacionTerritorial/Financiacion%20Autonomica/LOFCA%20consoli dada%2022_5_2012.pdf

―――, 1985. *Law No 7/1985, Reguladora de las Bases del Régimen Local* (Madrid), available at https://www.boe.es/buscar/act.php?id=BOE-A-1985–5392

―――, 2003a, *Organic Budget Law of the State, Law No 47* (Madrid), available at http:// www.boe.es/boe/dias/2003/11/27/pdfs/A42079–42126.pdf

―――, 2003b, *Autonomy Statutes (equivalent to regional Constitutions)*, available at http://www.congreso.es/consti/estatutos/

―――, 2012, *Ley Orgánica No 2/2012, de Estabilidad Presupuestaria y Sostenibilidad Financiera* (Madrid), available at http://www.boe.es/boe/dias/2012/04/30/pdfs/BOE-A-2012–5730.pdf

———, 2014, *Actualización del Programa de Estabilidad 2014–2017* (Madrid: Ministerio de Economía y Competitividad), available at http://www.mineco.gob.es/portal/site/mineco?lang_choosen=en

Statistics Canada, 2014, *Government Financial Statistics*, available at http://www5. statcan.gc.ca/subject-sujet/result-resultat?pid=3764&id=3766&lang=eng&type=CST& pageNum=1&more=0

Switzerland, 2014, *Competencies and Responsibilities of the Federal Audit Office*, available at http://www.efk.admin.ch/index.php?lang=en

United States, 2014, *Economic Report of the President* (Washington), available at http://www.whitehouse.gov/administration/eop/cea/economic-report-of-the-President/2014

Zipfel, F., 2011a, "German finances: Federal level masks importance of Länder," *Current Issues*, May 27 (Frankfurt: Deutsche Bank Research).

———, 2011b, Stability Council: Financial inspector of Germany's Länder, *Economics & Politics Research Briefing*, September 15 (Frankfurt: Deutsche Bank Research).

5 Financing of central and subnational governments

Geremia Palomba, Eva Jenkner,
Jeta Menkulasi, and Sergio Sola

I. Introduction

Financing arrangements between central and subnational governments vary across fiscal federations, shaped by history and specific institutional designs (Table 5.1). The previous chapters have discussed how transfers from the central government may finance subnational deficits in a sample of federations (Chapter 1) and how the center may at times impose borrowing constraints on subnational governments (Chapters 3 and 4). This chapter focuses on the financing of residual deficits and more particularly on the role of intergovernmental financing arrangements in normal circumstances.[1] The financial support by the center provided on a one-off basis, in times of crisis, is the subject of the next chapter (Chapter 6).

This chapter is organized as follows: Section II briefly reviews how debt and fiscal balances are distributed across levels of government in fiscal federations. Section III investigates the different channels through which central and state government financing interact and reviews special arrangements that occurred during the formation of federal states. Section IV describes prevalent financing practices, instruments, and financing costs of central and state governments. Section V draws parallels to current and proposed financing arrangements in the European Union. Section VI concludes.

II. Debt and fiscal balances across levels of government

The degree of financial centralization and revenue capacity affects the allocation of debt and fiscal imbalances across different levels of government. In general, the largest share of debt and deficits is held at the central level, although the share held by SNGs (subnational governments) tends to increase with their capacity to finance expenditure with own revenue (Figure 5.1).

In our sample, in 2000–11, subnational government debt averaged about 18 percent of national GDP and only about one third of central government debt. However, in more decentralized federations, where SNGs have larger revenue capacity (including Canada, the United States, and Switzerland), subnational government debt averaged almost 30 percent of GDP and reached more than three quarters of central government debt (Figure 5.2 Debt chart and Table 5.2). As for debt, local fiscal imbalances tend to be limited, although again relatively larger, on average,

Table 5.1 Overview of subnational financing frameworks across countries

Country	Subnational Entity	Fiscal Rules on Debt/Deficits	Other Borrowing Constraints[1]	Transfer Dependence[2]	Own Source Revenue/ SNG Revenue[3]	Composition of SNG Debt (2011)
Argentina[4]	23 Provinces (and Gran BA)	N		N/A	N/A	30% bonds, 70% loans (SG)
Australia[5]	Six states (and two territories)	N/Y	Y	44.1	21.2	N/A
Austria	Nine bundeslaender	Y	N	45.0	1.0	91% loans, 9% bonds
Belgium	Three regions	Y	Y	64.1	16.2	68% loans, 32% bonds
Brazil	26 states (and a federal district)	Y	Y	25.2	65.1	90% loans, 10% other (SG)
Canada[6]	Ten Provinces and three Territories	N/Y	N	16.5	59.7	59% bonds, 41% other
Germany	16 Bundeslaender	Y	Y[7]	54.2	11.1	57% loans, 43% bonds
India	25 states (and seven union territories)	Y	Y	31.3	49.3	50% loans, 37% bonds, 13% other (SG)
Mexico	31 states and a federal district	N	Y	88.6	1.1	80% loans, 15% bonds, 5% other
South Africa	Nine provinces	Y	N	70.4	1.1	N/A
Spain	17 autonomous communities	Y	Y/N[8]	49.7	37.4	63% loans, 37% bonds
Switzerland	26 cantons	Y	Y[9]	14.9	59.3	54% loans, 28% bonds, 18% other
United States	50 states and D.C.	Y	N	18.3	52.2	80% bonds, 20% other

Sources: Chapter 3; OECD, 2009; Plekhanov and Singh, 2007; Sutherland et al., 2005; Haver; Eurostat; national sources; and staff calculations.

[1] Borrowing constraints include budget frameworks set by the Australian Loan Council or the Belgian High Finance Council, and India's requirement of prior approval.
[2] Transfer dependence is defined as (grants + revenue sharing)/total SNG revenue. Data for 2005.
[3] "Own source revenue" refers to the share of SNG tax revenue regarding which the SNG has autonomy in determining the rate (OECD definition). Data for 2005.
[4] Suspended in 2009.
[5] Depends on state: only New South Wales and Queensland have numerical rules.
[6] Depends on province: Ontario, Quebec, British Columbia, and Alberta have budget balance rules.
[7] Restricted merely by the rules set up by the Länder themselves – primarily in their constitutions.
[8] All regions required authorization of debt issuance and foreign currency operations. Authorization for other credit operations depends on whether there is budgetary compliance. Authorization for debt issuance and foreign currency operations. Authorization for other credit operations depends on whether there is budgetary compliance. Data for 2005.
[9] There is no federal constraint on deficit financing, except that all tiers of government have no access to borrowing from the Central Bank, but cantons restrict themselves.

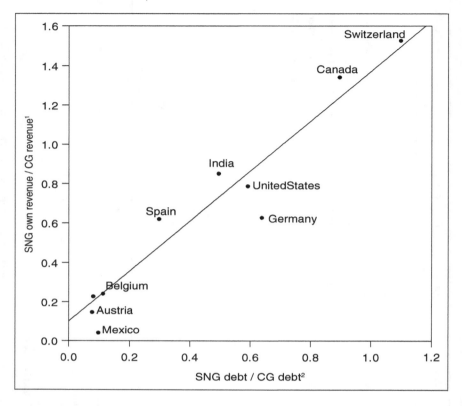

Figure 5.1 Debt allocation and tax capacity

[1]Own revenue for SNG are available only for 2005.
[2]2000–08 average

in federations where SNGs have larger local revenue capacity to finance their expenses (Figure 5.2 Fiscal Balance chart).

The recent crisis affected general government debt dynamics, including by making it harder for SNGs to borrow. With the exceptions of Switzerland and Canada, central government deficits and debt rose significantly more than subnational deficits during the recent crisis (Panel 5.1). This highlights the center's role in stabilizing the economy, but also reflected a drying up of financing for SNGs as investors' appetite for risk diminished.

III. Central and subnational government financing linkages[2]

Central government institutions provide financial support to states through a variety of channels. Apart from transfers, central governments can help finance state governments' deficits and provide guarantees both directly and indirectly through public financial institutions and special purpose vehicles (SPVs). They can also help set up

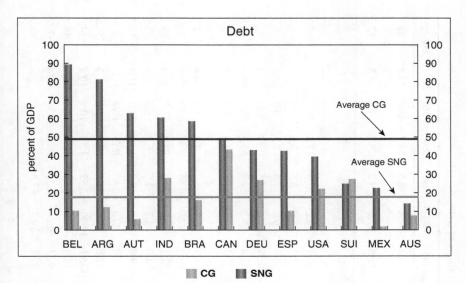

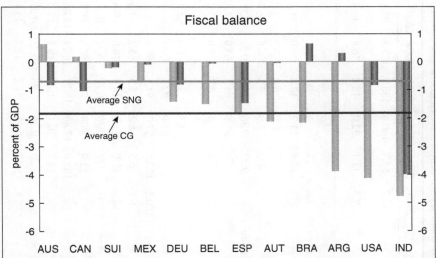

Figure 5.2 Average debt and fiscal balance by level of government, 2000–11 (percent of GDP)[1]

Sources: IMF staff calculations based on OECD, Eurostat, GFS, statistics Canada, Haver analytics, and Ministry of Finance and Public Credit of Mexico data.

[1]Data coverage is limited for the following countries and series: Argentina (deficits 2002–04); Australia (debt 2001–10; deficits 2000–09); Austria (debt 2002–11); Brazil (debt and CG deficit 2001–11); Canada (debt 2000–08; deficit 2000–10); Germany (debt 2002–11); India (deficits 2000–10); Mexico (CG debt 2000–10; SNG debt 2001–10; deficits 2003–10); Switzerland (debt 2000–10); US (CG debt 2000–10).

Table 5.2 Central and subnational government gross debt in selected federations, 2000–2011 (share of GDP)

Country	Source	Sector	2000	2001	2002	2003	2004	2005	2006	2007	2008	2009	2010	2011	Average
Argentina[1]	Finance Ministry	CG	45.7	53.7	166.4	138.9	127.4	87.1	76.2	67.4	58.5	58.7	48.4	44.5	81.1
	Finance Ministry	SG	7.5	11.1	22.0	18.8	16.8	14.8	12.8	11.0	9.2	9.2	7.8	6.5	12.3
		SNG	...	...	...	...	...	...	...	...	...	...	...	...	...
		SNG share	...	...	...	...	...	...	...	...	...	...	...	...	...
Australia[2]	ABS	CG	...	14.4	13.2	12.0	12.0	11.2	10.3	9.2	13.5	17.3	20.3	...	13.3
	ABS	SG	...	7.3	6.9	6.4	5.9	5.9	5.7	6.0	6.5	7.5	9.0	...	6.7
	ABS	SNG[3]	...	8.3	7.9	7.3	6.8	6.8	6.6	6.9	7.4	8.5	9.9	...	7.7
		SNG share	...	0.37	0.38	0.38	0.36	0.38	0.39	0.43	0.35	0.33	0.33	...	0.37
Austria	Eurostat	CG	...	...	65.8	65.5	65.0	64.5	57.8	55.2	59.3	63.3	66.1	66.0	62.8
	National Statistics	SG	2.3	3.3	2.4	2.3	2.6	3.0	3.3	3.4	3.7	4.8	5.9	5.9	3.6
	Eurostat	SNG	...	...	5.3	4.7	5.0	5.3	4.9	5.0	5.2	6.3	8.5	8.8	5.9
	Eurostat	SNG share	...	...	0.69	0.67	0.66	0.64	0.60	0.60	0.58	0.57	0.59	0.60	0.62
Belgium	Eurostat	CG	100.5	100.0	97.0	91.1	86.8	85.6	82.2	79.0	84.0	87.9	87.7	89.9	89.3
	Eurostat	SG	6.8	6.5	6.2	5.5	5.2	4.4	4.0	3.7	4.0	6.2	6.5	6.6	5.5
	Eurostat	SNG[4]	12.0	12.0	11.3	10.6	10.6	9.6	9.0	8.5	8.3	10.9	11.3	11.4	10.5
		SNG share	0.11	0.11	0.10	0.10	0.11	0.10	0.10	0.10	0.09	0.11	0.11	0.11	0.10
Brazil	BCB	CG	...	52.9	56.8	57.7	56.8	58.4	58.8	59.6	58.1	62.9	61.2	61.3	58.6
	BCB	SG	...	16.66	17.80	16.72	16.24	14.86	13.91	12.96	12.52	11.55	10.9	10.4	14.0
	BCB	SNG[3]	...	18.7	20.1	19.0	18.5	17.0	15.9	14.9	14.4	13.4	12.6	12.0	16.1
		SNG share	0.11	0.26	0.26	0.25	0.25	0.23	0.21	0.20	0.20	0.18	0.17	0.16	0.21
Canada	Statistics Canada	CG	58.8	58.7	54.1	51.2	47.7	44.1	42.3	39.7	37.8	...	...	...	48.3

Country	Source	Measure													
	Statistics Canada	SG	44.5	45.2	42.9	41.8	40.8	40.1	40.2	39.7	41.0	...	...	...	41.8
	Statistics Canada	SNG	45.8	46.8	44.6	43.7	42.2	41.5	41.6	41.1	42.9	...	...	...	43.3
		SNG share	*0.44*	*0.44*	*0.45*	*0.46*	*0.47*	*0.48*	*0.50*	*0.51*	*0.53*	*...*	*...*	*...*	*0.48*
Germany	Eurostat	CG	...	...	37.0	38.7	40.4	41.9	41.9	40.2	40.7	45.3	52.8	51.2	43.0
	GFS	SG	17.2	18.1	19.2	20.5	21.5	22.3	21.6	20.4	22.1	24.9	25.8	...	21.2
	Eurostat	SNG	...	...	23.1	25.4	26.2	27.0	26.5	25.2	26.3	29.4	30.3	30.0	26.9
		SNG share	*...*	*...*	*0.38*	*0.40*	*0.39*	*0.39*	*0.39*	*0.39*	*0.39*	*0.39*	*0.36*	*0.37*	*0.39*
India	RBI	CG	59.6	63.6	67.0	66.1	65.5	63.9	61.4	58.9	58.6	56.5	52.8	51.9	60.5
	RBI	SG	27.4	29.4	31.1	31.8	31.3	31.1	28.9	26.6	26.1	25.5	23.5	22.7	28.0
		SNG	...	...	...	...	...	...	...	...	...	...	...	...	...
		SNG share	*...*	*...*	*...*	*...*	*...*	*...*	*...*	*...*	*...*	*...*	*...*	*...*	*...*
Mexico	OECD	CG	21.2	20.5	21.9	22.1	20.7	20.3	20.6	20.9	24.4	28.1	27.5	...	22.6
		SG	...	...	...	...	...	...	...	...	...	...	2.7	...	
	Central Government	SNG	...	1.9	2.0	1.7	1.6	1.6	1.6	1.7	1.7	2.1	2.5	...	1.8
		SNG share	*...*	*0.08*	*0.08*	*0.07*	*0.07*	*0.07*	*0.07*	*0.08*	*0.07*	*0.07*	*0.08*	*...*	*0.07*
South Africa	IMF Staff Reports	CG	...	43.6	42.7	35.3	35.1	33.5	30.7	28.5	27.2	33.0	36.0	...	34.6
		SG	...	...	...	...	...	...	...	...	...	...	...	...	...
		SNG	...	...	...	...	...	...	...	...	...	...	...	...	...
		SNG share	*...*	*...*	*...*	*...*	*...*	*...*	*...*	*...*	*...*	*...*	*...*	*...*	*...*

Note: SNG share is calculated as share of CG plus SNG debt

(*Continued*)

Table 5.2 (Continued)

Country	Source	Sector	2000	2001	2002	2003	2004	2005	2006	2007	2008	2009	2010	2011	Average
Spain	Eurostat	CG	49.9	46.3	44.0	40.8	39.4	36.4	33.0	30.1	33.7	46.3	52.3	58.0	42.5
	Eurostat	SG	6.3	6.4	6.4	6.3	6.2	6.4	6.0	5.8	6.7	8.7	11.4	13.1	7.5
	Eurostat	SNG[4]	9.4	9.4	8.7	9.1	9.0	9.0	8.7	8.5	9.3	11.7	14.8	16.5	10.3
		SNG share	*0.16*	*0.17*	*0.17*	*0.18*	*0.19*	*0.20*	*0.21*	*0.22*	*0.22*	*0.20*	*0.22*	*0.22*	*0.20*
Switzerland	OECD	CG	25.6	24.8	28.2	28.3	28.1	28.1	25.2	23.2	22.4	20.7	20.2	…	25.0
	GFS	SG	…	…	19.7	20.2	20.1	17.9	16.2	15.6	12.6	12.8	12.2	…	16.4
	GFS	SNG[3]	…	…	31.9	32.0	31.7	29.5	26.6	25.3	23.1	23.6	23.1	…	27.4
		SNG share	…	*0.53*	*0.53*	*0.53*	*0.51*	*0.51*	*0.51*	*0.52*	*0.51*	*0.53*	*0.53*	…	*0.52*
United States	OECD	CG	33.9	32.4	33.2	34.9	36.0	36.1	36.0	35.7	40.2	53.6	61.3	…	39.4
		SG	…	…	…	…	…	…	…	…	…	…	…	…	…
	Haver	SNG	15.4	16.2	17.3	17.8	24.8	24.6	24.2	24.4	24.4	26.0	25.8	24.7	22.1
		SNG share	*0.31*	*0.33*	*0.34*	*0.34*	*0.41*	*0.40*	*0.40*	*0.41*	*0.38*	*0.33*	*0.30*	…	*0.36*

Sources: Eurostat, OECD, GFS, Haver analytics, IMF Staff Reports, Statistics Canada, Reserve Bank of India, Brazilian Central Bank, Ministry of Finance and Public Credit of Mexico, Ministry of Economy and Public Finance of Argentina, Australia Bureau of Statistics and Statistik Austria.

Note: SNG refers to state and local governments.

[1] Argentina debt that was not exchanged is included in the total.
[2] Refers to total liabilities (GFS), excluding unfunded superannuation liability and other employee entitlements for better cross-country comparability.
[3] Unconsolidated.
[4] 2000 and 2001 unconsolidated.

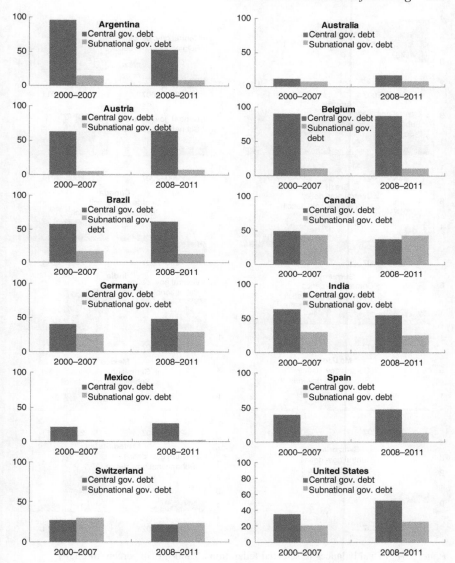

Panel 5.1a Debt in selected federations, 2000–11 (in percent of GDP)

Sources: Eurostat, OECD, GFS, Haver analytics, IMF Staff Reports, Statistics Canada, Reserve Bank of India, Brazilian Central Bank, Ministry of Finance and Public Credit of Mexico, Ministry of Economy and Public Finance of Argentina, Australia Bearu of Statistics and Statistik Austria.

budget stabilization funds, so-called rainy day funds and, in cases of financial distress, provide financial help and bailouts (Table 5.3 and Appendix A.5.1).[3]

• Central governments do not usually finance state governments directly, although a few notable exceptions arise. Central governments in Australia,

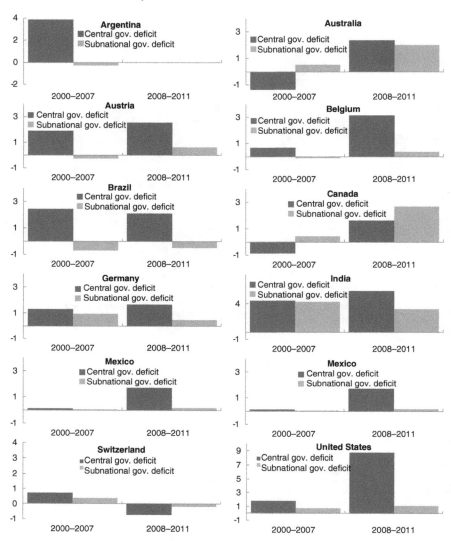

Panel 5.1b Fiscal balances in selected federations, 2000–11 (in percent of GDP)

Sources: Eurostat, OECD, GFS, Haver analytics, IMF Staff Reports, Statistics Canada, Reserve Bank of India, Brazilian Central Bank, Ministry of Finance and Public Credit of Mexico, Ministry of Economy and Public Finance of Argentina, Australia Bureau of Statistics and Statistik Austria.

Canada, Germany, and the U.S. provide small specific-purpose loans to states to finance selected programs. Programs mainly focus on housing and infrastructure (Australia, Germany) and unemployment compensation (United States). In India, over the last few years the central government has been phasing out its large direct loans to states (reflected in still large holdings of states' debt), and in 2011–12, central loans covered about 0.5 percent of

Table 5.3 Financial linkages between central and subnational governments in fiscal federations[1]

	Direct Financing	Indirect Financing (Through State Owned Entities)		Guarantees	Ad hoc Interventions[2]	
		Financial Institutions	SPVs and Others	(Direct/Indirect)	One Off Guarantees	Bailouts
Argentina	Yes	Yes (Banco de la Nación)	Yes (Fund for Provincial Development, Fund for Regional Infrastructure)	Yes/Yes	Yes	Bailouts 1992–94, 2001–2002, and 2003–2004
Australia	Limited (specific-purpose loans)	No	No	No/No	Guarantee scheme, 2009–10 (33 billion Australian dollars)	Bailout and centralization of debt in 1931
Austria	Yes (direct loans)	No	No	No/No	No	No
Belgium	No	No	No	No (only under particular circumstances)/No	No	No
Brazil	No	Yes (via BNDES and other public FIs)	No	Yes (guarantees for state projects and IFI loans)/No	No	Bailouts 1989, 1993, and 1997
Canada	Limited (specific-purpose loans)	No	No	No/No	No	Bailout 1940s
Germany	Limited (specific-purpose loans/joint bonds)	No	No	Limited/No	No	Bailout 1994-2004
India	Yes (direct loans and advances)	Yes (RBI overdraft)	Yes (EPFO, Employees' Provident Fund Organization; other funds, and NSSF)	Limited/No	Guarantees for state bonds to rescue SOE	Ongoing debt restructuring and relief
Mexico	No	Yes (via Banobras)	No	Yes/Yes	Yes, during 2004–06 bailout	Bailouts 1995 and 2004–06

(Continued)

Table 5.3 (Continued)

| | Direct Financing | Indirect Financing (Through State Owned Entities) | | Guarantees | Ad hoc Interventions[2] | |
		Financial Institutions	SPVs and Others	(Direct/Indirect)	One Off Guarantees	Bailouts
South Africa	No	Yes (via DBSA, Development Bank of South Africa)	No	No/No	No	1997–98: Takeover of provinces' departments to keep services running 2011–12
Spain	No	No	No	No/No	No	Quasi-bailout through advanced transfers 2012; Fund to Finance Payments to Suppliers (FFPP); and establishment of FLA in October 2012 (18 bn euros)
Switzerland	No	No	No	No/No	No	No
United States	Limited (to finance unemployment compensation)	No	No	No/No	No	No state bailouts, only NYC 1975; D.C. 1995; state fiscal stabilization fund 2009 ($54 billion)

[1]See Appendix A.5.1 for more detailed information and sources. Subnational governments cover only one level below the federal governments (e.g., states, provinces).
[2]See Chapter 6.

states' annual fiscal deficits.[4] Austria is the only notable exception of central-ized borrowing. The Austrian federal government's debt management agency is tasked by law to raise debt and on-lend to states through direct loans. While the stock of these loans is not large (about 2.5 percent of GDP in 2011), it covers about one third of states' financing needs (Table 5.4).

• In some federations, central governments indirectly finance states by chan-neling financing through centrally owned entities, although this is not very common (Table 5.5). Indirect financing is mainly used, to varying extent, in emerging market economies. In 2011–12, centrally-run funds in India (such as the pension fund EPFO and a small savings fund NSSF) provided for about one quarter of Indian states' financing needs (and owned about *half* of their debt), although their role is declining. On a more moderate scale, cen-trally owned development banks provide project-related financing to SNGs in Mexico (Banobras), Argentina (Banco de la Nación and others), Brazil (BNDES, et al.), and, with a very limited role, in South Africa (DBSA).

• Central governments also provide guarantees to states directly and through centrally owned institutions, although the amounts are generally limited. As for indirect financing, central guarantees are often used in emerging market economies. In Mexico, Banobras provides guarantees to states for the financ-ing of infrastructure projects, amongst other things (Nuñez, 2012), with total guarantees of about 0.1 percent of GDP (about 3 percent of states' debt) in mid-2012 (Banobras, 2012).[5] In India, the federal government used to guar-antee the payment obligations of state electricity boards, now eliminated.[6]

Table 5.4 Stock of direct federal loans to states in selected federations, 2011–12

	Percent of GDP	*Percent of CG Gross Debt*	*Percent of States' Gross Debt*	*Purpose*
Argentina	3.6	8.0	55.4	Debt restructuring and current financial support
Australia	0.2	1.2	2.6	Housing and infrastructure
Austria[1]	2.4	3.6	31.9	General budget financing and borrowing on behalf of states
Canada[1]	0.2	0.5	0.5	General budget financing
Germany	0.3	0.6	1.2	Housing and infrastructure
India	1.8	3.4	7.9	General budget financing
United States[1]	0.3	0.5	1.1	Unemployment compensation

[1]For Austria, states including Vienna; for the U.S., central, state, and local government debt in 2010; for Canada, state debt in 2008.

Table 5.5 Stock of indirect public loans to states in selected federations, 2011–12

	Percent of GDP	Percent of CG Gross Debt	Percent of States' Gross Debt	Vehicle
Argentina[1]	1.4	3.1	21.1	Banco de la Nación, TFPD, TFRI
Brazil[2]	1.1	1.8	9.1	Public financial institutions
India	11.7	22.5	50.3	EPFO, other Funds, NSSF
Mexico[3]	0.6	2.3	23.5	Banobras
South Africa	0.03	0.1	n/a	DBSA

[1]Banco de la Nación public sector loans and provincial debt to TFPD and TFRI at end 2011.
[2]Refers to SNGs.
[3]Central debt for 2010 and SNG debt for 2011.

In Brazil, the federal government can by law guarantee states' borrowing to finance projects that meet specific eligibility criteria. In all these countries, the central government either guarantees IFIs' loans to states or borrows on their behalf. Amongst advanced economies, only the German federal government provides guarantees, although on a very limited scale, to Länder for projects in agriculture, fishery, and social infrastructure (in 2011, such guarantees were less than €1 billion).[7]

• In a few federations, SNGs can rely on budget stabilization funds (or rainy day funds) to absorb temporary shocks or smooth out volatile revenue flows. While the majority of rainy-day funds are funded at the local level, in some countries funds are centrally financed.[8] Centrally financed funds operate in Canada where the Canadian Fiscal Stabilization Program was established in 1967, and in Mexico, where the FEIEF (Fondo de Estabilizacion de Ingresos de Entidades Federativas), administered by Banobras and financed with oil revenue, helps protect states against volatility in federal revenue transfers. Apart from rainy day funds, centrally financed crisis-emergency funds were also set up in Australia in 2009–10 and Spain in 2012 (see Chapter 6).

The various channels central governments use to provide financial support to states are reflected in the composition of SNG debt holdings (Panel 5.2). Most central governments do not directly hold significant shares of states' debt, with the exception of Austria where in 2011 the central government held about 32 percent of states' debt (Table 5.4 and Appendix A.5.1).[9] In India, the central government holds still a large, but rapidly declining, share of states' debt (about 8 percent in 2011).[10] However, central governments hold states' debt indirectly through national financial entities. In India, over the last few decades, public schemes such as the NSSF and Provident Funds have largely replaced central government financing and in 2011 held a combined share of about 50 percent of states' debt.

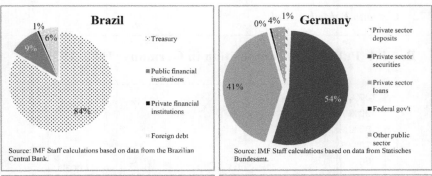

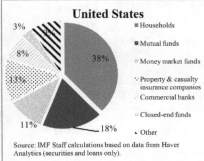

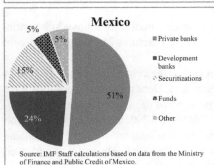

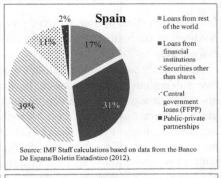

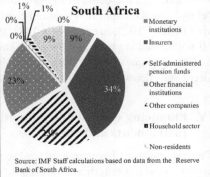

Panel 5.2 State debt by holders in selected federations, 2011[1]

[1]Data for Brazil, the U.S., and Mexico cover both state and local governments, for South Africa only locals.

Box 5.1 Public debt composition in Germany: 1880–1939

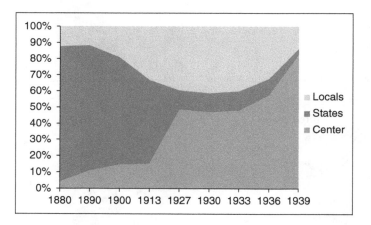

Source: Statistisches Bundesamt and Bundesministerium für Finanzen (2009)

In Argentina, Brazil, and Mexico, public financial institutions have substantial holdings of subnational government debt as well, reaching 21, 9 and 24 percent respectively in 2011.[11]

At the early stage of the creation of federations, the center has sometimes taken over sub-entities' debt on a one-off basis (Box 5.1). Debt takeover operations have always been associated with new revenue powers. In the United States, for example, the federal government took over states' debts in 1790, as the new constitution assigned the main revenue source (i.e., tariffs) to the center. Similarly, in Canada, the new Confederation created in 1867 assumed provincial debt and was endowed with a revenue-raising capacity. In Italy, the new unitary government created in 1860 inherited the debts of the previously independent states, including the large debt of the Kingdom of Piedmont-Sardinia and imposed new taxes immediately after (Tanzi, 2012). In contrast, in 1871, the new federal German government started off without taking over any debt, and states maintained their debt and control over their taxes (James, 1997). However, during the German re-unification in 1990, East Germany's debts were fully assumed by the federal government (Mai, 2002).

IV. Financing central and subnational governments: Instruments and costs[12]

Central and state governments tend to rely on different combinations of instruments to meet their financing needs. Central governments finance their debt mainly by issuing securities, while state governments tend to contract direct loans and use less security issuances. In 2011, for example, central governments in our sample of federations owed on average about four fifths of their debt in securities while state governments kept only about two fifths of their debt in securities, preferring instead to contract loans (covering about half of their debt) (Figure 5.3).[13] The different combination of financial instruments used by central and state governments may reflect several factors including tighter borrowing rules at state level (e.g., in some federations states can only use bonds to finance investment), close links of state governments with local state banks (e.g., in Germany), and still relatively underdeveloped SNG security markets.[14]

However, there are significant differences in the pattern of states' financing across federations (Figure 5.4). In the United States and Canada, for example, state governments finance about 70–80 percent of their debt through securities, only a bit less than their central governments do, and much more than in most of the other federations.[15] These different financing strategies are likely the outcome of institutional features, historical preferences for market over bank financing, financial market development, and fiscal incentives.[16] As a result, they tend to evolve slowly over time, although states in Belgium, India, and Germany have come to rely increasingly on securities over the last decade.[17]

Institutional characteristics of fiscal federations matter for market perceptions of the creditworthiness of lower levels of government. These perceptions

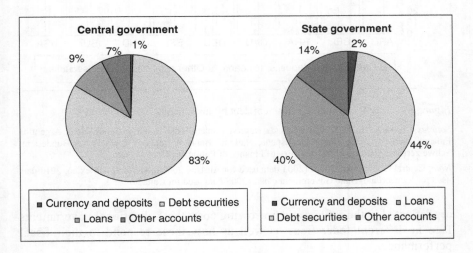

Figure 5.3 Central and state government debt by instruments, 2011.

Countries included: India, Spain, Canada, Germany, Brazil, Belgium, Argentina, United States, and Switzerland.

Sources: Eurostat, OECD, Statistics Canada, Reserve Bank of India, Brazilian Central Bank, Argentina Finance Ministry Banco De España, National Bank of Belgium, Statistisches Bundesamt, Schweizerische National Bank.

Note: Central Government Chart (2010 data used for Switzerland), State Government Chart (2008 data used for Canada).

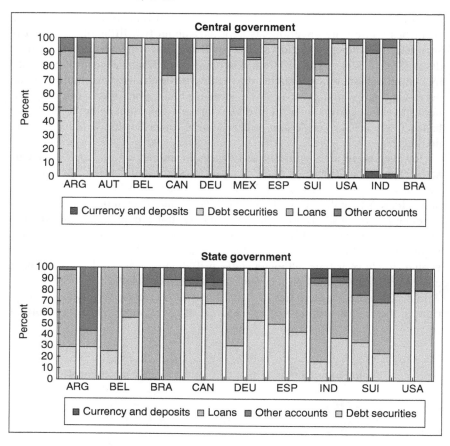

Figure 5.4 Central and state government debt by instrument, 2002 and 2011

Sources: Eurostat, OECD, Statistics Canada, Reserve Bank of India, Brazilian Central Bank, Argentina Finance Ministry World Banco De España, National Bank of Belgium, Statistisches Bundesamt, Schweizerische National Bank, Ministry of Finance of Public Credit of Mexico.

Note: Central Government Chart (2003 data used for Austria, 2006 data used for Mexico, 2010 data used for Switzerland) State Government Chart (2008 data used for Canada).

are reflected in the ratings and borrowing costs that subnational governments face in different federations as well as how these respond to their fiscal performance.

Higher transfer dependency tends to be associated with a lesser dispersion of ratings between the central and subnational levels. In general, markets for subnational debt tend to be less liquid than markets for sovereign bonds, which contributes to higher financing costs for SNGs.[18] However, in federations characterized by large reliance on central government transfers (e.g., Austria, Belgium, and Germany), the debt ratings of state governments tend to be more similar to, and less dispersed around, the ratings of the sovereign (Figure 5.5).

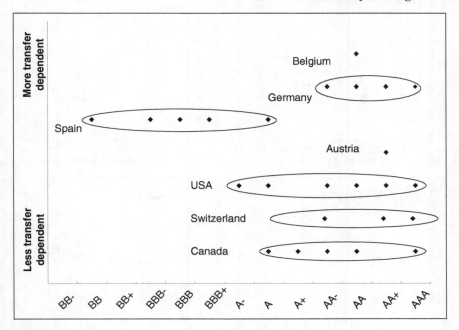

Figure 5.5 Credit ratings in selected federations, September 2012

Source: Standard and Poor's.

Note: Countries are ranked according to the degree of transfer dependency.

Also, the ratings of state governments in these federations are less responsive to states' fiscal performance. For example, the ratings of provinces and states in both Canada and Germany reflect the performance of basic fiscal indicators (Figure 5.6), but states in Germany, which benefit from higher fiscal transfers than do their Canadian counterparts, seem to achieve the same rating as Canadian provinces with much poorer fiscal indicators.[19] This supports the conjecture that markets view high transfer dependency as a form of implicit bailout guarantee, improving the rating of the subnational entity.

In the same vein, state governments usually borrow at higher interest rates than central governments, and the premiums are larger in more decentralized federations.

- Using primary market data for subnational governments in Canada, Germany, and Spain, Schuknecht et al. (2009) show that states borrowed at higher interest rates than did central governments during 1991–2005. This evidence continues to hold for the period 2005–11.[20] Over this period, primary market spreads on long-term bonds averaged about 85 basis points (Figure 5.7).
- Country specific evidence from both primary and secondary markets suggests that states and local governments face higher spreads if they are part

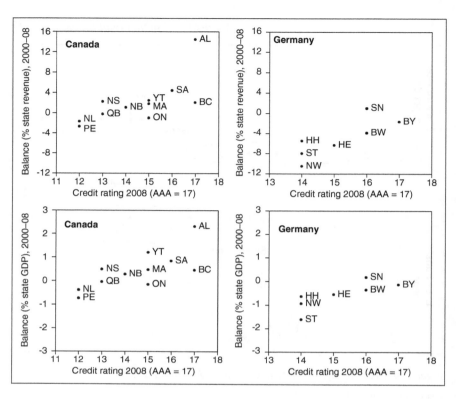

Figure 5.6 State government ratings and fiscal performance in Canada and Germany

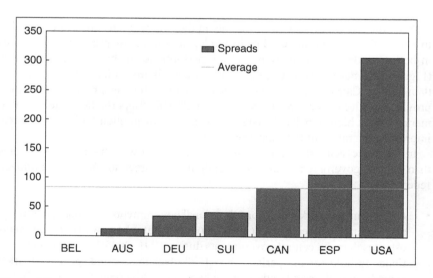

Figure 5.7 Average spreads on the primary market for SNG bonds (average spread at issuance for bonds of maturity >10 years: 2005–2011)

Source: Dealogic.

of a more decentralized federation. In Canada, for example, where SNGs enjoy relatively more fiscal autonomy, primary market data for 2007–12 suggest that the average cost of borrowing at maturities above seven years was about 80 to 100 basis points (bps) higher for states and local governments than for the central government. In contrast, German states that rely more on central transfers paid a lower premium of 20 to 60 bps over the same period.[21] The same holds for bonds with maturities shorter than three years, while the evidence is more mixed for bonds with intermediate maturity (Figure 5.8).[22]

• Spreads constructed using information from the secondary market at constant maturity confirm the previous findings (Figure 5.9).[23] Data on constant maturity yield curves for state governments are available for a subset of the countries in our sample. These data allow us to compute the spread that each state government pays over the central government's borrowing cost for a given maturity. Comparing Canada and Australia – a relatively more centralized fiscal federation – it turns out that, at least until the onset of the 2008 crisis, the dispersion of interest rate spreads on state bonds was larger in the more decentralized Canadian federation. After the 2008 crisis, however, this evidence is more mixed, potentially due to different liquidity conditions.

Recent empirical studies suggest that expectations of bailouts can unduly suppress spreads for SNGs and add a risk premium to sovereign borrowing. In the case of Swiss cantons and municipalities, for example, Feld et al. (2011) find that the creation of a credible no-bailout regime of cantons versus their municipalities (with a 2003 Supreme Court decision) reduced the cantonal risk premium by about 25 bps. Schuknecht et al. (2008) show that Canadian provinces which are systematically net recipients of the equalization grants are not necessarily penalized by markets for running large budget deficits, as being subsidized is seen as a form of guarantee from the center. On the other hand, financial market discipline is likely to be more effective in federations where the federal government is not expected to bail out subnational debtors – for instance, the U.S.

These stylized facts hide simultaneous relationships, and more extensive research is needed to fully disentangle the role of different factors. For example, the relationship between institutional arrangements of federations' and states' ratings and yield spreads may well be linked to the different fiscal performances across federations rather than to the presence of an implicit bailout guarantee. As shown, more centralized fiscal federations tend to have relatively lower levels of SNG debt and deficits. This in turn could either be the result of systematic differences between the degree of transfer dependency and the strength of fiscal rules, or be related to the fact that in more centralized fiscal federations central governments borrow "on behalf" of SNGs, therefore contributing to their fiscal performance.

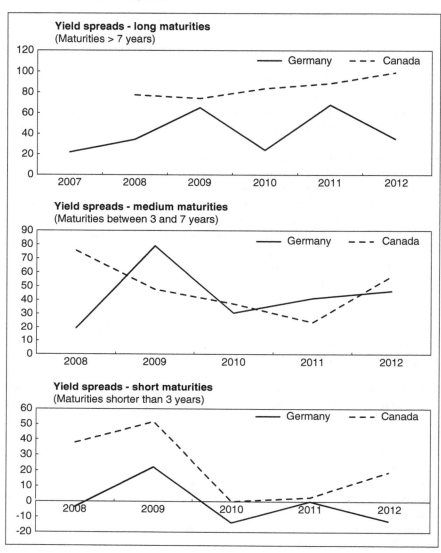

Figure 5.8 Yield spreads on subnational government bonds by maturity at issuance: Germany and Canada, 2007–12

V. Financing arrangements in the European Union

Existing supranational financing arrangements in the European Union (EU) play a limited role compared to those in federations. Financial transfers are limited to structural funds that, given the small size of the EU budget, amount to only 0.5 percent of the area GDP. There is no central direct financing of national governments,

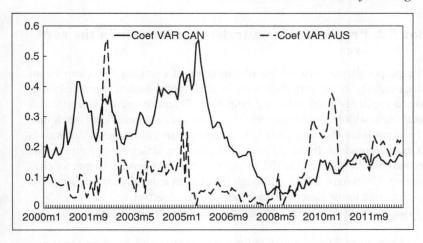

Figure 5.9 Coefficient of variations of spreads (std. dev. of sovereign spreads / average spread)

but some indirect financing is available through the European Investment Bank (EIB).[24] In response to the recent crisis, a permanent crisis resolution fund for euro members (ESM) was set up to provide for greater risk sharing at the supranational level and create a fiscal backstop for a banking union (see Chapter 6).

While intra EU financing arrangements are limited, several proposals are being discussed to create greater fiscal coordination and integration for euro area countries. Differently from the practices in most fiscal federations, attention has been focused primarily on creating mechanisms for direct central financing (e.g., via centralized borrowing). More in line with experience in existing federations, proposals also include the creation of a common insurance fund for euro area members (Enderlein et al, 2012), which would be comparable to the budget stabilization funds in place in many federations (and discussed in Section III).

- **Direct financing:** Several proposals have focused on centralized borrowing through the issuance of common European bonds. The aim would be to reduce borrowing costs for some member states by pooling risks. It could however weaken incentives for national fiscal discipline (a typical moral hazard problem). Specific proposals include euro bills, the red-blue bond scheme, and ESBies. These different proposals mostly differ in the way they seek to contain the weakening of incentives for national fiscal discipline and the pursuit of structural reforms (Box 5.2).
- **Rainy day fund:** A proposal to create a cyclical adjustment insurance fund for euro members aims at alleviating cyclical fiscal imbalances (Enderlein et al., 2012).[25] Akin to rainy day funds, countries would pay into the fund when the cyclical component of their growth is significantly larger than the euro area average and could draw on it during severe downturns. The fund

Box 5.2 Proposals for centralized borrowing in the euro area

The proposals put forward for the issuance of common European bonds differ mainly in the way they seek to limit moral hazard. Joint liabilities would explicitly pool risks and help lower average country-specific risk premiums, which could encourage a relaxation of national fiscal discipline. The main issue thus becomes how to strengthen governments' incentives to pursue prudent fiscal policies and advance structural reforms while reconciling the spirit of the EU Treaty's no-bailout clause with greater risk-sharing (Claessens, 2012). Although fiscal rules exist already, enforcement mechanisms in the Euro area have been largely ineffective.

The main options under consideration to date are as follows:

- **Euro-bills** (Hellwig and Philippon, 2011) would be short-term euro securities issued on behalf of euro-zone countries by a joint debt management office (DMO), for which countries would be jointly liable. Countries would issue demand schedules to the DMO, which would then issue bonds on their behalf, based on auction mechanisms. Excess amounts would be bought by the ECB. The moral hazard problem would be addressed by asking countries to pay a penalty rate if they do not meet fiscal prerequisites and by capping the amount of issuance.
- **The Blue-Red bond scheme** (Von Weizsäcker and Delpla, 2011, and the European Commission) would create a euro-wide "blue bond" that would have joint liability and cover up to 60 percent of each country's GDP, and a "red bond" for any debt issued beyond this threshold and for which countries would remain individually responsible. The two types of bonds will also be different in seniority: blue bonds will be senior while red bonds will be junior. Blue bond creditors would only be subordinate to the IMF. Moreover, red bonds would not be eligible for refinancing operations of the ECB and would have higher risk weights for financial sector capital requirements. The allocation of blue bonds would take place on an annual basis, on the basis of a proposal by an independent stability council and approval by national parliaments. Allocation of blue debt by the council would be decided on the basis of the principles of the SGP and fiscal sustainability analysis. Should parliaments fail to adopt the proposal, the country could temporarily leave the blue bond scheme.
- **ESBies** (Euro-nomics group) would involve the creation of safe assets through a securitization vehicle, the European Debt Agency (EDA). The EDA – initially financed by capital provided by member states – would buy the debt of euro area member states up to 60 percent of each country's GDP, and use it as collateral to issue two securities: a senior tranche – the European Safe Bonds (ESBies) – and a junior

tranche – the European Junior Bonds (EJBs). It would function as a passive manager, buying debt on the secondary market in proportion of each country's GDP. In contrast to the other proposals, no shared or joint liability would be required, but due to pooling and tranching the ESBies would be effectively a safe asset. Because of their zero risk weight, they would be held by banks, therefore breaking the link between sovereign risk and financial sector fragility. Moreover, the ESBies could be used as collateral by the ECB for repo operations. Because of the absence of joint liability, this proposal does not require a fiscal union or modifica-tion of the EU Treaty (Brunnermeier et al., 2011).

would be automatic and rules-based, financed by national budget contri-butions, and controlled by national parliaments. Over the medium term, it should be of neutral benefit to participating states.

These and other proposals on redesigned euro area supranational fiscal arrange-ments are still under discussion, and it is not clear to what extent EU member states outside the euro zone could opt to participate in such financing schemes.

VI. Conclusions

Evidence shows that institutional arrangements matter in shaping central and sub-national governments' financing strategies in fiscal federations. Debt and deficit allocations across different levels of government tend to follow governments' tax capacity, with more autonomous subnational governments borrowing more. Historical episodes also confirm that, conversely, the centralization of debt has tended to be associated with a transfer of tax authority.

In most cases, the center does not provide significant direct support to finance states' fiscal balances. However, in less advanced countries, the center tends to help covering states' financial requirements through other national institutions and by providing guarantees – either directly or indirectly. One-off debt central-izations have also occurred during the formation of several unitary states, when subnational entities' debts were taken over by the center (for example, in the United States and Canada).

Financial and risk-sharing ties between the center and SNGs have an impact on the borrowing costs of both sovereign and subnational entities. In more finan-cially centralized federations with implicit bailout expectations, states (particu-larly those that are less fiscally sound) benefit from an implicit subsidy resulting from sharing risks with the central government. In turn, sovereigns may be paying an implicit risk premium in light of their expected responsibilities vis-à-vis their subnational units.

Empirical evidence suggests that bailout expectations are likely to dominate fiscal fundamentals in determining entities' interest rate spreads, limiting market discipline. This is in line with the risk re-assessment that occurred since the start of the European debt crisis, when markets greatly reassessed the probability of bailouts of weaker governments within the euro area.

Supranational financing mechanisms in the European Union are still limited but are likely to evolve further, particularly for euro area countries. With the ongoing euro crisis, several proposals have been put forward supporting centralized borrowing and a joint cyclical adjustment insurance fund (akin to rainy funds), in addition to the creation of a permanent crisis resolution fund (ESM). It is not clear to what extent the scope of these new mechanisms would include non-euro member states.

Appendix A.5.1
Country case studies

This Appendix provides detailed information on direct and indirect financing and guarantees that central governments provide to subnational governments in selected federations. Table 5.3 and Section III provide a summary of the Appendix findings.[26]

A. Argentina

Background: The federal government has a long history of providing financial support to provinces often as part of rescue packages. During the 1980s, provinces routinely financed excessive deficits with federal loans. During 1992–94, the federal government bailed out seven provinces by issuing treasury bonds and granting loans amounting to about US$800 million (Bordo et al., 2011). In 1995, Cordoba province received extraordinary transfers, and during the 1990s all provinces received extraordinary financing via advanced transfers, loans from the state-owned Banco de la Nación Argentina, loans from the Trust Fund for the Provincial Development, and re-discounts by the central bank to the provincial banks. In 2001–03, the federal government had to bail out provinces again, taking over US$9.7 billion in provinces' bank debt and US$2.5 billion of central bank liabilities (Chapter 6). Currently, revenue transfers from the federal government serve as a guarantee for repayment of past loans to the federal government.

Direct financing: The Federal Government provides direct financing to provinces. Over the last few years, federal loans to provinces have continued at a lower scale as provinces are regaining market access (Province of Buenos Aires, 2010). As of June 2012, outstanding federal loans to provinces amounted to US$15 billion (55 percent of provincial debt and 8 percent of total federal debt) (Ministry of Economy and Finance, 2012). Federal financial support is highest in the provinces of Buenos Aires and Cordoba. In June 2012, province of Buenos Aires' debt to the federal government amounted to US$7 billion (almost 50 percent of its total debt), and the province of Cordoba owed the federal government just over US$1 billion (or 46 percent of its total debt).

Indirect financing: The Federal government provides indirect financing to provinces, although to a smaller extent than in the past. The main vehicles of indirect financing are the Banco de la Nación, the Trust Fund for Provincial

Development (TFPD), and the Trust Fund for Regional Infrastructure (TFRI). During the early 2000s, the federal government used the TFPD to assume and restructure provincial debt and issued guaranteed bonds. In 2011, total provincial debt to the TFRI and the TFPD was US$335 million and US$290 million, respectively – about 2 percent of total provincial debt (Ministry of Economy and Finance, 2012), and public sector loans from Banco de la Nación amounted to about 21 percent of provinces' total debt.

Guarantees: The federal government provides direct guarantees to provinces, usually limited to loans from IFIs. In June 2012, the federal government reported guarantees to provinces of almost US$2 billion (about 1 percent of federal gross debt), of which 92 percent related to IFI loans (Ministry of Economy and Finance, 2012).

B. Australia

Background: Legislation on the linkages between central and subnational government financing has changed over time. In the 1927 Financial Agreement between the commonwealth and the states, the commonwealth was empowered through the Loan Council to manage and take over state debts and borrow on their behalf. States accepted this reduction in their financial autonomy in return for the commonwealth guaranteeing their debts. In 1931, the Commonwealth Debt Conversion Act authorized the central government to convert all existing central and state debt into new debt. Loan Council domination of the commonwealth was further strengthened by states' exclusion from indirect taxation and the commonwealth's monopoly on income tax from 1942 (Von Hagen et al., 2000). In 1984, reforms of the Loan Council enabled the states to take greater responsibility for their borrowing and securities and loans previously raised for them by the commonwealth (Ter Minassian, 1997). From 1990, the commonwealth ceased to be responsible for states' new borrowing, and the 1994 Financial Agreement Act states were to progressively redeem the debt that had been issued on their behalf.

Direct financing: The commonwealth government provides small specific-purpose loans to states, territories, and local governments, mostly related to housing and infrastructure. In June 2011, the stock of commonwealth government's loans to states amounted to AUS$3.4 billion (about 2.5 percent of states' gross debt and 1.2 percent of the commonwealth's gross debt – Australian Bureau of Statistics, 2012).[27]

Indirect financing: No instances of indirect financing are known.

Guarantees: There is no federal guarantee to states (Government of Australia, 2012a).

Others:

Ad-hoc interventions: In response to the recent financial crisis, in 2009 the government launched the Australian Government Guarantee of State and Territory Borrowing scheme to support states' access to capital markets at lower rates. Guarantees for new and existing non-complex, domestic currency-denominated securities were issued for a fee. Only New South Wales and Queensland have issued guaranteed bonds of about AUS$31 billion. The scheme was closed at end-2010 (Government of Australia, 2012b), and since then both states have sought to reduce their guaranteed debt outstanding (Reserve Bank of Australia, 2011).

C. Austria

Direct financing: The federal government provides direct financing to states under the federal financing law (*Bundesfinanzierungsgesetz*) and enters into contracts with states for swap operations on their behalf. The federal government operates through the Austrian debt management agency (*Oesterreichische Bundesfinanzierungsagentur,* OeBFA) that raises debt and on-lend the funds to states through direct loans. In 2011, the stock of these loans amounted to €7.2 billion (about 32 percent of states' (including Vienna) total debt in 2011[28]), up from €6 billion at end-2010 (Bundesrechnungshof, 2012; Statistik Austria 2012).

Indirect financing: No instances of indirect financing are known. However, some banks taken over by the federal government in 2009 still have loans to state governments outstanding (Hypo Alpe-Adria, Oesterreichische Volksbanken AG).

Guarantees: There are no federal guarantees to states (Bundesrechnungshof, 2012).

D. Belgium

Background: Since 1993, Belgium is a Federal State composed of two main types of federated bodies: Regions and Communities. There are three regions (Walloon, Flemish, and the Brussels Capital) and three communities (the French, the Flemish, and the German speaking communities). In Flanders, the community and regional institutions have been merged. Only the Regions have significant fiscal autonomy. Both the Communities and the Regions can contract loans though (LSF, Article 49, §1, January 1989).[29]

Direct financing: No instances of direct federal financing to regions and communities are known.

Indirect financing: No instances of indirect financing are known.

Guarantees: Provinces and Communities do not benefit directly from the guarantee of the Federal State (LSRI, Article 15).[30] However, if the Federal government pays dues late or only partially, then Regions can contract loans under a federal government's guarantee (LSF, Article 54, §2). No instances of indirect guarantees are known.

Others:

Local governments. Regions can issue guarantees for debt contracted at the local level. Guaranteed debt "refers to all bonds issued by regional or local institutions to meet their financial needs. These loans are guaranteed in the region for all that concerns the payment of interest and/or amortization" (Federation Wallonia-Brussels, 2011).

E. Brazil

Direct financing: The federal government does not provide direct financing to states. The 2000 Fiscal Responsibility Law (FRL) prohibits any lending from one level of government to another (in addition, the law does not allow SNGs to issue bonds until 2020). The Federal government holds large amounts of state debt as a result of the large bailout packages implemented during 1995–2000 (Banco Central do Brasil, 2012).

Indirect financing: The federal government provides financing to states indirectly through a federally owned development bank (Banco Nacional de Desenvolvimento Econômico e Social, BNDES) (Fitch, 2012a) and other public financial institutions. BNDES provides financing to both states and municipalities, with states accounting for the larger share of BNDES' loans (BNDES, 2011). In 2011, total loan disbursements to states (covering 25 states) amounted to US$1.4 billion (0.7 percent of states' debt). The ten states receiving the largest disbursements were Ceará, Bahia, Rio Grande do Sul, Sergipe, Pernambuco, Rio de Janeiro, Espírito Santo, São Paulo, Paraíba, and Amazonas. As part of the World Cup infrastructural building, BNDES has also contracted loans to different states of about US$259 million for the construction of stadiums (BNDES, 2011). Total public sector loans to states and municipalities amounted to 9 percent of SNG debt in 2011 (Banco Central do Brasil, 2012).

Guarantees: The federal government can provide guarantees to the financing for selected states' projects that respect some publicly defined criteria; however, no guarantee has been so far provided. In theory, an eligible project may receive a federal guarantee when the fiscal position of the state is sufficiently robust to insure repayment capacity (the fiscal position is assessed on a "score" system based on a several different fiscal indicators). However, there are some exceptionality clauses; for instance, a project may be deemed eligible and be centrally guaranteed if it is of particular interest to the federal government or contributes to improving revenue administration capacity. A project may be also granted a guarantee if the SNG offers counter-guarantees (what can count as counter-guarantee is also legislated). If guarantees are activated, states cannot borrow further (Fiscal Responsibility Law 2000 and Ordinance no. 306 September 10th 2012).The Federal government provides direct guarantees on all debt that states contract with International Organizations (e.g., IDB). No instances of indirect guarantees are known.

F. Canada

Direct financing: The federal government provides very limited direct financial support to provinces and territories. In 2011, loans and advances to provincial and territorial governments, made under various legislation, amounted to CAN$3.5 billion (about 0.5 percent of provincial debt) (Government of Canada, 2012).[31]

Indirect financing: There is no indirect federal financing (Federal-Provincial Relations Division, Ministry of Finance).

Guarantees: There are neither direct nor indirect federal guarantees (Federal-Provincial Relations Division, Ministry of Finance).

Others:

> *Local governments.* Federal and provincial governments issue guarantees to privately held companies. In the event that the firm fails, a debt guarantee becomes a claim on government revenues. In 2012, Federal Government's guarantees amounted to US$249.4 billion (Government of Canada, 2012). Provinces also provide similar guarantees although no recent information is available (Gabel and Veldhuis (2004) reports that in 2001/02, provinces' debt guarantees were about US$81 billion).

G. Germany

Direct financing: The federal government does not directly finance states' budgets, except for small specific-purpose loans (e.g., for housing and public infrastructure). In 2011, these loans amounted to €7.5 billion (1.2 percent of states' total debt) (Bundesministerium der Finanzen, 2012a, Statistisches Bundesamt, 2012).

Indirect financing: No instances of indirect financing are known.

Guarantees: The federal government provides limited direct guarantees to states. To illustrate, the 2011 federal budget included about €112 billion in guarantees and only just under €1 billion was directly referred to state's programs (e.g., in agriculture, fishery, and social infrastructure). The federal government also guarantees half of any contingent losses facing the State of Bavaria for hosting the Olympic and Paralympic Games in 2018 (Bundesministerium der Finanzen, 2012b). No instances of indirect guarantees are known.

Others:

> *Joint bond.* The German federal government also issued a joint bond (of 3 billion euros, *Bund-Laender-Anleihen*) with ten Länder in June 2013,[32] of which it assumed liability for only its own share of 13.5 percent, however. Borrowing costs were about 50 bps higher for the federal government, whereas a few Länder (Berlin, NRW) faced lower costs vis-à-vis their stand-alone emissions (Frankfurter Allgemeine Zeitung, 2013).
>
> *Local governments.* The majority-federally owned bank KfW provides small, subsidized loans to municipalities, mainly for energy efficiency and communal infrastructure.

H. India

Direct financing: Since 2004, the federal government has been phasing out historically high direct financing to states.[33] The federal government used to provide for a significant part of states' financing needs through direct loans and advances. In the late 1990s, federal government's loans used to meet about half of states' financing needs and, in 1999, the federal government held about half of states' total debt. In 2004, the Twelfth Financing Commission recommended to phase out this intermediation and force states to rely to a greater extent on markets (Government of India, 2004). By 2011, central government holdings of states' debt had fallen to 8 percent of states' debt, and in 2011–12 federal loans to states covered only 0.5 percent of states' gross fiscal deficits (Reserve Bank of India, 2012).

Indirect financing: The federal government provides financing to states indirectly through a number of central government-run schemes. For example, states borrow from the Employees Provident Fund (EPFO), other public funds, and the National Small Savings Fund (NSSF) (in 2011, about 24 and 26 percent of total states' debt, respectively; Reserve Bank of India, 2012; Ianchovichina et al., 2006). Financing from these sources accounted for about 24 percent of the financing of states' gross deficits in 2011–12. At the same time, market borrowings in 2011 increased to 37 percent of total states' debt and covered more than two thirds of states' gross deficits (ICRA, 2012).

Guarantees: The central government provides guarantees for IFI loans channeled to states (through the central Ministry of Finance's Aid Account & Audit division) and used to guarantee payment obligations of states' electricity boards (Government of India, 2012)

Others:

> *One-off interventions.* In the past, states were granted debt relief in return for fiscal consolidation, without facing penalties for any breaches (Purfield, 2004). In September 2012, the central government approved a bailout for state electricity boards that could amount to up to INR2 trillion (about US$36 billion).

I. Mexico

Direct financing: No instances of direct financing are known.

Indirect financing: The federal government provides indirect financing to subnational governments mainly through the federally owned development bank, the National Bank of Public Works and Services (Banobras). In 2010, its loan portfolio was more than US$10 billion and its loans to states and municipalities amounted to about US$7 billion in 2011 (Banobras, 2012). The federal government is Banobras' majority shareholder (owning 99.5 percent of the bank's capital) and, as stated under its organic law (Article 11), it is explicitly responsible for Banobras' liabilities with domestic or foreign institutions (Fitch Report, 2012b).

Guarantees: The federal government provides direct guarantees for loans which subnational governments' contract with international organizations (e.g., IDB). The federal government also guarantees indirectly states' loans via Banobras that, in turn, guaranteed about 3 percent of states' debt directly in 2012, and uses federal revenue transfers to collateralize state governments' loans (Bano-bras, 2012). The Fondo de Aportaciones para la Infraestructura Social (FAIS) and the Fondo de Aportaciones para el Fortalecimiento de las Entidades Federativas (FAFEF) do not directly provide guarantees but their transfers can be used as collateral for SNGs' borrowing.[34] In 2011, about 6 percent of SNG debt was guaranteed by FAIS/FAFEF, 72 percent by revenue sharing transfers from the center (participaciones) (Secretaria de Hacienda y Credito Publico, 2012).

J. South Africa

Background: The national government is not allowed to bail out or provide guarantees to provinces and municipalities (Government of South Africa, 2011), with the sole exception represented by Article 100(a) and Article 100(b) of the South African Constitution. According to those provisions, in fact, "When a province cannot or does not fulfill an executive obligation in terms of the Constitution or legislation, the national executive may intervene . . . assuming responsibility for the relevant obligation in that province to the extent necessary to maintain essential national standards or meet established minimum standards for the rendering of a service; maintain economic unity; maintain national security; or prevent that province from taking unreasonable action that is prejudicial to the interests of another province or to the country as a whole." The actions under these provisions are conditional to the fact that the financial powers/authority delegated to the Provincial Government be withdrawn and are temporarily taken over by the National Government. It is important to notice, in addition, that the constitution expressly requires the intervention to be limited in time and amount (". . . to maintain essential national standards or meet established minimum standards . . . .")

Direct financing: No instance of direct national government financing to provinces is known. The constitution does not foresee any direct financing across different levels of governments apart from transfers.

Indirect financing: The national government provides limited indirect financing to provinces through the Development Bank of Southern Africa – DBSA (DBSA is 100 percent owned by the national government; Fitch, 2011). In 2011 12, DBSA's development loans amounted to US$4.9 billion (93 percent of its total assets), and about 2.5 percent of these loans were directed to national and provincial governments. Of these latter, about 43 percent of DBSA's loans were disbursed to local governments, 28 percent to public utility companies, 22 percent to private sector intermediaries, and the rest to development and educational institutions (DBSA, 2012).

Guarantees: There are no direct guarantees to lower levels of government (Government of South Africa, 2011), and no instance of indirect guarantee is known. However, Article 5 of the 1996 Borrowing Powers of Provincial Governments Act, while setting a general principle of no federal guarantee, allows for exceptions as it states that: "Notwithstanding anything to the contrary in this or any other law, no guarantee shall be furnished by the national government in respect of the fulfillment of a financial commitment incurred or to be incurred by a provincial government pursuant to the raising of bridging finance or conclusion of a loan denominated in rand" (Government of South Africa, 1996).

Others:

Ad hoc interventions. In December 2011, the National Cabinet approved a 17 million rand rescue package for the bankrupt province of Limpopo under the provision of article 100(a) and 100(b) of the Constitution.[35] Gauteng, Free State, and Eastern Cape also received transfers in 2011–12, and Eastern Cape and Kwazulu-Natal previously had in 1997–98 (see Chapter 6).

K. Spain

Direct and indirect financing and guarantees: No instance of central government direct or indirect financing or guarantee is known.

Others:

Ad hoc interventions. During the recent European debt crisis, the central government has taken steps to provide liquidity to regions. By September 2012, autonomous regions owed the central government about €18 billion (or 11 percent of their total debt) under the Fund to Finance Payment of Suppliers (FFPP). In October 2012, the government set up a regional liquidity fund (FLA) amounting to €18 billion after an emergency credit line and advance transfers of €10 billion announced in January 2012 did not suffice. Autonomous regions can obtain loans under strict conditions, including on reporting and fiscal consolidation. Funds are to be used primarily to service debt obligations; remaining surpluses can be used for 2012 financing needs and to pay suppliers (Ministry of Finance and Public Administration, 2012).

L. Switzerland

Direct and indirect financing and guarantees: The federal government does not provide any form of direct or indirect financing to cantons, and does not guarantee cantonal debt (nor do cantons guarantee municipal debt). A Supreme Court decision in 2003 relieving the cantons from assisting municipalities in fiscal distress confirmed a fully credible no bailout regime on all levels (Feld et al., 2011).

M. United States

Background: The states that comprise the United States have the largest subnational debt market. About US$400 billion are issued on average each year, in a market of about US$1.12 trillion (December 2005), accounting for about 10 percent of the U.S. domestic bond market, and 26 percent of U.S. public sector bonds (Young, 2012). Individual investors are the largest holders of U.S. subnational bonds, followed by mutual funds, bank trust accounts, banks, insurance companies, and corporations (Maco, 2001).

Direct financing: The federal government provides limited direct financing to cover states' current expenditure for unemployment compensation. As of February 2011, 31 States and the U.S. Virgin Island had borrowed about US$43 billion through trust fund loans from the Federal Government (about 1 percent of total state and local government debt). For some states, this form of indebtedness is particularly large (e.g., California owes about US$10 billion, 23 percent of total federal lending for unemployment compensation) (Maguire, 2011).

Indirect financing: No instance of federal indirect financing to states is known.

Guarantees. No instance of federal direct or indirect guarantee to states is known.

Others:

> *Local governments.* The federal and state governments provide indirect financing and guarantees to municipalities through "State Revolving schemes" and bond banks. Under revolving schemes, federal and state governments provide loans (usually at a subsidized rate) to local governments through a fund, which then re-lends the loan repayments to other borrowers. It is also relatively common to have issuances of local government bonds being carried out through bond banks that carry state guarantees. Bond banks are entities whose main purpose is to pool loans to municipalities from a portfolio and sell shares of it back to the market. Formally, bond banks are financial intermediaries. A few states have credit guarantees either on the instruments issued by bond banks or on the underlying loans to the local governments. The state of New Hampshire, for instance, provides a direct guarantee on the underlying bonds of the local governments. However, the majority of the states do not do so, because of statutory limitations on the amount of general-obligation debt they can issue or because they prefer to retain that debt capacity for statewide investments (Kehew et al., 2005). The H.R. 344 *Fiscal Responsibility Effective Enforcement Act* of 2011 forbids the Federal Reserve Board from buying short-term municipal securities.

Notes

Ari Binder and Asad Zaman provided excellent research assistance.

1 For details on the sample of federations, see Introduction and Overview. In this chapter, the term "subnational government" (SNG) includes state and local governments. However, discussion of financing instruments and costs focuses on state governments.
2 Discussion in this section focuses on one level of government below the federal level (e.g., states, provinces, Länder), generally defined as states, hence excluding local governments.
3 For detailed information on financial linkages between different levels of government in fiscal federations, see Appendix 5.1. For a detailed discussion of bailout experiences, see Chapter 6.
4 Through the 1980s and 1990s, the central government in India provided loans to finance approximately half of states' deficits (e.g., in 1997–98, the central government financed about 52 percent of states' deficits).
5 In addition, SNGs can use general revenue transfers (participaciones) as well as transfers through some federal funds (FAIS, Fondo de Aportaciones para la Infraestructura Social, and FAFEF, Fondo de Aportaciones para el Fortalecimiento de las Entidades Federativas) as collateral. In 2011, about six percent of SNGs' debt was collateralized by FAIS/FAFEF and 72 percent by revenue sharing transfers from the center (Secretaria de Hacienda y Credito Publico, 2012).
6 The 2012–13 Union Budget reports no remaining stock of these guarantees (Government of India, 2012).
7 In June 2013, the German federal government issued a first joint bond (*Bund-Laender-Anleihen*) with ten Länder (Berlin, Brandenburg, Bremen, Hamburg, Mecklenburg-Vorpommern, NRW, Rheinland-Pfalz, Saarland, Sachsen-Anhalt, Schleswig-Holstein). The federal government assumed liability for only its own share (13.5 percent of total amount), however, without any obligation to step in should any Länder fail to meet its obligations. The joint bond issue aimed at reducing borrowing cost of Länder, however, yields at issuance were about 50 bps higher for the federal government, whereas a few Länder faced lower costs vis-à-vis their stand-alone emissions (FAZ, 2013).
8 Locally financed rainy day funds are widespread in the United States, for example. States started creating stabilization funds after the crisis of the early 1980s; deposit and withdrawal rules and funds' size differ across states. During the recent financial crisis, states drew on these funds and other reserves, with the aggregate balance decreasing from 4.5 percent of states' spending in 2006 to 1.5 percent by 2011 (Center on Budget and Policy Priorities, 2011). In Canada, the fiscal stabilization fund of New Brunswick aims to preserve budget balance year-to-year, and Alberta has a trust fund to save royalties from resource depletion for future generations.
9 Lack of a detailed breakdown of holdings prevents us from including Austria in Panel 2.
10 In Brazil, large federal holding of SNG debt (84 percent) reflects bail out operations carried out in the 1990s rather than ongoing financing. In Argentina, the large central government's stock of provincial debt (55 percent) is also mainly the result of debt restructurings, although more limited support to provinces continues. In Spain, the central government held 11 percent of autonomous regions' debt in September 2012 through the Fund to Finance Payments to Suppliers (FFPP), set up in reaction to the crisis (Panel 2).
11 SNG debt securities are formally accepted as collateral in major central banks (such as the U.S. Fed, the ECB, and the Bank of Canada). However, there are no significant central bank holdings of SNG debt.
12 This section focuses on a subset of our sample of countries for which detailed state level data on debt, ratings, and yield spreads are available.
13 The same conclusion is reached when looking at consolidated state and local governments' debts, which have only a slightly higher share of loans.

14 The United States remains the largest subnational bond market, with annual issuances of about US$400 billion, which was more than half of annual SNG bond issuances in 2009. Germany, Japan, Canada, China, and Spain accounted for about 85 percent of the remaining SNG bond issuances (about US$310 billion) (Canuto and Liu, 2011).

15 For the U.S., only SNG data is available.

16 For instance, the U.S. federal government provides a tax exemption for state and local debt. The exemption is estimated to cost about US$162 billion over 2010–14 (U.S. Congress, 2010).

17 Since 2005, states in Germany, Canada, and Spain have substantially expanded their total bond issuances. While for Germany this reflects a shift towards greater market reliance in the composition of financing, for Spain and Canada it appears to be mainly driven by higher deficits and financing needs, with the share of security financing in total financing actually declining. In emerging economies, the development of subnational bond markets is a relatively new phenomenon, often linked to the need for large-scale infrastructure investments (Canuto and Liu, 2010; Liu and Waibel, 2008).

18 For example, during the recent financial crisis, primary markets spreads of SNGs vis-à-vis the sovereign increased sharply, in particular at short maturities, as liquidity for subsovereign debt dried up amid reduced appetite for risk (Canuto and Liu, 2010). SNG financing costs have again come down since mid-2009, however.

19 Similar results hold for the other two countries with significantly large SNG bond markets: U.S. and Spain. In both cases there exists a positive relationship between the ratings and the budget balance. Moreover, in the U.S. – where states depend relatively less on federal transfers than in other federations– higher ratings are achieved through larger fiscal efforts, while in Spain – a relatively more centralized fiscal federation – regions can achieve high ratings with poorer fiscal performances.

20 Given the relatively small sample size of primary market data, we use both state and local bonds to have a more robust inference.

21 Canada and Germany are among the most liquid bond markets and, besides the U.S., are the fiscal federations for which the Dealogic reports the largest number of observations. In this analysis, we focus on Canada and Germany because – due to the favorable fiscal treatment of subnational government bonds in the U.S. – spreads of subnational government bonds over the corresponding benchmark bonds issued by the federal government are a poor measure of risk premiums.

22 Yields to maturity from the secondary market show that this is not the rule for the Municipal Bonds (MUNIS) in the U.S. This can be due to the extremely favorable fiscal treatment that they enjoy with respect to bonds issued by the federal government.

23 Spreads have been constructed for Canada, Australia, and the United States comparing the borrowing cost of individual states to central government bonds for a five-year maturity. In this analysis, we focus on Canada and Australia. For the United States, the favorable fiscal treatment of subnational bonds causes spreads over the federal government bonds to assume negative as well as positive values, which makes the coefficient of variation a very poor measure of dispersion.

24 The EIB is the financial arm of the European Commission. Similar to development banks in existing fiscal federations, the EIB provides loans to European public institutions, banks, corporations, and sovereigns in line with established priorities, such as environmental protection or transportation. Loans are exclusively for project financing and are usually guaranteed by public institutions or banks. As of end-2011, the EIB's total portfolio amounted to about 3 percent of EU GDP, and one quarter of total loans were either held or guaranteed by sovereigns (Fitch Ratings, 2012c).

25 This was one among other proposals put forward by the Tommaso Padoa-Schioppa Group.

26 Selected fiscal federations include: Argentina, Australia, Austria, Belgium, Brazil, Canada, Germany, India, Mexico, South Africa, Spain, Switzerland, and the United States. This appendix considers one level below the federal level (e.g., states, provinces, and Länder).

27 Gross debt excludes the unfunded superannuation liability from total liabilities.
28 According to Maastricht criteria (Statistik Austria, 2012).
29 Loi Spéciale du Financement des Communautés et des Régions (LSF).
30 Loi Special de Reformes Institutionelles (LSRI).
31 Historically, the federal government had provided loans to provinces and municipalities under the "Relief Acts" of the 30s and the 40s.
32 Participating Länder were Berlin, Brandenburg, Bremen, Hamburg, Mecklenburg-Vorpommern, NRW, Rheinland-Pfalz, Saarland, Sachsen-Anhalt, Schleswig-Holstein.
33 Throughout the 1980s and 1990s central government loans provided around half of states' financing needs.
34 FAIS (constituted in 1997) provides, among other activities, transfers to states and municipalities to finance infrastructure and social investment projects in part financed via Banobras' loans (Banobras-FAIS program). Twelve percent of FAIS's funding is transferred directly to the states to support regional and inter municipal programs implemented at the state level (Wellenstein et al., 2006). FAFEF (created in 2006) disburses funds mainly to finance physical infrastructure, public debt reduction programs, civil protection, education, and research in part financed via Banobras' loans. In 2009 the total of the resources made available to subnational governments was US$1.77 billion (or 6.1 percent of SNG debt) (Secretaria de Hacienda y Credito Publico, 2009).
35 Media Statement: Joint Ministerial Team on Limpopo Section 100 Intervention.

References

Australian Bureau of Statistics, 2012, *GFS 2010–11* (Canberra).
Banco Central do Brasil, 2012, available at http://www4.bcb.gov.br/fis/dividas/dividas.asp
Banobras, 2012, *Informe Annual 2012,* SHCP March 2013, Mexico D. F.
BNDES, 2011, *Annual Report for 2011,* available at http://www.bndes.gov.br/SiteBNDES/bndes/bndes_en/Institucional/The_BNDES_in_Numbers/Annual_Report/annual_report2011.html
Bordo, M., A. Markiewicz, and L. Jonung, 2011, "A Fiscal Union for the Euro: Some Lessons from History," NBER Working Paper No. 17380.
Brunnermeier M., L. Garicano, P. Lane, M. Pagano, R. Reis, T. Santos, S. Van Nieuwerburgh, and D. Vayanos, 2011, "ESBies: A Realistic Reform of Europe's Financial Architecture," VoxEU.org, October 25th.
Bundesministerium der Finanzen, 2012a, *Vermoegensrechnung des Bundes 2011* (Berlin: BMF).
———, 2012b, *Haushaltsrechnung 2011* (Berlin: BMF).
Bundesrechnungshof, 2012, *Bundesrechnungsabschluss 2011, Teil 1* (Bonn).
Canuto, O., and L. Liu, 2010, S*ubnational Debt Finance: Make It Sustainable* (Washington: World Bank).
———, 2011, "Subnational Debt Finance and the Global Financial Crisis – Economic Premise Note Number 13," 2010 (Washington: World Bank).
Center on Budget and Policy Priorities, 2011, "Why and how states should strengthen their rainy day funds," February 3, available at http://www.cbpp.org
Claessens, Stijn, 2012, "Overview of the Proposals, Some Criteria to Use, and a Summary," Bruegel-IMF conference on Common Euro Area Sovereign Debt (Bruxelles).
Collet, Stephanie, 2012, "A Unified Italy? Sovereign Debt and Investor Scepticism," Job Market paper, Universite Libre de Bruxelles.
DBSA, 2012, "DBSA and DF Annual Report 2011–12," available at http://www.dbsa.org/EN/About-Us/Publications/Pages/DBSA-Annual-Reports.aspx

Enderlein, Henrik, et al., 2012, "Completing the Euro – A Road Map Towards Fiscal Union in Europe," Report of the Tommaso Padoa-Schioppa Group, June.

Frankfurter Allgemeine Zeitung, 2013, *Teure Bund-Laender-Anleihe*, June.

Feld, L.A. Kalb, M. Moessinger, and S. Osterloh, 2011, "Sovereign Bond Market Reactions to Fiscal Rules and No-Bailout Clauses – The Swiss Experience," Centre for European Economic Research (ZEW) and University of Freiburg, November.

Federation Wallonia-Brussels, 2011, "Public Debt Annual Report 2011 Federation Wallonia-Brussels," April, available at http://www.budget-finances.cfwb.be/

Fitch Ratings, 2011, *Fitch Ratings Report on DBSA 29th November 2011* (New York: Fitch Ratings).

———, 2012a, *Fitch Ratings Report on BNDES February 2, 2012* (New York: Fitch Ratings).

———, 2012b, *Fitch Ratings Report on BANOBRAS, November 21 2012* (New York: Fitch Ratings).

———, 2012c, *Fitch Ratings Report on European Investment Bank, June 29 2012* (New York: Fitch Ratings).

Gabel, Todd, and Niels Veldhuis, 2004, "A guide to the indebtedness of Canada and the Provinces," Vancouver: The Fraser Institute, June 11).

Government of Australia, 2012a, *Australian Budget Paper No.1 and No. 3, Appendix B: Debt Transactions* (Canberra, 2012).

———, 2012b, *Description of the Commonwealth of Australia* (Canberra, 2012), available at http://www.guaranteescheme.gov.au/australia/pdf/commonwealth-australia-24102013.pdf

Government of Canada 2012, Public Accounts of Canada 2012, available at http://epe.lac-bac.gc.ca/100/201/301/public_accounts_can/pdf/2012/index.html

Government of India, 2004, *Twelfth Financing Commission Report*, Ministry of Finance, Government of India, 2004.

———, 2012, "Union Budget 2012–13."

Government of South Africa, 1996, Borrowing Powers of Provincial Governments Act.

———, 2011, "Local Government Budget and Expenditure Review: 2006/2007 – 2012/2013," National Treasury, available at http://www.treasury.gov.za

Hellwig, Christian, and Thomas Philippon, 2011, "Eurobills, not Eurobonds," available at http://voxeu.org

Iantchovichina, E., L. Liu, and M. Nagarajan, 2006, "Subnational Fiscal Sustainability Analysis: What Can We Learn from Tamil Nadu?" World Bank Policy Research Working Paper No. 3947.

ICRA, 2012, "Debt burden of state governments remains considerable," ICRA Rating Feature, Gurgaon, India, February.

James, Harold, 1997, "Monetary and Fiscal Unification in Nineteenth-Century Germany: What Can Kohl Learn from Bismarck?" *Essays in International Finance* No. 202 (Princeton: Princeton University)

———, 2012, Alexander Hamilton's Eurozone Tour, Project Syndicate, March 5, 2012, available at http://www.project-syndicate.org

Kehew, Robert, Tomoko Matsukawa, and John Petersen, 2005, "Local Financing for Sub-sovereign Infrastructure in Developing Countries: Case Studies of Innovative Domestic Credit Enhancement Entities and Techniques," The World Bank Infrastructure, Economics and Finance Department.

Liu, L., and M. Waibel, 2008, "Subnational Borrowing, Insolvency and Regulation," in *Macro Federalism and Local Finance*, edited by Anwar Shah (Washington: The World Bank).

196   *Geremia Palomba, et al.*

Maco, Paul S., 2001, "Building a Strong Subnational Debt Market: A Regulator's Perspective." *Richmond Journal of Global Law and Business* 2 (1): 1–31.

Maguire Steven, 2011, "State and Local Government Debt: An Analysis," Congressional Research Service Report for Congress, available at http://fas.org/sgp/crs/misc/R41735.pdf

Mai, Karl, 2002, "Zur Hoehe der Staatsverschuldung infolge der deutschen Vereinigung," in *Ostdeutschland zwischen Währungsunion und Solidarpakt II : eine Retrospektive kritisch-alternativer Ökonomen.*(Berlin: Trafo-Verlag, 2006), pp. 235–254.

Di Matteo, Livio, 2012, "A Debt Interpretation of Canadian Confederation" (blog post), available at http://worthwhile.typepad.com/worthwhile_canadian_initi/2012/07/a-debt-interpretation-of-canadian-confederation.html

Ministry of Economy and Finance, 2012, Deuda Publica, available at http://www.mecon.gob.ar/finanzas/sfinan/?page_id=37

Ministry of Finance and Public Administration, 2012, "Note clarifying the application of the Regional Liquidity Fund," MFPA, Madrid, Spain, October 19.

Neumark, Fritz, 1977, *Handbuch der Finanzwissenschaft*, Mohr Verlag, Tuebingen.

Nowlan, George, 2001, "Initiatives to Develop Canadian Capital Markets: A Case Study," University of Toronto Munk School of Global Affairs, G20 Information Center, provided by the G20 Research Group.

Nuñez Barba, 2012, "FAIS y FAFEF como Garantia o Fuente de Pago de Obligaciones Financieras," *Federalismo Hacendario No. 175*, Marzo-Abril.

OECD, 2009, "Explaining the Sub-National Tax-Grants Balance in OECD Countries," OECD Network on Fiscal Relations across Levels of Government, Paris, France.

Plekhanov, I., and R. Singh, 2007, "How Should Subnational Government Borrowing Be Regulated? Some Cross-Country Empirical Evidence," IMF Staff Papers, Vol. 53, No. 3.

Purfield, Catriona, 2004, "The Decentralization Dilemma in India," IMF Working Paper, 04/32.

Randall Henning, C. and Martin Kessler, 2012, "Fiscal Federalism: US History for Architects of Europe's Fiscal Union," *Bruegel Essay and Lecture Series*, Brussels.

Reserve Bank of Australia, 2011, "The Australian Semi-Government Bond Market," *Bulletin – September Quarter*, RBA, Sydney.

Reserve Bank of India, 2012, *RBI Monthly Bulletin June*, RBI, Mumbai.

Schuknecht, Ludger, Jurgen von Hagen, and Guido Wolswijk, 2009, "Government Risk Premiums in the Bond Market: EMU and Canada," *European Journal of Political Economy*, 25 (2009), pp. 371–384.

Secretaria de Hacienda y Credito Publico, 2009, "Informe del Resultado de la Fiscalización Superior de la Cuenta Pública 2009," SHCP, México D.F.

———, 2012, "Obligaciones Financieras de Entidades Federativas y Municipios," SHCP, México D.F.

Statistik Austria, 2012, *Oeffentliche Schulden*, Wien.

Statistisches Bundesamt and Bundesministerium für Finanzen (2009), *Schulden der öffentlichen Haushalte in Deutschland von 1881 bis 1980, GESIS Datenarchiv, Köln*.

Statistisches Bundesamt, 2012, *Finanzen und Steuern-Schulden der Oeffentlichen Haushalte 2011*, Wiesbaden.

Sutherland, Price, and I. Joumard, 2005, "Sub-Central Government Fiscal Rules," *OECD Economic Studies*, No. 41 2005/2.

Tanzi, Vito, 2012, "A Century and a Half of Public Finances in Italy," Lectio Marco Minghetti (Torino: IBL Libri, 2012).

Ter-Minassian, Teresa, ed., 1997, *Fiscal Federalism in Theory and Practice* (Washington D.C.: International Monetary Fund).

U.S. Congress, 2010, "Estimates of Federal Tax Expenditures for Fiscal Years 2010 to 2014," Joint Committee on Taxation, JCS 3–10, December, Washington D.C.

Von Hagen, J., M. Bordignon, M. Dahlberg, B. Grewal, P. Petterson, and H. Seitz, 2000, "Subnational Government Bailouts in OECD Countries: Four Case Studies," *Research Network Working Paper* R-399 (Washington: Inter-American Development Bank).

Von Weizsäcker, and Jakob and Jacques Delpla, 2011, "Eurobonds: The Blue Bond Concept and its Implications," Bruegel Policy Brief, Brussels.

Wellenstein, Anna, Angelica Nunez, and Luis Andres, 2006, "Social Infrastructure: Fondo De Aportaciones Para la Infraestructura Social (FAIS)," in *Decentralized Service Delivery for the Poor* (Washington: World Bank).

Young, Samuel, 2012, "Market-Oriented Subnational Debt Regimes: Empowering the Developing World to Construct Infrastructure," *Vanderbilt Journal of Transnational Law*, 45: 917.

6 Subnational fiscal crises

Till Cordes, Martine Guerguil,
Laura Jaramillo, Marialuz Moreno-Badia,
and Sami Ylaoutinen

I. Introduction

Over the past three decades, subnational fiscal crises have occurred in many feder-ations. This chapter looks at 16 such episodes across nine advanced and emerging market federations. This list is not exhaustive, in the sense that it does not include cases where subnational financial difficulties were resolved without central sup-port (i.e., through adjustment) or cases where support may have been provided but not reported. It should thus not be taken as strict evidence of the frequency and size of subnational financial crises. It still illustrates, however, the diversity of approaches adopted by the central government to respond to subnational fiscal crises and helps to shed some light on the benefits and limitations of alternative crisis resolution mechanisms.

This chapter is structured as follows. Section II gives an overview of the sub-national fiscal crises included in the sample. Section III discusses crisis resolution mechanisms, followed by a review of conditionality in Section IV. Section V dis-cusses crisis prevention mechanisms whose introduction was instigated by fiscal crises. Section VI compares the recent crisis response in the euro area with crisis resolution schemes in the sample. Section VII concludes.

II. Subnational fiscal crises: Stylized facts

A fiscal crisis can be characterized as a situation whereby the state/local govern-ment loses market access or faces rising financing costs that undermine its capac-ity to deliver essential services. We draw on the sovereign debt crisis literature (Reinhart and Rogoff, 2008; Manasse et al., 2003) to define subnational fiscal crises as those cases where financing constraints at the subnational level resulted in a state default or ad hoc central government support.[1] Based on these criteria, 16 episodes of fiscal crises across nine countries were identified over the last thirty years (Table 6.1).

A. Triggers

Subnational fiscal crises have been triggered by exogenous and endogenous fac-tors. In some cases, the trigger was an external shock that resulted in interest rates

Table 6.1 Case studies of subnational fiscal crises

Country	States involved	Year	Trigger	Financing Situation	Resolution	Fiscal Costs to the Center	Conditionality
Argentina	Almost all	1992–1994	Convertibility plan leads to more stringent financing conditions	Median deficit to revenues of 10 percent, with a maximum of close to 60 percent.	Federal loans, direct transfers	Loans of close to US$750 million	Yes, but not enforced
Argentina	Buenos Aires, Chaco, Formosa, Mendoza, Misiones, Rio Negro, San Juan, Santiago del Estero, and also the city of Buenos Aires (65 percent of GDP)	2001–2002	End of convertibility regime	Average overall cash deficits of 2.5 percent of national GDP.	Debt restructuring		No
Argentina	Buenos Aires, Catamarca, Cordoba, Corrientes, Chaco, Chubut, Formosa, Jujuy, La Rioja, Mendoza, Misiones, Neuquén, Rio Negro, Salta, San Juan, Santa Cruz, Tucuman, and Tierra del Fuego (90 percent of GDP)	2003–2004	End of convertibility regime	Debt to national GDP of close to 3 percent with banks, plus bonds circulating as "quasi-money"	Federal loans	Federal government takes over US$9.7 billion of bank debt of the provinces, and a liability of US$2.4 billion with the Central Bank	No

(Continued)

Table 6.1 (Continued)

Country	States involved	Year	Trigger	Financing Situation	Resolution	Fiscal Costs to the Center	Conditionality
Australia	Queensland, New South Wales (51 percent of GDP)	2009–2010	2008–09 global financial crisis and bank guarantee	Queensland: 17 % debt to GDP; New South Wales: 18% debt to GDP (2009); Abrupt increase in refinancing costs with spreads to Australian government bonds doubling in December 2008	Debt guarantees	Bonds of about 33 billion Australian dollars guaranteed	No, only a fee for the guarantee
Brazil	Almost all	1989	Fiscal mismanagement coupled with exchange constraints	Nominal overnight rate of 2,407 percent (1989)	Federal loans	R$10.5 billion refinanced	Yes, but not enforced
Brazil	Almost all	1993	Fiscal mismanagement	Nominal overnight rate of 3,059 percent (1993)	Federal loans (refinancing of subnational debt with federal public banks); central bank support (1994)	R$39.4 billion refinanced	Yes, but not enforced
Brazil	Almost all (25 out of 27 states)	1997	Fiscal mismanagement	Nominal overnight rate of 24.8 percent (1997)	Federal loans, public bank intervention (1995)	R$87 billion restructured (without resources used to reform the state banks)	Yes, enforced

Country	Subnational entity	Years	Cause	Debt	Type of support	Details	No-bailout rule
Germany	Bremen, Saarland (2.3 percent of GDP)	1994–2004	Local economic decline resulted in steady erosion of revenue base	Debt in 1992: Bremen 44 percent of GDP; Saarland 39 percent of GDP; Unsustainable interest payments to revenue ratios in 1996: Bremen 26.3 percent; Saarland 19.8 percent	Extraordinary federal transfers	Bremen: EUR 8.5 billion from 1994–2004; Saarland: EUR 6.6 billion from 1994–2004; Total of about 0.7 percent of GDP	Yes, enforced
India	All states	1980–2012	Mismatch of revenues and expenditure responsibilities	High average interest rate on outstanding liabilities of 11.2 percent, subnational debt to GDP at 26.1 percent in 2000	Federal loans (and debt relief); central and public bank intervention	Federal loans and advances from central government 45 percent of subnational debt in 2000, debt relief of more than 6 percent of GDP since 1974	Yes
Mexico	Almost all	1995	Tequila crisis and devaluation of the peso	Median debt to subnational GDP ratios of 3 percent, up to a maximum of 9 percent of GDP; debt servicing costs close to 10 percent of total expenditure.	Debt restructurings with domestic banks; extraordinary federal transfers	Extraordinary cash transfers to states of about 0.5 percent of GDP between 1995 and 1998	Yes, but not enforced
Mexico	Estado de Mexico, Guerrero, Tabasco, Queretaro (16 percent of GDP)	2004–2006	Weak fiscal accounts	Debt to subnational GDP ranging from 1 to 5 percent.	Federal transfers	Up to 25 percent of government fund, which holds 1.4 percent of federal revenue sharing	Yes, enforced

(Continued)

Table 6.1 (Continued)

Country	States involved	Year	Trigger	Financing Situation	Resolution	Fiscal Costs to the Center	Conditionality
Spain	Most provinces (86 percent of GDP)	2012	Weak fiscal accounts, European debt crisis	In 2011, subnational debt of 20 percent of GDP and aggregate subnational fiscal deficit at almost 3 percent of GDP; unable to access markets	Federal loans	Rescue fund with federal loans of EUR18bn (1.4 percent of GDP) for nine regions, loans for payment of outstanding commercial debt of EUR18bn (1.4 percent of GDP) for 14 regions	Yes, enforced
South Africa	Eastern Cape and KwaZulu-Natal (23 percent of GDP)	1997–98	Fiscal mismanagement	Funding deficit, banks refuse to extend overdraft facilities	Federal transfers	Transfers of 0.3 percent of GDP	Yes, enforced
South Africa	Limpopo, Gauteng, Free State, Eastern Cape (54 percent of GDP)	2011–2012	Fiscal mismanagement	Funding deficit of four provinces, banks refuse to extend overdraft facilities	Federal transfers	Transfers of about 1 percent of GDP	Yes, enforced
United States	New York City (0.009 percent of GDP)	1975	Fiscal mismanagement	New York City: $6 billion in short-term debt; operating deficit of at least $600 million, unable to access private credit markets or only at high interest rate of more than 10 percent	Federal loans	Credit line of $2.3 billion for New York City	Yes, enforced
United States	District of Columbia (0.003 percent of GDP)	1996	Fiscal mismanagement	District of Columbia: budgetary deficit of more than $500 million (1996), downgrade below investment grade	Federal loans	Direct borrowing from the Treasury	Yes, enforced

spikes, exacerbating underlying subnational fiscal weaknesses. This was the case in the aftermath of the Great Recession, with borrowing costs rising sharply for subnational governments in Australia (Figure 6.1). Similarly, the Tequila crisis resulted in financing difficulties not only for Mexican states but also for Argentine provinces. In other cases, the central government itself has been the source of the shock on subnational governments, for example with the end of convertibility plan in Argentina in early 2000s or exchange constraints imposed in Brazil in the 1980s. However, more often, the fiscal crisis had its roots in local factors, reflecting state-specific economic problems or fiscal mismanagement (Germany, Brazil, South Africa, India, and the United States).

In some cases, the crisis was precipitated when banks were no longer willing to extend credit because of high deficits (United States,[2] South Africa, and Spain). In a few cases, the situation was exacerbated by weak banks unable to roll over debt in the face of liquidity constraints and high exposures to subnational governments (Argentina and Brazil). But more often, the increase in the debt service to a level perceived to be excessive prompted federal intervention. The threshold varied, from 15 percent of revenue in Brazil to over 25 percent in Germany and 35 percent in India.[3]

B. Magnitude and spillovers

Among the cases surveyed, fiscal crises tended to affect a significant portion of subnational governments with the notable exceptions of Germany and the United States (Figure 6.2). This likely reflects incentive problems in the design of intergovernmental relations, very often stemming from high transfer dependency (Chapter 1),

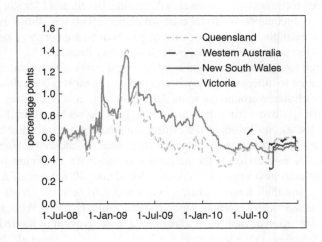

Figure 6.1 Australia: State bond spreads (percentage points)[1]

Sources: Bloomberg and authors' calculations.

[1]Ten-year maturity, Australian dollars.

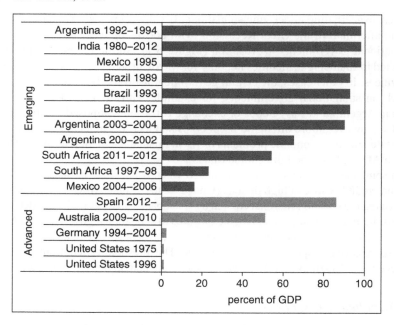

Figure 6.2 Size of subnational governments under fiscal stress (percent of GDP)

Source: Authors' calculations.

which in time results in the parallel buildup of fiscal pressures across states. Crises have also been recurrent as in the cases of Argentina, Brazil, and Mexico. Moreover, it has not been uncommon for fiscal crises to be persistent, sometimes over several decades. For example, in Germany, central government support was needed over the course of ten years; and in India, over close to four decades.

It is difficult to ascertain the extent to which fiscal stress in some states may have been transmitted to other (seemingly healthy) states as most crisis episodes within a country are clustered around the same date. However, in several cases there were clear negative spillovers from the states to the banking sector (Brazil) and public enterprises (India). Spillovers to the central government, on the other hand, have been more limited as the size of the subnational debt or federal transfers involved is small relative to the size of the national economy.[4] An exception was Brazil, where subnational governments accounted for almost 40 percent of total public debt in 1997, and their large financing needs and debt servicing costs ultimately threatened the federal government's macro stabilization program. Also, many have argued that subnational fiscal woes contributed to the erosion of the federal fiscal position in Argentina in the lead-up to the 2001–02 crisis (Torre et al., 2003).[5]

III. Crisis resolution mechanisms

When facing a financing crisis, subnational governments have been rarely allowed to default on their private creditors. In fact, when debt restructurings have occurred, they mainly involved smaller political entities or cases where the federal government debt itself was restructured. Pre-set crisis resolution frameworks such as bankruptcy procedures are indeed absent for subnational governments, with only a few exceptions. Instead, the federal government has provided financial support in times of crisis through a range of ad hoc mechanisms involving guarantees, loans, and transfers, but not through standing facilities.

A. State debt restructuring

Subnational debt restructurings with the private sector have been relatively rare. The United States is the only country in the sample that ever let states default without providing additional financial support. In the 1840s, at least 22 states defaulted on their debt (Hempel, 1971; English, 1996). The refusal of Congress to assume state debt is widely seen as the establishment of a credible no-bailout norm in the United States (Henning and Kessler, 2012). In other countries, state debt restructurings have happened mostly when both the subnational and the central governments faced large financing pressures (Argentina in 2001–02, Mexico in the mid-1990s). In these cases, the resolution of fiscal crises at the federal level largely determined the resolution for the subnational level as well. It is important to note, however, that even in cases of default, the federal government still had to finance ongoing subnational deficits at a later stage (in the form of transfers or loans).

B. Pre-set crisis resolution frameworks

Very few federations in our sample have established pre-set crisis resolution frameworks. Even when they existed, they have seldom been used and, again, did not preclude the provision of financial support from the federal government.

- In the United States, Chapter 9 of the Bankruptcy Code provides a formal bankruptcy procedures for municipalities (Box 6.1). However, states and the District of Columbia are explicitly restricted from using it. In addition, only 24 out of 50 states currently allow local governments to file for bankruptcy (Fitch, 2012). Furthermore, Chapter 9 has not been invoked in the case of some large municipalities such as New York City (NYC) in 1975 or Cleveland, Ohio in 1978 (Moody's, 2012).
- Mexico set up a Fund for Strengthening of Mexican States (FAFEF) in 2006, which annually holds 1.4 percent of federal revenue sharing. The funds can be used to pay down subnational debt stock as part of an exchange offer or serve as collateral for subnational borrowing. A handful of states have used the framework to restructure their debts (Secretaría de Hacienda y Crédito Público de México, 2005, 2007). However, this framework did not preclude the federal government from putting in place an additional, temporary financing mechanism in the context of the 2008–09 financial crisis to compensate subnational governments for the drop in their share of federal revenue (Fitch, 2011).

Box 6.1 United States: Chapter 9

Chapter 9 is a debt restructuring mechanism for political subdivisions and agencies of U.S. States (which include cities, towns, villages, counties, taxing districts, municipal utilities, and school districts). States and the District of Columbia cannot file for relief under the U.S. Bankruptcy Code.

The first municipal debt provisions under federal bankruptcy law were enacted in 1934 during the Great Depression as emergency legislation for the relief of distressed minor subdivisions of the states. Major changes were enacted in the wake of New York City's financial crisis in 1975, to update procedural mechanisms that were generally believed to be inadequate to govern the reorganization of a major municipality like New York, including in particular the requirement that the petitioning municipality obtain the prior consent of owners of 51 percent of its outstanding securities before the bankruptcy court could approve the petition as properly filed (New York City did not file for bankruptcy).

The current version of Chapter 9 provides the procedural machinery whereby a debt restructuring plan acceptable to a majority of creditors can become binding on a dissenting minority. Only debtors may file for Chapter 9. In order to be eligible to file, the debtor municipality must be authorized to file under state law in its capacity as a municipality. It must be insolvent and it must have (a) obtained agreement to a reorganization plan by a majority of creditors; (b) demonstrated that it has negotiated in good faith with creditors and failed to obtain agreement; or (c) proven that negotiation is impracticable.

Chapter 9 does not provide for the liquidation of a municipality's assets and distribution thereof to the creditors. Instead, it provides a legal mechanism through which municipalities may be protected from the claims of their creditors as they attempt to develop and negotiate a plan to adjust their debts. In this way, Chapter 9 has similarities to Chapter 11 reorganizations that apply to companies. However, a municipality retains more control in a Chapter 9 case than does the debtor in a Chapter 11. The oversight and involvement of the bankruptcy court is quite limited: it cannot interfere with the municipality's political or governmental powers, its property or revenues, or its use or enjoyment of its income-producing property.

The debtor is expected to negotiate a business plan for rehabilitation with its creditors who ultimately vote to accept or reject it. The process is designed to facilitate consensus. The Code, and judicial oversight, establishes parameters designed to promote debtor rehabilitation and maximize the bankruptcy estate for distribution among creditors.

Since 1980, the number of Chapter 9 filings per year has averaged less than eight.[1] The vast majority have been filed by small government agencies like municipal utilities, school districts, or entities established for a single project such as a hospital or convention center. Orange County, California, was reorganized under Chapter 9 in 1994. More recently, Chapter 9 was filed by Jefferson County, Alabama, in 2011, San Bernardino, California, in 2012 and Detroit, Michigan, in 2013.

Sources: Pettit (2011); Jeweler (2007); Liu and Waibel (2008); and Canuto and Liu (2010).

[1]See http://www.abiworld.org/Content/NavigationMenu/NewsRoom/Bankruptcy Statistics/Bankruptcy_Filings_1.htm.

C. Ad hoc financial support from the central to the subnational level

In most cases where the central government provided financial support to subnational entities under stress, it was provided in an ad hoc manner, including through federal guarantees, direct or indirect loans, and extraordinary transfers. In a few cases, the central government opted to step up (although by a large amount) the resources it was providing to the subnational government under its regular arrangements (discussed in the previous chapter). But most frequently, the central government used a vehicle that was different and separate from that used in its regular transactions with the subnational government.

Federal guarantees for states in a fiscal crisis

Federal governments can introduce guarantees of subnational debt at a time of crisis. This form of intervention has been rarely used in the cases surveyed, probably because it applies only in cases where states retain market access. Federal guarantees represent limited upfront costs to the federal government, though there could be an impact on the sovereign risk premium, and explicit contingent liabilities can be large. Implicit liabilities can also be significant as the federal government would likely be expected to cover subnational debt not explicitly falling under the guarantee scheme.

Argentina, Australia, and India have used guarantees to the debt of subnational governments facing financing difficulties. Australia's guarantee scheme, established at the onset of the Great Recession, proved to be largely preventative: no guarantees were called, states maintained market access, and the central government's risk premium did not rise. In contrast, the Argentine and Indian schemes were insufficient to alleviate subnational financing pressures and had to be complemented by other forms of support.

Indirect financing through the central and public banks

In a few cases, the federal government has provided exceptional financing to subnational governments indirectly through public sector entities, either the central or public banks. This limited upfront costs to the federal government but did not avert the need for further federal financing down the road. Emergency central bank financing has been used in India, where states repeatedly exceeded their overdraft facilities at the Reserve Bank of India (RBI) through the 1970s and 1980s, and in Brazil, where the federal government authorized the temporary swapping of unmarketable state bonds for central bank bonds in 1994 to prevent spillovers to the rest of the financial system. In addition, when Brazilian states lost market access in the 1990s, public banks were heavily relied on to channel resources to subnational governments, both directly (through the provision of emergency credit lines by the Caixa Economic Federal, a federal bank) and indirectly (through the mandatory underwriting of unmarketable state bonds and the capitalization of interest payments). Indian state banks were also used to provide financial support to subnational governments facing financial stress.

Federal loans

Direct federal loans have been used more frequently to relieve subnational fiscal stress. Modalities have ranged from rather straightforward lending to more complex instruments, sometimes used on a recurring basis. The terms of federal lending were uniformly more favorable than those the subnational entity would have obtained from the market. They usually included longer maturities, a grace period, and in most cases lower interest rates. In a number of cases, explicit cost-recovery provisions were attached to the loans, for example through withholding of future revenue-sharing transfers. However, in several instances repayment was postponed or restructured.

- Under the simplest form, the federal government provides a loan to enable the subnational authorities to service their debt. Examples include U.S. federal lending to New York City in 1975 and to the District of Columbia in 1996; and the rescue fund (Fondo de Liquidez Autonómica) set up in 2012 by the Spanish government to lend to regions.
- Alternatively, the federal government can assume the debt of the subnational entity in distress, which in turn incurs a matching liability to the federal government.[6] This option was followed repeatedly in Brazil in the late 1980s and 1990s (Box 6.2), Argentina, in the early 2000s, and in Spain in 2012 (via a special fund, the Fondo de Financiacion del Pago a Proveedores).
- In Argentina, federal loans have been part of more complex financing transactions. In the early 1990s, the federal government provided close to 0.3 percent of GDP in federal bonds (BOTESOs) to provinces facing financial difficulties; the provinces placed the BOTESO bonds gradually in the market, and agreed to repay the federal government through ten-year loans (Sanguinetti, 1999). In 2003, the federal government provided the central bank with 0.6 percent of GDP in bonds to finance the conversion to actual currency of subnational "quasi-monies" (Fernández et al., 2006).
- The restructuring of subnationals' outstanding liabilities to the federal government is another way to provide financial relief. It has been used in Brazil in 1993 (Box 6.2), and recurrently in India since 1974, through a variety of schemes involving the consolidation of loans on common terms, lower

interest rates, moratoria on interest and principal payments, write-off of loans, a debt swap scheme, and most recently the establishment of a Debt Consolidation and Relief Facility (Reserve Bank of India, 2012).

Ad hoc federal transfers

In several instances, central governments provided emergency transfers on top of what was already disbursed under the pre-set transfer system. These extraordinary transfers were seldom one-offs, as the federal government had to continue providing financing to subnational governments over consecutive years.

Extraordinary transfers were used to support subnational governments in Argentina from 1992 to 1994, Mexico between 1995 and 1998, and Germany since 1992. In Germany and Mexico, transfers amounted to 0.5–0.7 percent of GDP. In both cases, they were conditioned to the adoption of fiscal consolidation plans.[7]

Box 6.2 Brazil: State government financial support

Brazil experienced three major state-level crises during the late 1980s and 1990s. In each of the crisis episodes, most states faced a precarious fiscal position with high levels of personnel spending and unsustainable levels of borrowing. In all the cases, the central government responded by federalizing the state debts.

- In 1989, the federal government formally assumed much of the subnational external debt (Rs. 10.8 billion or 1.4 percent of state GDP on average)[1] with the states incurring an equal liability to the federal government in domestic currency but with a longer maturity, a five-year grace period, and an interest rate equivalent to the original contracts (plus inflation correction).
- With much of the fiscal imbalances unresolved, in 1993 the federal government once again assumed the debt of the states, this time owed to federal financial institutions (for Rs. 39.4 billion or 7.25 percent of state GDP on average), which the states had stopped paying for a few years. The new liability of the states to the federal government had a longer maturity (20 years) but the interest rate remained that specified in the original contracts plus inflation correction. In addition, the amount of annual debt service arising from all of rescheduled debts was capped at 11 percent of net revenues, with any excess capitalized. The combination of grace periods, rescheduling, and debt service caps provided substantial yet unconditional debt service relief largely in the form of postponement.
- Finally, after several years of negotiations, a standardized framework was agreed upon in 1997 to change the financial terms of state debts

through new contracts between the federal government and each state. The restructuring was more comprehensive, in that it also included securitized debts and state debt to banks. The new debt was divided into two parts: (1) an amount equivalent to 20 percent of the total (the so called *Conta gráfica*) was to be amortized before December 1998 with the proceeds from the privatization of state assets; (2) the rest was restructured with maturities up to 30 years and an annual interest rate of 6–9 percent (plus inflation). Annual debt service payments were capped at 13–15 percent of net revenues, with all debt service exceeding this cap automatically capitalized. The contracts involved a subsidy element (as the interest rate was substantially lower than the real interest rates at which the federal government was likely to finance its debt during the contract period).[2] They also included debt forgiveness for securitized debt. Thus, unlike previous attempts, the aim was to permanently reduce the debt service rather than merely postponing it. These contracts were signed by 25 states (out of 27) for a total amount of Rs. 87 billion (about 11.75 percent of state GDP on average). States agreed to three-year fiscal programs monitored by the Treasury with targets for debt/revenue ratio, primary surplus, revenue measures, and wage/revenue ratio.

Sources: Alleyne (1998); Dillinger (1998); Lopreato (2000); Bevilaqua (2002); Rodden (2006).

[1]The bailout was, however, more important for the states in the Northeast region, with the amounts involved exceeding 6 percent of state GDP in the case of Ceará, for example.
[2]In 1997 the interest rate subsidy would have amounted to some 10.5 percentage points (given an average overnight rate of 24.6 percent in 1997) or some Rs. 8 billion (1 percent of GDP) in annual accrued interest.

D. Cost of alternative financing vehicles

Schemes with the least cost for the federal government are limited in scope. The success of a guarantee scheme, the least expensive form of intervention if the guarantee is not called, relies on the ability of subnational governments to retain market access. But guarantees are unlikely to be sufficient when the fiscal situation of subnational governments hinders their ability to service their debt. Indirect financing through central or public banks can provide temporary respite at what can appear to be little upfront cost to the federal government. However, as the case studies show, this often does not avert the need for a more sizeable federal involvement at a later stage.

Transfers look like the most costly option for the federal government because unlike loans, their repayment is not expected. In practice however, the line between loans and transfers can be blurred. In both cases, the federal government faces large upfront financing needs and therefore needs to maintain steady market access. Additional costs could arise if the sovereign risk premium increases, especially if the impact on the debt-to-GDP ratio is sizeable. Furthermore, both schemes set a precedent for governments to provide support to states, which could result in potentially large implicit contingent liabilities. Federal loans and transfers can both suffer from lack of accountability, either because they are left at the full discretion of the executive branch (transfers in Argentina and Mexico) or because the conditions are continually revised (loans in the cases of Brazil and India). Finally, both loans and transfers may create distortive incentives for subnational governments and lenders unless strict conditionality is attached.

IV. Conditionality

A. *How has conditionality been used?*

Conditionality has typically been included in crisis resolution frameworks, though with varying degrees in terms of its spectrum, comprehensiveness, and effectiveness. For government guarantees, no conditionality was introduced but for extraordinary transfers and federal loans states had to comply with some policy conditionality, and in some extreme cases the federal government implemented direct administrative controls.

No conditionality

Crisis resolution mechanisms implemented without conditionality just rely on market discipline and for that reason have been relatively rare. Their success relies primarily on market perceptions of the probability of a federal bailout. In Australia, federal guarantees were granted without conditions, but subnational deficits remained moderate, and market financing ensured subnational discipline to some extent. In contrast in Mexico, Hernández-Trillo and Smith-Ramirez (2009) conclude that market discipline was weakened by the perception that the federal government would ultimately provide additional financial support.

Policy conditionality

Conditionality has typically sought to achieve a reduction in deficits over the short run, and in a few cases sought to advance structural reform. Conditionality has included deficit targets (Mexico), debt-to-revenue targets (Brazil in 1997), expenditure ceilings (Germany and Brazil), and a freeze on the number of public employees (Argentina in the mid-1990s). Additionally, conditionality may have sought to reduce financing needs, for example through the privatization of state assets (Brazil in 1997). In some cases, strict limits were set on access to new debt financing, for example requiring that all new debt had to be authorized by the federal government (Spain), prohibition on contracting new debt (Argentina in the 1990s) or through the privatization of public banks (Brazil in 1997). On the structural side, conditionality has included privatization of public enterprises (Brazil in 1997), subnational pension reform (Argentina in the 1990s),[8] and even passage of fiscal responsibility laws (India in 2005).[9]

One of the main limitations of conditionality has been its temporary nature – either because resources were disbursed up front, reducing the incentive to carry out proposed reforms, or because subnational governments were no longer bound by fiscal adjustment agreements once the financial support package expired. As a result, underlying fiscal vulnerabilities soon resurfaced after the crisis episode. For example, in Germany, Bremen and Saarland's nominal debt increased by almost fifty percent in the five years after the end of the financial support plan in 2004. In Brazil, the cap on debt service payments attached to the 1993 debt restructuring undermined the subnational governments' incentives to implement reform fully (Box 6.2). In some cases, conditions were simply unrealistic. For example, in Brazil in 1995, states were required to ensure actuarial equilibrium in their pension systems, establish comprehensive privatization programs, and implement centralized systems for their state enterprises – all within a quarter.

Direct administrative controls

Direct administrative controls of subnational governments by the center have been rare as they involve the loss of subnational fiscal autonomy. The few examples in our sample include the United States and South Africa (Box 6.3), where the federal government was allowed to approve the budgets and financing plans, and even personnel decisions and cash management (in NYC and DC), and the introduction of new public financial management procedures (South Africa).

B. How conditionality has been enforced

Even when conditionality has been imposed as part of a crisis resolution scheme, the degree of enforcement has varied, relying mainly on financial and administrative sanctions.

Sanctions for non-compliance can be financial or administrative. While it is generally accepted that financial sanctions may give rise to time inconsistency problems,[10] some countries have used them. For example, in Brazil, deviations from the agreed targets under state restructuring contracts are punishable with more burdensome financing costs. Transfers have also been withheld to guarantee the service of debt (Mexico and Brazil).[11] Administrative sanctions have included dismissal procedures, obligations to resign, fines or lower wages (Brazil, Spain). Among the case studies surveyed, tranching of disbursements – of the kind used, for example, for IMF conditionality – has not been used as an enforcement mechanism.

Importantly, experience shows that two pre-requisites are required for conditionality to work: the existence of a reasonably well-functioning subnational public financial management system (Chapter 4) and the availability of timely, reliable, and comprehensive information on subnational government operations, to enable the federal government to seek corrective action without delay. In Germany, Bremen and Saarland were required to report annually to the federal finance minister and state finance ministers, which kept the two states in line

Box 6.3 Three cases of direct administrative controls

Direct administrative controls have been relatively rare, as they infringe on a subnational governments' fiscal autonomy. Three examples illustrate this type of intervention:

- *District of Columbia (DC)*. In 1995, the federal government set up a financial control board (the DC Financial Responsibility and Management Assistance Authority) charged with approving the budget and financial plan, reviewing all legislation that affected the financial plan, and approving all labor contracts. Moreover, an independent chief financial officer was installed, responsible for preparing and monitoring the budget, multiyear financial plans, personnel control systems, and all public and invested funds. The financial control board suspended its operations in 2001 when all debt was repaid and DC had regained access to private credit markets at reasonable rates and achieved four consecutive years of balanced budgets. The control board can be re-established at any time if DC does not fulfill these conditions.
- *New York City*. In 1975, NYC faced US$14 billion in outstanding debt and an operating deficit of US$600 million (Dunstan, 1995). Because the procedural mechanisms of Chapter 9 were believed to be inadequate to govern the reorganization of a major municipality, New York State took over the public financial management of the city. As part of the package, the governor appointed an Emergency Financial Control Board (EFCB). The EFCB could control the city's bank accounts; issue orders to city officials; remove them from office and press charges against them; review and reject the city's financial plan and operating and capital budgets; contracts negotiated with the public employees union; and all municipal borrowing (Dunstan 1995). By 1978, NYC was without short-term debt. It regained market access in 1979, and ran a balanced budget in 1981.
- *South Africa*. The Constitution gives the central government the right to intervene if a province is unable to meets its constitutional obligations. The central government intervened in the provinces of Eastern Cape and KwaZulu-Natal in 1997–1998 (Ahmad, 2003)[1] and enforced stringent conditions, including spending controls and expenditure reduction. It also reformed public financial management procedures, establishing multiyear budgets and a monthly reporting system to the national treasury. In 2011–2012, the provinces of Limpopo, Eastern Cape, Gauteng, and Free State faced a funding deficit and were unable to pay salaries and suppliers. In line with faculties allowed under the Constitution, the central government placed several departments under its administration, including the public works, health, public transport, and education department, seeking to introduce new public financial management procedures and proper supply-chain management.

¹Provincial treasuries had only been established in 1994 and were unable to monitor or check departmental expenditures in the first years. Given the high expectations for the post-apartheid regime, over-spending in education, health and welfare was widespread. Health and education costs rose by 26 and 31 percent, respectively, from 1995/6–1996/7 (Ajam and Aron, 2007). Most of these costs were personnel-related expenditures that the provinces could not completely control because wages were set at the national level.

with conditionality. Spain introduced monthly budget reporting requirements in 2012 for the regions tapping the government rescue fund. In contrast, in Mexico during the mid-1990s, states did not follow a standardized plan of accounting, nor did they provide reliable fiscal data. Addressing this deficiency was a central tenet of the reform of the crisis prevention framework in the early 2000s. Brazil's 1997 contracts between the federal and state governments also addressed previous deficiencies in the capacity – both data and manpower – to monitor state finances.

V. Crisis prevention as a legacy of crises

Some countries have taken advantage of subnational fiscal crises to enshrine conditionality in a broader set of institutional reforms that would not have been politically feasible beforehand. These reforms did not necessarily crystallize in the immediate aftermath of a crisis; they usually took some time to implement because of the need to build consensus, including in the legislature. However, in about half of the countries in our sample, the experience of a crisis did raise support for stronger crisis prevention measures and shaped their content in three main directions: imposing borrowing constraints; strengthening the fiscal framework; and improving transparency.

A. *Imposing borrowing constraints*

Financial markets often fail to exert disciplinary influence on subnational governments due to the lack of timely and reliable data on subnational accounts, the expectations of financial support by the center, and the subnationals' privileged access to financing. Two approaches have been adopted to confront these problems in the aftermath of a crisis:

- At one extreme, *market-friendly regulations* have been introduced to spur financial institutions to fully internalize credit risk. For example in Mexico, in the aftermath of the Tequila crisis, a new borrowing framework was introduced that subjects state debts to the same borrower concentration limits as other types of borrowers (so as to facilitate appropriate risk assessments by banks) and establishes a link between the risk weighting of bank loans to subnational governments and those governments' credit ratings (Giugale et al., 2000).

• At the other extreme, *administrative controls* have been used to limit subnational governments' direct access to financing. In Brazil, the introduction of borrowing controls, coupled with the privatization of state-owned banks, limited the privileged access of states to bank credit, resulting in a sharp decline in subnational debt (Figure 6.3). In Argentina, privileged financing was also restricted when provincial banks were privatized in 1994–96, as a condition for the federal government to refinance provincial bank liabilities that had earlier been taken over by provincial governments (Burki et al., 1999).

B. Strengthening the fiscal framework

Some countries have gone one step further and tried to use the crisis resolution mechanisms as a springboard to improve the fiscal framework in a durable way through legal changes, for example local fiscal responsibility laws in India, an overarching national fiscal responsibility law in Brazil, and the introduction of a subnational balanced budget rule in the constitution in Germany (Liu and Webb, 2011; Finance Commission India, 2009; Margedant, 2003; Bundesverfassungsgericht, 1999; Enderlein et al., 2012). In Brazil, a national fiscal responsibility law (FRL) was introduced in 2000, applying to all levels of government. That framework reinforced the restrictions on personnel spending, deficits, and debt included in the state debt restructuring agreements and was supported by changes to the legislative framework. In particular, enforcement was stepped up through the Penal Law for Fiscal Crimes, which includes prison sentences for illegal efforts to issue public bonds. The law

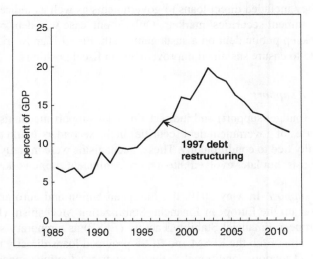

Figure 6.3 Brazil: Subnational net debt (percent of GDP)[1]

Sources: Bevilaqua, 2002; Giambiagi and Ronci, 2004; and Central Bank of Brazil.

[1]Including debt of states and municipalities.

also stipulates that the executive mandate of a mayor or governor may be stripped if debt limits or personnel expenditure ratios are exceeded. Moreover, debt and labor contracts in violation of the FRL are not legally valid (which could lead to lenders losing their money).[12]

Some countries supported the introduction of rules by creating institutions charged with ensuring fiscal discipline at the subnational level. A prime example is Germany, where a stability council, consisting of both federal and state finance ministers, was established in 2010. The council evaluates states' fiscal performance and can agree on a consolidation program if a state performs significantly worse than other states.

C. *Improving transparency*

The lack of timely and reliable data has been an obstacle for market discipline to work and for the effective implementation of conditionality. Brazil, India, and Mexico sought to improve transparency and accountability in the aftermath of subnational fiscal crises. In Brazil and in India, this was done through provisions in the fiscal responsibility laws. In the case of Mexico, states that do not publish fiscal data are subject to higher capital risk-weighting in the context of the new subnational borrowing framework (Giugale et al., 2000).

VI. The response to the euro area crisis

The mechanisms set in place to contain the sovereign debt crisis in the euro area bear some resemblance with those used during subnational crises in fiscal federations. They included direct loans to governments as well as indirect intervention in government securities' markets. Only in one case was debt restructuring required to keep public debt on a sustainable path. Fiscal frameworks were also strengthened to ensure sustained improvements in fiscal positions.

A. *Financial support*

Both direct (budget support) and indirect financial support mechanisms (central bank purchases of government debt securities in the secondary market) have been used, typically tied to conditionality. These mechanisms were initially set up on a temporary basis, but later evolved into a more permanent framework.

•   *Direct support.* In May 2010, the European Union and euro area member states set up the European Financial Stabilization Mechanism (EFSM) and the European Financial Stability Facility (EFSF) as temporary stabilization mechanisms. Both the EFSM and EFSF provided loans directly to countries for budget support, conditional on these countries adopting a macroeconomic adjustment program monitored by the European Commission (EC) in liaison with the European Central Bank (ECB) and the IMF. Building on the EFSF, the European authorities created the European Stability Mechanism (ESM) in

October 2010 as a permanent crisis resolution framework (entering into force in 2012). The ESM was given the mandate to (i) provide stability support loans within a macroeconomic adjustment program; (ii) participate directly in the recapitalization of financial institutions; (iii) provide precautionary financial assistance through contingent credit lines; and (iv) intervene in primary and secondary markets. ESM financing was tied to conditionality on macroeconomic and structural reforms – taking the form of a macroeconomic adjustment program, financial sector program, or enhanced surveillance under a precautionary program – monitored by the EC, ECB, and, where appropriate, the European Supervisory Authority and IMF. Through June 2013, five euro area countries had made use of this financing (Table 6.2). Nonetheless, the existence of the ESM did not preclude the use of bail-ins to reduce the size of financing needs, as occurred in Cyprus with the participation of bank creditors, including uninsured depositors, in bank recapitalization.

• *Indirect financial support.* In May 2010, the ECB launched the Securities Markets Program (SMP) as a temporary measure to alleviate pressures in government debt securities markets that hampered the monetary policy transmission mechanism. Under the SMP, the ECB intervened by buying euro area government securities on the secondary market, for a total amount close to €220 billion. In August 2012, the ECB announced its Outright Monetary Transactions (OMT) program to undertake purchases of sovereign bonds in the secondary market with no *ex ante* quantitative limits on the size. This was put forward as a more permanent mechanism, though the discretion to start or suspend the program lies with the ECB Governing Council. In contrast to the SMP, OMT requires strict conditionality tied to an appropriate EFSF/ESM program so as to preserve the ECB's price stability mandate and ensure that governments have an incentive to implement the required fiscal adjustment and structural reforms.

Although similar in concept, there are some notable differences between these mechanisms and those used in subnational crises analyzed:

Table 6.2 Lending programs (in billions of euro)

	EFSM	EFSF	ESM
Ireland	22.5	17.7	
Portugal	26	26.0	
Greece		144.6	
Spain			100.0
Cyprus			9.0
Total	48.5	188.3	109.0

Sources: ESM and European Commission.

Note: As of June 2013.

- The ESM has a permanent, institutionalized character that is relatively rare in fiscal federations. Relatedly, it is more comprehensive and complex, establishing several alternative forms of financing (loans, precautionary credit lines, bank recapitalization, and market intervention) not seen in other formal resolution frameworks for subnational crisis. This responds to a greater reliance by euro area countries on financing through debt securities, in contrast to the more prominent role of bank lending in most of the subnational crisis cases analyzed. The lending capacity of the ESM is also greater than that of the permanent mechanisms available to subnational governments in our sample, reflecting its supranational nature. Finally, unlike the experience in federations, tranching of disbursements has been used to enforce conditionality.
- While fiscal federations have at times used the central bank to provide direct financing to subnational governments, central bank intervention in the euro area crisis has relied mainly on purchases of securities in the secondary markets to alleviate pressures in government debt markets.
- As in subnational debt crises, there has been a reluctance to restructure the debt with private creditors in the euro area because of the perceived risk of contagion and to avoid moral hazard. Indeed, Greece is the only member state to have undergone debt restructuring.[13] However, in contrast to subnational debt crises where debt restructuring took place against the backdrop of severe pressures at the center (such as in Argentina and Mexico), debt restructuring in the euro area did not occur in the context of market pressures on the larger euro area member states. Rather, it was used to contain bailout expectations – similar to the United States in the 1840s – although, unlike the United States, the center did provide direct support.
- For countries under EU/IMF-supported programs, outstanding liabilities to the center have been restructured to improve the debt servicing profile, both through the reduction of interest rates in 2011 and extension of maturities in 2013. This parallels the cases of Brazil and India, though in the latter restructuring of debt to the central government has taken place on a more recurrent basis.

B. Fiscal framework

The crisis in the euro area set the stage for broader institutional reforms to help address weaknesses in the economic governance. Reforms – implemented through the "Fiscal Compact," "Six Pack," and "Two Pack" – strengthened the preventive and corrective arms of the Stability and Growth Pact.[14] In particular, they (i) introduced a new expenditure benchmark as a complement to the change in the structural balance; (ii) made a significant deviation from the adjustment path toward the medium-term budgetary objective a trigger for a corrective mechanism; and (iii) put the debt requirement on an equal footing to the deficit requirement. A gradual system of financial sanctions for euro area countries was added that could eventually reach 0.5 percent of GDP. Enforcement of sanctions was strengthened by the expanded use of "reverse qualified majority" voting.[15]

Certain requirements on domestic budgetary arrangements, procedures, rules and institutions were also imposed. These included, among others, the independent monitoring of budgetary rules and independent *ex ante* endorsement of macroeconomic forecasts, which in many countries is under the mandate of a fiscal council (Chapter 3).

These improvements in the fiscal framework are similar in nature to those implemented by federations in the aftermath of subnational crises. The euro area imposed a combination of fiscal rules (debt, deficit, and expenditure ceilings) as did Brazil (limits on debt, deficit, and personnel expenditure) and India (limits on revenue and fiscal deficits). In contrast to Brazil where sanctions for non-compliance with rules included administrative and legal penalties to public servants, sanctions in the euro area were mainly financial. Similar to the stability council in Germany, the European Commission and European Council were charged with the responsibility of overseeing compliance with fiscal rules.

VII. Conclusions

This chapter has shown that when facing a financing crisis, subnational governments are rarely allowed to default on their private creditors. In fact, when debt restructurings have occurred, they mainly involved smaller political entities or cases where the federal government debt itself was restructured. Pre-set crisis resolution frameworks such as bankruptcy procedures are notably absent when dealing with states. Instead, federal governments may provide financial support through a range of ad hoc mechanisms, including sovereign guarantees, direct loans, and extraordinary transfers. Several common elements emerge across case studies on subnational crisis resolution – most of them are also present in the response to the euro area crisis.

• *Federal governments typically provided financing to subnational governments, but this was only possible because the center retained market access and was in a strong political position.* Even in the case of default to private creditors, costs to the center were not avoided as federal governments provided financing to states at a later stage. The type of financing provided has taken different forms, dictated by country specific circumstances. In cases where federal financing was insufficient to align subnational governments' debt servicing profile with their income prospects, further interventions were needed down the road.

• *Crisis resolution has tended to be more successful when subnational governments took on the burden of solving their own underlying fiscal vulnerabilities, facilitated by effective and well-enforced conditionality.* The most successful adjustment programs have been those that were anchored in a realistic medium-term plan to improve the fiscal position over time and included specific enforcement mechanisms. Conditionality was better enforced when strong monitoring mechanisms where in place, supported by adequate and reliable subnational fiscal information.

- *Preset crisis resolution frameworks have been rare and often bypassed.* Despite their potential benefits (minimizing costs by serving as a deterrent and allowing the central government to address underperforming subnational governments early on), formal frameworks have been rare – although they occupy a prominent place in the response to the euro area crisis. The existence of formal frameworks has not precluded discretionary intervention by the center, as was the case of Mexico and the United States, suggesting that their adoption as well as their use tend to be hampered by significant political hurdles.
- *In many cases, the crisis itself has been a catalyst for broader institutional reform that emphasizes crisis prevention.* Though it took several years to develop, some countries used the crisis as a springboard for broader institutional reform that would have been politically difficult otherwise. Such reforms focused on imposing borrowing constraints, strengthening the fiscal framework, and improving transparency.

Notes

1 As mentioned, the list does not include the cases where the subnational government had to address financing constraints solely through fiscal adjustment, without default or external intervention. Our sample includes, however, United States' federal support for New York City in 1975 to illustrate the scope (and limitations) of formal bankruptcy procedures.
2 New York City in the mid-1970s and the District of Columbia in the 1990s lost access to financing when banks refused to roll over short-term debt. Similarly, the loss of access to bank overdraft facilities exposed severe fiscal stress in South African provinces. In Argentina, borrowing from provincial banks was lost when the Tequila crisis prompted a run on most provincial banks.
3 Debt service doubled to 9.5 percent of expenditures in Mexico between 1994 and 1995, and to around 15 percent of revenues by the mid-1990s in Brazil, in this latter case due to the indexation of the debt to short-term rates (Dillinger, 1998; Dillinger and Webb, 1999). In Germany, interest payments reached over 20 percent of revenues in the states of Bremen and Saarland in the early 1990s. In India, interest expenses trended upwards since the early 1980s reaching 35 percent of the states' own revenue by early 2000 (McCarten, 2003; Purfield, 2004). Finally, in Australia, state government bond spreads nearly doubled in December 2008 with almost no trading in the state bond market.
4 As noted in Chapter 5, subnational debt is generally much smaller than the debt of the central government.
5 Several provinces met financing needs through the placement of provincial bonds in domestic markets and the launch of their own small denomination paper. As a result, the total stock of quasi-monies reached about 26 percent of total pesos in circulation by the end of December 2001.
6 Historically, in the United States, as well as Canada, Germany, and Italy, the central government of the newly-formed union took over the debt of some of the member states. These cases are discussed in Chapter 5.
7 Almost all Argentine provinces received discretionary transfers from the federal government from 1992 to 1994, with no conditionality (Nicolini et al., 2002). In Mexico, transfers were conditioned to the approval of a fiscal consolidation plan and a debt rule, together with improved accounting, but no enforcement mechanism was in place (International Monetary Fund, 2004). In Germany, the federal government provided transfers to the states of Bremen and Saarland following a 1992 Constitutional Court

ruling that high interest payments represented extreme budgetary hardship for these two states and that they deserved federal support; transfers were provided for five years, and then another six years, against a set of conditions. While both states complied with these conditions, they still required additional extraordinary transfers in 2011.

8　In August 1993, the federal government negotiated a fiscal pact to reform provincial pension funds, in exchange for a higher guaranteed minimum of co-participation funds. Prior to 1995, only three provinces had signed the pact. As financing conditions worsened in the context of the Tequila crisis, many more provinces agreed to the pact (See Nicolini et al., 2002; Dillinger and Webb, 1999).

9　In some cases, conditionality on subnational governments took place alongside broader stabilization policies and structural reforms at the federal level (Argentina, Brazil, Mexico).

10　Fining a subnational government already in budgetary distress is not credible, as that government may require additional financial support in any event (Ter-Minassian, 2007).

11　In Brazil, the system was tested in 1999 when Minas Gerais announced a debt moratorium and precipitated the external crisis that led to the devaluation of the Real. The federal government's response was to withhold transfers in the same amount as the scheduled debt service and to decline to guarantee state loans.

12　See Chapter 4 for more details on the FRL.

13　The debt restructuring required both private and official sector involvement, generating cuts equivalent to 65 percent of GDP (International Monetary Fund, 2013). Other measures were undertaken to decrease the Greek debt burden including: (i) using EFSF funding to buy back debt at a deep discount; (ii) lowering interest rates on the Greek Facility Loan and EFSF loans; and (iii) remitting profits on Greek government bonds purchased by the ECB under the SMP.

14　Details are discussed in Chapter 3.

15　Under this voting system, an EC recommendation or proposal to the European Council is considered adopted unless a qualified majority of member states votes against it.

References

Ahmad, J., 2003, "Creating Incentives for Fiscal Discipline in New South Africa," in Rodden, J., G. S. Eskeland, and J. Litvack eds., *Fiscal Decentralization and the Challenges of Hard Budget Constraint* (Cambridge: The MIT Press).

Ajam, T., and J. Aron, 2007, "Fiscal Renaissance in a Democratic South Africa," *Journal of African Economies* Vol. 16, No.5, pp. 745–781.

Alleyne, T., 1998, "The Post-Real Fiscal Crisis in the States," in IMF Staff Country Report No. 98/24 (Washington: International Monetary Fund).

Bevilaqua, A. S., 2002, "State Government Bailouts in Brazil," Research Working Paper No. R-441 (Washington: Inter-American Development Bank).

Bundesverfassungsgericht, 1999, "2 BvF 2/98 vom 11.11.1999, Absatz-Nr. (1 – 347)," available at: http://www.bverfg.de/entscheidungen/fs19991111_2bvf000298.html

Burki, S. J., G. Perry, and W. Dillinger, 1999, "Beyond the Center: Decentralizing the State," World Bank Latin American and Caribbean Studies Viewpoints, July.

Canuto, O., and L. Liu, 2010, "Subnational Debt Finance: Make It Sustainable," in *The Day After Tomorrow – A Handbook on the Future of Economic Policy in the Developing World*, edited by Otaviano Canuto and Marcelo Giugale (Washington: The World Bank).

Dillinger, W., 1998, "Brazil's State Debt Crisis: Lessons Learned," *Economica,* Vol. CLIV No.3.

———, and Webb, S., 1999, "Fiscal Management in Federal Democracies: Argentina and Brazil," Policy Research Working Paper No. 2121 (Washington: The World Bank).

Dunstan, R., 1995, "Overview of New York City's Fiscal Crisis," California Research Bureau Note 3/1.

Enderlein, H., J. Fiedler, F. Schuppert, R. Geissler, F. Meinel, and C. von Mueller, 2012. "Gutachten zur Umsetzung der grundgesetzlichen Schuldenbremse in Baden-Württemberg" (Berlin: Hertie School of Governance).

English, W.B., 1996, "Understanding the Costs of Sovereign Default: American State Debts in the 1840's," *American Economic Review*, 86, 259–275.

Fernández, R.B., S. Pernice, J.M. Streb, M. Alegre, A. Bedoya, and C. Gonzalez, 2006, "The Development of Latin-American Bond Markets: The Case of Argentina," IADB – Latin American Research Network, May 24, 2006.

Finance Commission India, 2009, "Report of the Thirteenth Finance Commission 2010–2015," December 2009.

Fitch, 2011, "Institutional Framework for Mexican Subnational Governments," *Public Finance Special Report*, December.

———, 2012, "U.S. Local Government Tax-Supported Rating Criteria," *Fitch Public Finance Special Report*, August 14.

Giambiagi, F., and M. Ronci, 2004, "Fiscal Policy and Debt Sustainability: Cardoso's Brazil, 1995–2002," IMF Working Paper 04/156 (Washington: International Monetary Fund).

Giugale, M., F. Hernández-Trillo, and J.C. Oliveira, 2000, "Subnational Borrowing and Debt Management," in *Achievements and Challenges of Fiscal Decentralization: Lessons from Mexico,* edited by M. Giugale and S. Webb (Washington: World Bank Publications).

Hempel, G.H., 1971, *The Postwar Quality of State and Local Debt,* (New York: National Bureau of Economic Research, 1971).

Henning, C.R. and M. Kessler, 2012, "Fiscal Federalism: US History for Architects of Europe's Fiscal Union," Peterson Institute for International Economics Working Paper No. 2012–1.

Hernández-Trillo, F., and R. Smith-Ramirez, 2009, "Credit Ratings in the Presence of Bailout: The Case of Mexican Subnational Government Debt," *Economia* Vol. 10, No. 1, Fall, pp. 45–79.

International Monetary Fund, 2004, "Mexico: Selected Issues," IMF Country Report No. 04/418, December.

International Monetary Fund, 2013, "Greece: Staff Report," IMF Country Report No. 13/154, June.

Jeweler, R., 2007, "Municipal Reorganization: Chapter 9 of the U.S. Bankruptcy Code," Congressional Research Service for Congress, March 8.

Liu, L., and M. Waibel, 2008, "Subnational Insolvency: Cross-Country Experiences and Lessons," Policy Research Working Paper No. 4496 (Washington: The World Bank).

———, and S. Webb, 2011, "Laws for Fiscal Responsibility for Subnational Discipline," Policy Research Working Paper No. 5587 (Washington: The World Bank).

Lopreato, F.L., 2000, "O Endividamento Dos Governos Estaduais Nos Anos 90," *Economia e Sociedade*, Campinas (15), pp. 117–158.

Manasse, P, N. Roubini, and A. Schimmelpfennig, 2003,"Predicting Sovereign Debt Crises," IMF Working Paper 03/221 (Washington: International Monetary Fund).

Margedant, 2003, "Die Föderalismusdiskussion in Deutschland," available at: *http://www.bpb.de/apuz/27498/die-foederalismusdiskussion-in-deutschland?p=all*

McCarten, W.J., 2003, "Challenge of Fiscal Discipline in the Indian States," in *Fiscal Decentralization and the Challenges of Hard Budget Constraint*, edited by Rodden, J., G. S. Eskeland, and J. Litvack (Cambridge: The MIT Press).

Moody's, 2012, "US Municipal Bond Defaults and Recoveries, 1970–2011," Special Comment.

Nicolini, J. P., J. Posadas, J. Sanguinetti, P. Sanguinetti, and M. Tomassi, 2002, "Decentralization, Fiscal Discipline in Sub-National Governments and the Bailout Problem: The Case of Argentina," Research Working Paper No. R-467 (Washington: Inter-American Development Bank).

Pettit, C. A., 2011, "Chapter 9 of the U.S. Bankruptcy Code: Municipal Bankruptcy," Congressional Research Service for Congress, March 31.

Purfield, C., 2004, "The Decentralization Dilemma in India," IMF Working Paper 04/32 (Washington: International Monetary Fund).

Reinhart, C. M., and K. S. Rogoff, 2008, "This Time is Different: A Panoramic View of Eight Centuries of Financial Crises," NBER Working Papers 13882.

Reserve Bank of India, 2012, "State Finances – A Study of Budgets of 2011–2012," (Mumbai: Reserve Bank of India).

Rodden, J. A., 2006, *Hamilton's Paradox. The Promise and Peril of Fiscal Federalism* (New York: Cambridge University Press).

Sanguinetti, 1999, "Restricción de Presupuesto Blanda en los Niveles Subnacionales de Gobierno: El Caso Los Salvatajes en el Caso Argentino," *Económica, La Plata* Vol. XLV, No. 4, Agno 1999.

Secretaría de Hacienda y Crédito Público de México, 2005, "Diagnostico Integral de la Situacion Actual de las Haciendas Publicas Estatales Y Municipales 2005," available http://www.shcp.gob.mx/Estados/Paginas/DiagnosticoIntegral.aspx

———, 2007, "Diagnostico Integral de la Situacion Actual de las Haciendas Publicas Estatales Y Municipales 2007," available at http://www.shcp.gob.mx/Estados/Paginas/DiagnosticoIntegral.aspx

Ter-Minassian, T., 2007, "Fiscal Rules for Subnational Governments: Can They Promote Fiscal Discipline?" *OECD Journal on Budgeting* Vol. 6., No.3, pp. 108–120.

Torre, A., E. Levy Yeyati, and S. L. Schmukler, 2003, "Living and Dying with Hard Pegs: The Rise and Fall of Argentina's Currency Board," *Economía* Vol. 3, No. 2, Spring 2003, pp. 43–99.

7 Lessons from the crisis: Minimal elements for a fiscal union in the euro area

Céline Allard, John Bluedorn,
Fabian Bornhorst, and Davide Furceri

I. Introduction

The previous chapters examine the features of fiscal federalism in theory and in practice, describing the arrangements and experiences of a sample of federations from around the world and comparing them with the practices of the European Union. This chapter takes a different angle: focusing on the euro area, it looks back at the genesis and unfolding of the current crisis and draws lessons for future fiscal integration to prevent or minimize the depth of future crises.[1]

The euro area crisis has revealed critical gaps in the functioning of the monetary union. It has shown how sovereigns can be priced out of the market or lose market access altogether, and how private borrowing costs can differ widely within the union, despite a common monetary policy. It also has highlighted how contagion can set in, with deep recessions in some member states spilling over to the rest of the membership.

In response to that crisis, European leaders have taken positive steps to strengthen fiscal and economic governance. The Six-Pack went into force in December 2011; the Fiscal Compact in January 2013; and the Two-Pack regulation in May 2013, applying to the 2014 budgeting period.

In addition, in December 2012, the European Commission (EC) and the President of the Council, in close collaboration with the Presidents of the EC, the Eurogroup and the European Central Bank, both issued proposals for a roadmap toward greater fiscal integration (European Commission, 2012; European Council, 2012). This followed a call by euro area leaders, at their June 2012 summit, to issue proposals "to develop a specific and time-bound roadmap toward a genuine Economic and Monetary Union," including greater fiscal integration, so as to ensure the irreversibility of the Economic and Monetary Union (EMU). In any case, the idea of deeper fiscal integration for Europe is not a new concept: it was already developed in the 1970s in the famous MacDougall report (European Commission, 1977).

Yet, political backing for a clear roadmap is still missing, with views on the contours of a fiscal union differing widely among euro area members. Some argue in favor of greater solidarity between member states, while others point to the need to strengthen national fiscal policies as a first priority to prevent further stress. There is also concern that any debt mutualization would lead to moral hazard, sapping members' motivation to undertake prudent domestic policies in the future.

As a contribution to this ongoing debate, this chapter outlines a conceptual framework to assess the case for further fiscal integration for the euro area. To do so, this chapter analyzes the critical gaps in EMU architecture exposed by the crisis and derives from that analysis the minimal elements of a fiscal union to address them. It finds that four elements seem essential to make a future crisis less severe: (i) better oversight of national fiscal policies and enforcement of fiscal rules to build buffers and ensure common concerns are addressed; (ii) subject to strong oversight and enforcement of fiscal discipline, some system of temporary transfers or joint provision of common public goods or services to increase fiscal risk sharing; (iii) a credible pan-euro area backstop for the banking sector; and (iv) some common borrowing to finance greater risk sharing and a stronger back-stop and provide a common – albeit limited in size – safe asset.

The rest of the chapter is organized as follows. Section II looks at the critical gaps exposed by the crisis. The subsequent sections look in turn into the minimal elements for a fiscal union to ensure that future crises are less severe: section III focuses on risk reduction to address government failure and foster fiscal discipline, section IV looks at risk sharing options to insure against country-specific risks, and section V elaborates on the steps to dampen spillovers and stem contagion. Section VI concludes with a benefit and cost analysis and some immediate considerations.

II. Gaps exposed by the crisis – A conceptual framework

The crisis has exposed four critical gaps: While country-specific shocks have remained more prevalent than initially expected, the high degree of trade and, even more importantly, financial integration has created the potential for substantial spillovers. Furthermore, weak fiscal governance and the absence of effective market disciple have compounded these problems. Finally, sovereign and bank stresses have moved together, setting off a vicious circle with markets starting to price in both bank and sovereign default.

First, large country-specific shocks have remained prevalent. While it was recognized that countries joining the euro area had significant structural differences, the launch of the common currency was expected to create the conditions for further real convergence among member countries. The benefits of the single market were to be reinforced by growing trade and financial links – making economies more similar and subject to more common shocks over time (Frankel and Rose, 1998). In that context, these common shocks would be best addressed through a common monetary policy. Instead, country-specific shocks have remained frequent and substantial (Pisani-Ferry, 2012 and Figure 7.1). Some countries experienced a specific shock through a dramatic decline in their borrowing costs at the launch of the euro, which created the conditions for localized credit booms

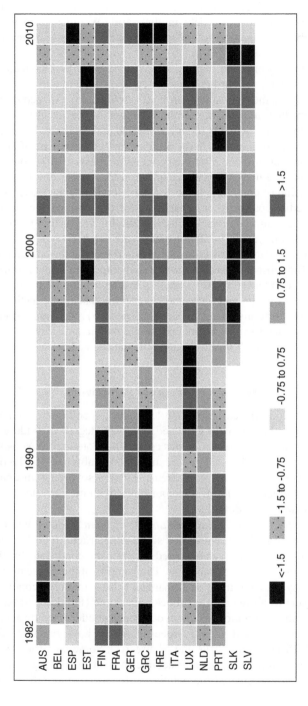

Figure 7.1 Country-specific growth shocks (percent)

Sources: OECD data and IMF staff calculations.

Note: The idiosyncratic growth shocks are derived as the part of the country-specific growth shocks that are not explained by euro area-wide growth shocks. Growth shocks (both for the euro area and individual countries) are computed as the residuals from a regression of the country's (euro area's) growth rate over two lags.

and busts. The impact of globalization was also felt differently across the euro area, reflecting diverse trade specialization patterns and competitiveness levels (Carvalho, forthcoming). These country-specific shocks have had lasting effects on activity. And divergences in growth rates across countries have remained as sizeable after the creation of the euro as before (Figure 7.2).

Second, the consequences of these shocks have been compounded by weak fiscal policies in some countries. In some cases, the shocks themselves were the result of idiosyncratic policies (e.g., Greece). More generally, the windfall from lower interest and debt payments were not saved, and higher revenues generated by unsustainable domestic demand booms were wrongly deemed permanent. By the time the crisis hit, countries had insufficient buffers to enable countercyclical support at the national level. Moreover, the European fiscal governance framework was too loosely implemented to ensure the appropriate management of public finances over the cycle. Government failure and political interference became especially evident when the Council decided to hold the Stability and Growth and Pact's procedure in abeyance for the two largest countries of the euro area in 2003.

Third, while country-specific shocks remained more frequent than expected, and imprudent national policies were pursued by some, there were few market forces to correct growing fiscal and external imbalances:

- **Labor market and price rigidities:** Unlike what would have been expected in an optimal currency area, prices and wages continued to display strong downward rigidities in many euro area countries, standing in the way of the timely real exchange rate adjustment that may be required after a negative shock (Jaumotte and Morsy, 2012). This allowed the accumulation of large intra-euro area imbalances that have been at the heart of the crisis. Likewise, labor mobility – even though increasing – continued to be lower than in other common currency areas (e.g., in federations such as the United States), because of both language and cultural barriers and institutional constraints – such as the inability to port pensions or unemployment benefits across borders – inhibiting rebalancing through migration.
- **Missing incentives for markets to enforce discipline:** A corrective mechanism against unsustainable national fiscal policies could have come from capital markets. In fact, the provision enshrined in the Maastricht Treaty to ensure that no member ends up assuming another fellow member state's fiscal commitments (Article 125 of the Treaty on the Functioning of the European Union, TFEU) – hereafter referred to as the "no bailout" clause – was meant to give financial markets an incentive to price default risk in a differentiated way across the euro area. However, general optimism about the region's growth prospects at the euro's inception blunted markets' scrutiny of national fiscal policies. Moreover, it also did not help that the clause lacked credibility: With few automatic mechanisms in place *ex ante* to support individual members in distress, markets could extrapolate that the crisis in the affected countries would be deep and that spillovers would be substantial enough for policymakers to prefer to bail out a member country *ex post* rather

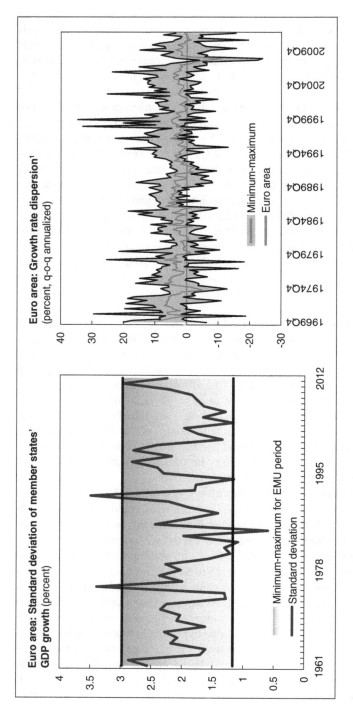

Figure 7.2 Persistent growth divergence within the euro area

Sources: Left panel, AMECO database and IMF staff calculations; right panel, OECD data and IMF staff calculations.

[1]Euro area is comprised of Austria, Belgium, Finland, France, Germany, Ireland, Italy, Luxembourg, the Netherlands, Portugal, and Spain until 2000, including new member states thereafter as they joined, with the exceptions of Malta and Cyprus.

than let it default. In other words, market discipline failed *ex ante* because the no-bailout option was not *ex post* credible. In turn, because *ex ante* market discipline was missing – and fiscal rules were not strictly enforced – some members borrowed excessively, taking on more debt than they would have if risks had been priced appropriately.

Finally, by fostering strong transmission channels, deeper financial integration also exacerbated contagion across countries once the crisis started. Indeed, when large adverse shocks hit at the end of the 2000s, they were left unmitigated, increasing the probability and impact of sovereign and bank distress. Domestic fiscal buffers were rapidly depleted. Meanwhile, with the advance of financial integration in the first ten years of EMU, some banks had extended themselves well beyond the capability of their national sovereigns to rescue them. Yet, many banks continued to hold a sizeable share of the debt issued by their domestic sovereign. This combination set the stage for an escalation of domestic stress, with problems in banks raising doubts about sovereign creditworthiness, and sovereign stress aggravating the pressure on banks' balance sheet – creating severe negative feedback loops between sovereigns and domestic banks (Figure 7.3). With no clear circuit-breaker in the system, markets could start pricing in default in a self-fulfilling way. In a highly integrated union, the deleterious impact of these shocks could travel fast across borders. Spreading through interconnected euro area banks, localized points of stress in 2010 were quickly amplified to a systemic level (Figure 7.4).

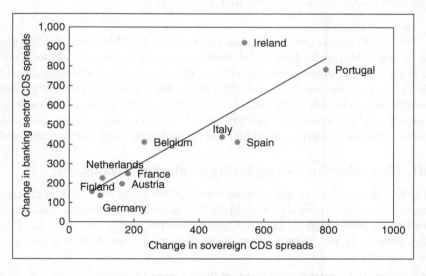

Figure 7.3 Sovereign-bank feedback loops: Change in sovereign and bank credit default swap (CDS) spreads, 2008-2012Q2 (basis points)

Sources: Bloomberg, Datastream, and IMF staff calculations.

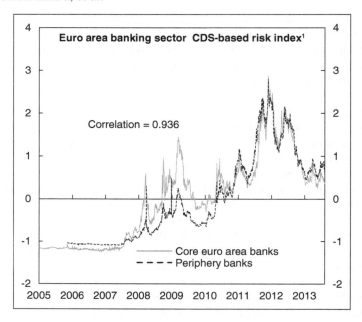

Figure 7.4 Financial sector interconnectedness

Sources: Bloomberg, Datastream, and IMF staff calculations.

[1]Normalized score from a principal component analysis on five-year senior bank CDS spreads, estimated over Jan. 2005 – Aug. 2013 for 23 banks in the core (Austria, Belgium, France, Germany, Netherlands) and 22 banks in the periphery (GRC, IRL, PRT, ESP, ITA).

How could greater fiscal integration address these gaps? Although the first step to dealing with country-level fiscal problems must be larger national fiscal buffers and stronger governance at the center, the size of shocks and their capacity to freeze up markets suggest a role for a zone-wide insurance mechanism. Fiscal integration can be that mechanism, providing an *ex ante* framework for enforced fiscal discipline, temporary transfers, and a common backstop for euro area banks – and hence also providing for more certainty that shocks will be contained.

III. Risk reduction: Strengthening fiscal policy making

The first pre-requisite to minimize the impact of future crisis is to reduce the risks created by imprudent fiscal policies in the euro area member countries. This entails addressing government failures and establishing the proper incentives for fiscal discipline, including, to the extent possible, through appropriate market scrutiny.

A. Addressing government failures at the national level

The euro area cannot afford a repeat of the imprudent fiscal and financial policies undertaken by some countries in the first decade of EMU. Debt is approaching dangerously high levels in some places, and confidence in the existing enforcement mechanisms embedded in the Stability and Growth Pact (SGP) is low. Steps toward improving fiscal governance and restoring the commitment to fiscal discipline should be guided by the following principles – which, for the most part, are already embedded in the recent steps to improve fiscal governance:

- **Smarter fiscal rules at the national level:** While a (structural) medium-term objective is also pursued, the binding target in the SGP applies to the headline fiscal balance and is therefore defined independently of the position in the cycle. This has proved suboptimal, with countries easily hitting an unambitious deficit of 3 percent of GDP under favorable economic conditions, but forced to unduly tighten during downturns to meet that same target. To some extent, the flexibility introduced in the 2005 reform of the SGP (through the "effective action" clause) and the Fiscal Compact allows for the focus to be put more on structural – instead of headline – fiscal balance targets. But that concept should be applied more systematically.
- **Robust corrective mechanisms:** Flexibility in the fiscal rules, however, will be credible only if fiscal policy is anchored in medium-term plans that clearly state the path back to lower debt levels. In particular, any accommodation for the cycle during downturns needs to be accompanied by plans to offset this over the medium term, possibly in an automatic way. When there are policy slippages, countries should have the incentive to take corrective measures systematically, with institutions in place to keep the potential for political interference to a minimum. While the establishment of such corrective mechanisms has, in principle, been agreed in the Fiscal Compact, they still have to be designed at the national level and made consistent across countries.
- **Independent forecasts:** Likewise, switching to structural targets will require a careful assessment of the position in the cycle – a difficult exercise to perform in real time. Furthermore, governments have tended to rely on overly optimistic forecasts to build their budgets. For all these reasons, relying on independent national agencies – in coordination with central oversight (see below) – to assess fiscal policy design and implementation would improve the process, as is now embedded in the "Two Pack" regulation.

B. Fostering fiscal discipline collectively

Chapter 3 discusses the various disciplining mechanisms that exist in a sample of federations. Market discipline at the subnational level can be underpinned by a credible "no bailout" rule and self-imposed budget constraints, as is the case in the United States, Canada, and to some extent in Switzerland.[2] Conversely, where bailout episodes of subnational governments have occurred in the recent past, discipline is often imposed through stronger central oversight, as has been the case in Brazil, and more recently in Germany. In intermediate arrangements, the federal government's authority over lower jurisdictions has been supported by a culture of dialogue and intergovernmental coordination (Australia, Belgium) or by direct democracy (Switzerland) – all cooperative features that have proved effective at instilling sound subnational fiscal policies. In addition, Chapter 6 has shown how crisis episodes not unlike the one currently experienced by the euro area tend to lead – at least for a time – to tighter borrowing constraints, stronger fiscal frameworks, increased transparency, and conditionality, including on the conduct of fiscal policy when financial support is provided.

So what are the options for the euro area in the steady state? Cooperative approaches to foster fiscal discipline have shown their limits in the first decade of EMU. Conceptually, this leaves two different options. One is to seek to restore the credibility of the "no bailout" clause, including through clear rules for the involvement of private creditors when support facilities are activated. But the transition to such a regime would have to be carefully managed and implemented in a gradual and coordinated fashion, so as to not trigger sharp readjustments in investors' portfolios and abrupt moves in bond prices. Another one is a center-based approach that relies less on market price signals. This would, however, come at the expense of a permanent loss of fiscal sovereignty for euro area members. In practice, the steady state regime might have to embed elements of both options, with market discipline complementing stronger central governance.

C. Transitional considerations

As argued earlier, while market discipline could be an important element to prevent future fiscal imbalances from emerging, it cannot be restored overnight, and certainly not in the midst of a crisis. Therefore, in the interim – and possibly as a long term solution too – the center will have to take a more active role. For now, while the other elements underpinning deeper fiscal integration are put in place, support from the European Stability Mechanism (ESM) to sovereigns under market stress continues to constitute the best line of defense against further systemic shocks. Credible rules in the form of conditionality will be needed to preserve the incentives to reform and ensure decisive implementation of adjustment measures at the country level.

To ensure enforcement in a "center-based" approach, greater involvement in national fiscal decisions could take various forms, along the following lines:

• **Legal challenges at the national level:** With fiscal rules enshrined into national legislation, enforcement will also become a national matter. In that setting, it might be possible to bring cases of infringement to domestic courts, depending on the domestic legal tradition of the member, and on the specific provisions of the domestic legal instruments implementing fiscal rules. European Union (EU) court jurisdiction over compliance of national domestic rules could also be considered. However, this would likely require treaty changes, and it remains to be seen whether such a deterrent would be effective in generating enforcement in real time.

- **Leverage to sanction with a larger central budget:** The case for controls on national fiscal policies would be even stronger in the context of greater risk sharing between the euro area countries (see further on). For example, if a larger euro area budget were to emerge, member states could be under threat of losing some transfers from the center in cases of non-compliance with relevant rules or policy recommendations. Such a mechanism, in triggering more systematic sanctions, possibly deferred over time, could act as a more credible device to generate conformity with the rules. In the same vein, some in Europe have suggested the introduction of targeted transfers to countries that implement beneficial structural reforms. Conditions could also be applied for access to a rainy day fund or to existing crisis mechanisms, such as the ESM. While this approach has merit in encouraging reforms by making central transfers contingent on compliance, the main drawback would be to reduce the automatic stabilization effect of these transfers. In addition, it might be politically difficult to cut transfers in such a pro-cyclical way.
- **A veto power from the center:** The "Two Pack" envisages that national authorities may be requested to revise their budgets if plans are not deemed to be in accord with common principles for the euro area. Yet, this does not give the center the power to enforce compliance. Consideration should be given to stronger powers for the center, either to set national spending and/or borrowing plans or to veto national fiscal decisions, when they breach commonly agreed rules. While very intrusive, such an arrangement would be able to provide timely and pre-emptive intervention when budget plans are clearly inconsistent with the targets derived from fiscal rules. However, it would also require treaty changes and a significant loss of national sovereignty. To mitigate this concern, a gradation in the loss in sovereignty could be considered, depending on the degree of non-compliance with the fiscal rules. Significant loss in fiscal autonomy and extensive fiscal custody would be reserved to the most extreme cases of rule violation and when financial support is being extended – variations of which can be found in countries such as Brazil and Germany.

Down the road, and regardless of the exact set of long-term solutions that are chosen, certain conditions would have to be fulfilled to provide markets with sufficient incentives to exert discipline on fiscal policy choices, including to minimize the spillover effects of sovereign financial distress. These conditions include:

- **A minimum of fiscal risk sharing:** With a minimum of fiscal risk sharing in place, a country facing severe financial distress would not be deprived of essential government services, social security, and financial stability. This would contain the social and economic costs of the crisis. Country-specific shocks would then be less likely to damage the economies of other members of the euro area, alleviating the need for *ex post* financial support and hence making the no-bailout rule more credible. Approaches to achieving greater risk sharing are the focus of the next section.

- ***Ex ante* rules involving private actors in bailouts:** A complementary approach should be to combine the existing crisis support facilities for distressed sovereigns with predictable resolution mechanisms when these facilities are activated. This would help markets better assess, and therefore price, sovereign risks and would strengthen incentives for debtor and creditor countries to avoid excessive sovereign borrowing, even in the presence of bailout arrangements. The requirement in the ESM treaty for all new euro area government bond issuances with maturity above one year to include aggregated collective action clauses as of January 2013 is a step in that direction.

Finally, a larger role for the center raises difficult questions about political and democratic accountability for European and euro area decision bodies. Existing fiscal unions are also political unions, and moving toward deeper fiscal integration in the euro area may not be possible without changes in the political organization of the union. While the issue of the steady-state political regime for the euro area is beyond the scope of this chapter, it will be essential to ensure that the political bodies implementing and enforcing fiscal rules at the central level are mandated to do so with the euro area's collective interest in mind – rather than individual members' national interests.

IV. Risk sharing: Insuring against country-specific shocks

A. *Rationale for risk sharing*

A stronger fiscal governance framework and larger fiscal buffers at the national level would help lower the incidence of policy-induced shocks and dampen the impact of country-specific shocks in the euro area (risk reduction). But given the size and potential for contagion of country-specific shocks, some insurance mechanisms (risk sharing) at the euro area level would also be beneficial, on top of the governance reforms already in progress. These would give individual countries the means to smooth demand in the face of negative income shocks – and, as a consequence, better insulate other euro area members from damaging spillovers. Such mechanisms take on an added importance in a currency union, where countries have no independent currency and so cannot use monetary policy tools to respond to country-specific shocks.

Cross-country risk sharing can be provided by markets and governments, through three broad channels:

- **Cross-border credit markets** can help countries smooth consumption and output through saving and borrowing internationally. However, a country's ability to borrow in credit markets is often inhibited when negative income shocks hit (see below). Recessions are typically associated with heightened market uncertainty, which can make banks, and more generally credit markets, reluctant to lend. Moreover, since asset prices tend to fall in down-turns, the ability to use other assets (such as real estate) as collateral for loans may also be negatively affected. Credit markets can effectively become closed off if these forces are strong enough, short-circuiting their use as tools for consumption smoothing.

- **Insurance through private capital markets** can be obtained by households or governments, either implicitly, through holding a portfolio of international investment assets with diversified income streams, or explicitly, through mechanisms such as outright insurance against some kinds of income shocks (for example natural disasters). However, insurance through portfolio hold-ings is often limited, as private investors tend to hold more domestic assets than would be optimal from a diversification perspective (a feature that is referred to as "home bias"). Additionally, markets may be unwilling to pro-vide explicit insurance due to moral hazard and adverse selection problems inherent to any insurance contract. These problems can be especially acute when the income risks against which insurance is sought are large, as would be the case if euro area country governments tried to insure against GDP shocks.

- **Fiscal risk sharing arrangements** can act as an important supplement when access to insurance through credit or capital markets is limited or no longer available. Cross-country risk sharing can be either *ex ante*, through common fiscal arrangements, or *ex post*, through mechanisms implemented only in the context of crises. Drawing from the experience of fiscal federations described in previous chapters, specific options include:

  (i) common tax and transfer mechanisms, particularly those sensitive to output cycles – such as a universal floor for unemployment insurance – which would help offset country-specific shocks;

  (ii) centralized provision of public goods and services, possibly including, among other instruments, common infrastructure investments (which would be insulated from potentially pro-cyclical decisions at the country level);

  (iii) bailout agreements or other forms of *ex post* financial support that kick in after crises (including deposit insurance to reduce the likelihood of system-wide spillovers from an isolated bank failure and a common fis-cal backstop to shoulder the costs of bank resolution).

B. Risk sharing in the euro area

International comparisons of the degree of risk sharing, and fiscal risk sharing in particular, tend to show that the euro area lacks the degree of risk sharing seen in existing federations (Figure 7.5).[3]

- **Little overall insurance:** While federations such as the U.S., Canada, and Germany manage to smooth about 80 percent of local shocks, the euro area

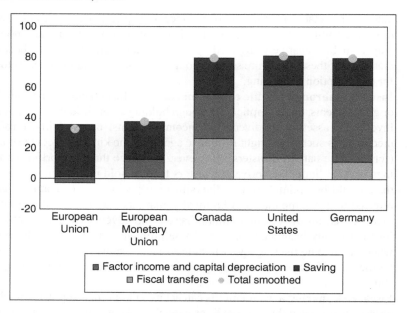

Figure 7.5 Overall risk-sharing (percent of regional income shock smoothed by channel)

Sources: Hepp and von Hagen (2013) for Germany; Sorensen and Yosha (1998) for the U.S.; Balli, Basher, and Rosmy (2011) for Canada; and Afonso and Furceri (2008) for the European Monetary Union and the European Union.

manages to insulate only half of that amount – in other words, when GDP contracts by 1 percent in one of the euro area countries, households' consumption in that country is depressed by as much as 0.6 percent (as opposed to 0.2 percent in the U.S., Canada, or Germany).[4]

•   **Little market-based insurance:** Capital markets in the euro area play much less of an insurance role than elsewhere, in part because cross-border ownership of assets within the euro area remains more limited than, for example, across states of the U.S. or across German Länder – despite the single market. To the extent that there is insulation from negative shocks in the euro area, it occurs primarily through cross-border saving and borrowing.

•   **Little fiscal risk sharing:** Cross-country fiscal risk sharing is almost nonexistent, both in the EU and the euro area. This is not surprising given the small size of the EU budget, its focus on harmonizing living standards (through the structural and cohesion funds) as opposed to providing risk sharing, and the overall limited transfer of fiscal authority to the EU level.

Digging deeper into these findings, we investigate how risk sharing among euro area members has changed across time and over the business cycle (Furceri and Zdzienicka, 2013). For a panel of 15 European countries (Austria, Belgium, Estonia, Finland, France, Germany, Greece, Ireland, Italy, Luxembourg,

Netherlands, Portugal, Slovak Republic, Slovenia and Spain) over 1979–2010, the analysis shows that:

* The degree of income shock smoothing within this group of countries has *decreased* over time (Figure 7.6). Twenty-year rolling window estimates suggest that the share of GDP shocks that remains unsmoothed has risen over time (from 58 percent over 1979–99 to 66 percent over 1990–2010). This largely reflects a decline in cross-country smoothing via credit markets after the creation of the euro area – in other words, credit flows have been more pro-cyclical post- than pre-EMU. Such a decline in the use of credit markets for risk sharing purposes may have arisen from the fall in saving and the underpricing of risks by markets that characterized the first decade of EMU, in a context of over-optimistic growth expectations. In parallel, the number of income shocks smoothed via international capital markets has risen somewhat, a likely reflection of increasing financial integration within the euro area prior to the current crisis.
* Risk sharing mechanisms provided through private markets are found to be particularly ineffective *during downturns*.[5] The share of shocks unsmoothed in recessions become significantly larger than during normal times (Figure 7.7). The deterioration is in part driven by the sharp decline in saving and borrowing in international credit markets. International credit markets

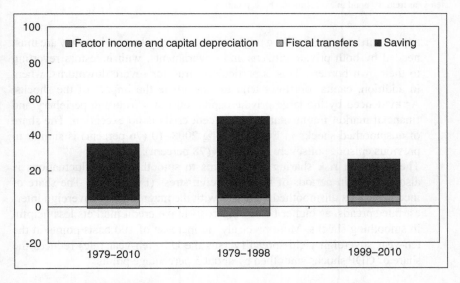

Figure 7.6 Risk sharing in the euro area over time (percent of regional income shock smoothed over time)

Source: Furceri and Zdzienicka (2013).

Note: The sample split between pre-1999 and post-1998 characterizes the changes in risk sharing that occurred after the introduction of the euro.

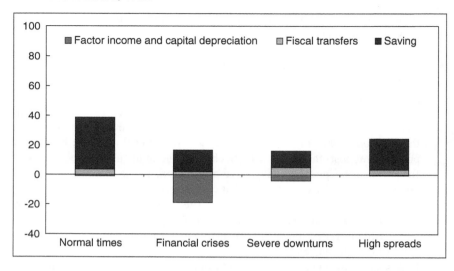

Figure 7.7 Risk sharing in times of stress (percent of regional income shock smoothed)

Source: Furcieri and Zdzienicka (2013).

Note: Normal times = full sample; financial crises = current, sovereign debt and banking system crises, from Laeven and Valencia (2012); severe downturns = periods of recession as identified by the Harding and Pagan (2002) algorithm; high spreads = spread of ten-year government bond to U.S. ten-year treasury bond in excess of 300 basis points.

appear particularly unwilling to grant cross-country loans when they are most needed by both private citizens and governments, with investors reverting to their own borders. This is particularly true for severe downturns, when, in addition, capital outflows tend to exacerbate the impact of the shocks. As evidenced by the large private capital outflows from the periphery and financial market fragmentation, the recent crisis is no exception. The share of unsmoothed shocks in Europe during 2008–10 (76 percent) is similar to previous episodes of severe downturns (78 percent).

- The ability of risk sharing mechanisms to smooth income fluctuations is also reduced in periods of high sovereign stress (Figure 7.7). The share of income shocks unsmoothed increases with the magnitude of sovereign interest rate spreads, as higher borrowing costs make credit markets less helpful in smoothing shocks. More precisely, an increase of 100 basis points in the ten-year sovereign yield spread (versus the U.S. ten-year rate) reduces the share of GDP shocks smoothed by about 5 percentage points.

Overall, the analysis indicates that the euro area would benefit from larger overall smoothing of country-specific income shocks. But what policies could play a role in increasing risk sharing going forward?

- **Crisis management measures:** Financial support through the EFSF and the ESM has provided some elements of fiscal risk sharing, while the Target2 system has cushioned against the sharp reversal in private capital outflows since the beginning of the crisis. Yet, these measures have come *ex post*, namely once the crisis had already severely impacted the economy, with a high cost in terms of lost output.

•   **Banking union:** The creation of a banking union would help reinforce the role of credit markets in providing risk sharing. In particular, it would help develop banking services in a truly integrated way and prevent financial market fragmentation along national borders, especially in times of stress (IMF, 2013a).

•   **Capital market (re-)integration:** While the widening in Target2 positions has prevented a sudden stop, the impact of the shocks has still been amplified, rather than attenuated, by capital market movements. A reversal of the recent financial de-integration, let alone further capital market integration, will take time to materialize. The functioning of capital markets in the euro area could also be improved through common financial market reporting standards and further harmonization of financial market regulations.

•   **A role for fiscal risk-sharing:** In that context, and going forward, fiscal risk sharing could play a complementary role beyond crisis mechanisms, both by providing a minimum amount of smoothing, when other channels break down, and by serving as a catalyst for investors' behavior (Fahri and Werning, 2012). Knowing that there is a floor on the impact of negative shocks, private markets would view countries under stress as less risky than they do currently and hence be more willing to support them through market-based mechanisms. In other words, the existence of a credible form of government insurance would catalyze the provision of market insurance. In that respect, it is worth pointing out that countries with slightly higher *fiscal* risk sharing than the euro area, such as the U.S. and Germany, also exhibit significantly higher *market-based* risk sharing.

If (and when) the union provides a safety net in case of an accident, countries may be tempted to implement riskier policies ("free-riding" or moral hazard), which calls for reinforced governance. Indeed, international experience shows that stronger risk-sharing and stronger governance typically go hand in hand (Figure 7.8). This implies that a prerequisite for any increase in fiscal risk sharing in the euro area should be further strengthening of governance and enforcement provisions.

C. Specific options to increase risk sharing going forward

In practice, there are a number of options to ensure better common insurance against country-specific shocks, with various degrees of centralization and requirements in terms of legislative changes. We elaborate below on three options for the euro area.

A rainy-day fund

The simplest way of organizing temporary transfers to deal with adverse shocks at the country level would be through a common, dedicated "rainy-day fund,"

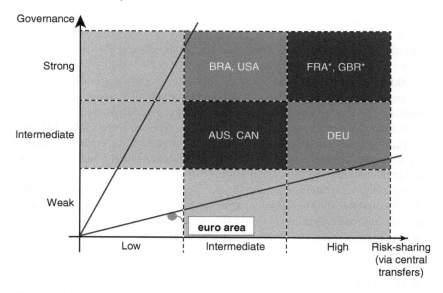

Figure 7.8 Nexus between risk sharing and governance

Note: *denotes unitary countries (FRA, GBR), where administrative units are defined by the central government and exercise powers at the central government's discretion. The remaining countries (AUS, BRA, CAN, DEU, USA) are federations, where the subnational states' existence and powers cannot be changed unilaterally by the central government. The risk-sharing classification is based on estimates from the literature of the share of income shocks to subnational entities that are absorbed by central transfers . The governance classification is based on a review of each country's codified rules and an assessment of their effectiveness in constraining subnational budgets.

similar to the one suggested by the Report from the Tommaso Padoa-Schioppa Group (2012).[6]

- **General features:** Such a fund would collect revenues from euro area members at all times and make transfers to countries when they experience negative shocks. With a dedicated and guaranteed flow of revenues, the fund might even be able to borrow at low cost to smooth the impact of downturns throughout the union.
- **Size of the fund:.** While any such evaluation comes with numerous caveats, we estimate that if the fund had existed since the inception of the euro, annual contributions of the order of 1.5 to 2.5 percent of GNP would have been sufficient to provide a level of overall income stabilization comparable to that found within Germany – where 80 percent of regional income shocks are smoothed, as compared to the 40 percent currently smoothed in the euro area (IMF, 2013b). While still limited, these amounts are larger than the resources transferred under the existing EU budget and could be underestimates if the risk of contagion were to increase. Any misidentification of the nature of shocks (see below) would also lead to higher transfers. In comparison, the total resources devoted to the euro area firewalls (ESM

and EFSF), at their maximum, will amount to about 7.5 percent of GNP (euro 700 billion).

- **Pros:** Unlike the ESM, it would provide *ex ante* support – namely before the shocks have turned into funding crises. But like the ESM, it would be lighter to manage than a full-fledged euro area budget and would not involve any devolution of spending responsibilities to the center. Furthermore, in addition to providing cross-country insurance – against idiosyncratic shocks – the fund would allow for region-wide counter-cyclical fiscal policy responses, with contributions saved in good times and paid out to the contributing countries in tough times – in times of common shocks, or when idiosyncratic shocks have spilled over to other euro area countries.

- **Cons:** The main practical challenge in such a scheme would be to correctly detect the events warranting the activation of the insurance scheme, and hence transfer payments. While technical methods exist to identify negative growth shocks, they are not free of errors and are complex to implement in real time, making it hard to disentangle temporary from permanent shocks, and exogenous shocks from policy shocks. The parameters of intervention could also be difficult to communicate to the public, raising challenging issues of transparency and accountability. As with any insurance scheme – that is, without any conditionality – "free-riding" would remain a risk, especially if the scheme ends up delivering more permanent transfers than warranted: countries could be less inclined to build fiscal buffers at the national level or implement difficult adjustment measures, knowing that ultimately, the rainy-day fund would provide support.

Common unemployment insurance

Social protection could also be a candidate for more fiscal risk sharing. More specifically, moving a minimum level of provision of unemployment benefits to the euro area level would naturally provide insurance against individual income risk across the union. Indeed, as discussed in Chapter 1, in most existing federations, unemployment insurance is centralized. Even in the case of the U.S. where states also finance part of the unemployment benefits, the role of the federal government typically increases in the event of severe negative shocks (IMF, 2013b). Such a scheme should go hand-in-hand with efforts to enhance and harmonize labor market arrangements across countries.

- **Pros:** The funding (via social security contributions) and provision of unemployment benefits are highly related to the cycle. A common scheme would also require a minimum amount of harmonization in labor taxation, as well as, potentially, pension rights – a beneficial step on its own toward a Single Labor Market. Finally, by focusing on unemployment, a highly identifiable variable, a common social security fund would be more understandable and acceptable to the public than a rainy-day fund. With *ex ante* defined parameters, transfers in the form of unemployment benefits would also have the advantage of automaticity.

- **Cons:** Unemployment reacts with lags to activity shocks, so the transfers may not be sufficiently timely. In addition, given the wide variation in long-term unemployment levels across the euro area, the focus should be restricted to short-term unemployment benefits, which are directly connected to negative shocks – as opposed to long-term unemployment – which are more closely linked to labor market and other structural rigidities. Providing insurance against long-term unemployment from the center would immediately give rise to permanent transfers from low-unemployment level regions to high-unemployment regions. This would be akin to redistribution, and not risk sharing, and could provide disincentives to reform labor markets in recipient countries. Focusing on short-term unemployment insurance would, however, reduce the amount of smoothing – although it would still enable the immediate mitigation of adverse shocks to employment.

A euro area budget

A full-fledged budget at the euro area level would allow for risk sharing both through revenues – as countries hit by negative shocks would automatically contribute less – and through spending – as countries hit by negative shocks and in compliance with relevant rules and policy recommendations would still benefit from the same amount of centrally-provided public services. An example of such jointly provided services is public infrastructure, where the central government retains an important role in many existing federations, often using such outlays as a counter-cyclical tool.

- **Pros:** The extent of risk sharing would increase with the extent of centralization of fiscal revenue and spending responsibilities. Along that dimension, the euro area budget would therefore be superior to the other options explored above. In addition, it would facilitate the coordination of the fiscal stance at the euro area level and foster some fiscal harmonization for those taxes that are dedicated to fund the common budget and those spending responsibilities moved to the center.
- **Cons:** Setting up a dedicated full-fledged euro area budget would require more extensive loss of fiscal sovereignty at the national level than other options – as this would require transferring some taxation and spending responsibilities to the center. At this stage, such a move is unlikely to have the support of the constituent electorates.

V. Mitigating contagion

A. A common backstop for the banking union

While more prudent fiscal policies accompanied by some insurance mechanisms to smooth the impact of country-specific shock would go a long way toward reducing the prospects for contagion within the euro area, those measures would not address the potent negative spillovers transmitted through the banking sector. There, an effective common macro-prudential supervisory framework would help prevent the buildup of financial imbalances. In addition, a single resolution mechanism covering all banks regardless of their nationality, including a common fiscal backstop, would provide a powerful tool to sever the adverse feedback loop between sovereigns and domestic banks at play in times of stress. It would also provide a mechanism to internalize home-host concerns and reach agreement on cross-border resolution and burden sharing. As such, it would naturally complement the single supervisory mechanism being put in place and avoid protracted and costly resolutions.

As resolution involves sensitive choices over the distribution of losses, clear *ex ante* burden sharing mechanisms – as envisioned in the Bank Resolution and Recovery Directive – are necessary to achieve least-cost resolution, while they also help provide the right incentives for investors and foster market discipline. At the same time, when systemic risks prevail, exceptional treatment may require recourse to taxpayer money, and hence a fiscal backstop from the center (IMF 2013a). Indeed, in no existing federation has the responsibility for resolving or providing deposit insurance for troubled banks – especially systemic ones – fallen on the subnational level in this crisis.[7] And even though no *ex ante* national bank resolution fund existed prior to the crisis, these funds have all been put in place, with public means, as ad hoc crisis responses (see IMF 2013a).

- **Funding from the industry:** Contributions from the industry – in the form of a resolution fund – should be used first to finance resolution. The fund would build resources over time through levies on the industry, as is common for existing national deposit insurance schemes or resolution funds. Use of the funds could also be complemented by arrangements to recoup net losses through *ex post* levies on the industry. In the steady state, the recently agreed Single Resolution Fund for euro area members will fulfill this requirement.
- **Fiscal backstop:** But insofar as private sector contributions and loss allocation across uninsured and unsecured claimants would be insufficient in a systemic crisis, a common fiscal backstop would need to be tapped, including through a credit line from the ECB – with appropriate safeguards – to ensure adequate liquidity. Even if such a backstop would be tapped only in exceptional circumstances, the mere existence of a common backstop would help anchor confidence in the euro area banking system. The ESM can provide a bridge to such permanent fiscal backstops, as is considered with ESM direct bank recapitalization. But ultimately, a credit line from pooled fiscal resources would provide the best insurance against financial risks.

B. Pooled debt instruments

Large reversals in capital flows going to sovereign bonds can also amplify and propagate shocks. With very few sovereign bonds still considered safe assets, the risk of sharp portfolio shifts between sovereigns will persist in the future. The existence of common debt (in the sense of debt incurred by euro area bodies) could provide some relief against this channel of contagion – nonetheless small initially – and a more stable source of funding.

But pooled debt instruments would have to come with pooled resources and responsibilities. As discussed in Chapter 5, the issuance of common debt to fund subnational budgets is not a feature in existing federations. Instead, provided that the appropriate governance structure is in place, and fiscal revenues have been assigned to the center – be it in a dedicated fund or through a full-fledged budget – a euro area debt instrument backed by those revenues could help finance temporary transfers and spending responsibilities that are moved to the center, and/or provide a credible, common backstop to the banking union. Finally, while any spending responsibility at the center would have to be backed by revenue, borrowing from the center could increase the counter-cyclical nature of these instruments, by also providing intertemporal risk sharing. However, any common bonds would require the creation of entities at the center able to issue debt on their own behalf (for example, a euro area Stabilization Fund, a euro area Unemployment Fund, or an entity managing the euro area budget).

VI. Pros, cons and immediate considerations

The ultimate scope and shape of further fiscal integration in the euro area will remain a matter of social and political preferences. But as just argued, four elements seem essential to make a future crisis less severe: (i) better oversight of national fiscal policies and enforcement of fiscal rules to build buffers and ensure that common concerns are addressed; (ii) subject to strong oversight and enforcement of fiscal discipline, some system of temporary transfers or joint provision of common public goods or services to increase fiscal risk sharing; (iii) a credible pan-euro area fiscal backstop for the banking sector; and, (iv) some common borrowing to finance greater risk sharing and a stronger backstop and provide a common – albeit limited in size – safe asset.

The benefits from further fiscal integration would accrue both in the short and long term. In the steady state, with these elements in place, the likelihood of future crises will be decreased, and when they occur, are likely to be less severe and less prone to systemic spillovers. But spelling out today a roadmap toward further fiscal integration would have immediate effects in raising confidence in the viability of the union, by itself supporting current crisis management efforts. In addition, a shared approach with some elements of centralized fiscal policy would allow for better fiscal coordination. It would expand the scope of available counter-cyclical tools when national policies are constrained by limited market access or fiscal rules – avoiding, for example, excessively restrictive fiscal stances during severe recessions. In these circumstances, it would more than offset the loss of some stabilization capacity at the country level resulting from stronger control on national budgets and the transfer of some fiscal responsibility to the center.

Yet, there are also costs to deepening fiscal integration:

- **Political costs:** Political hurdles to ceding some national sovereignty over budgets are considerable, and they would require extensive public debate. Many steps may necessitate legal changes. In some cases, where existing EU treaties provide only a limited legal basis for euro area-specific reforms, strengthening the legal framework over time would help clarify the role of euro area versus EU members – but it would require approval by all EU countries. Alternatively, intergovernmental treaties outside the EU framework could be considered, where feasible, as was done with the Fiscal Compact and the Single Resolution Fund.
- **Operational challenges:** The mechanisms suggested here could be complex to put in place. Mistakes in the identification of temporary shocks could lead to more permanent transfers than desirable. The costs of a fiscal union could also be financial if centralized fiscal oversight proves ineffective in curbing moral hazard and instilling policy discipline. In addition, fiscal risk sharing would have a headline cost in terms of transferred revenues to central institutions – although deeper fiscal integration would also mean transferring some spending responsibilities to the center.

That being said, the current approach to dealing with the crisis *ex post* instead of *ex ante* does not come without costs. First, there is the cost in terms of lost output and increased unemployment, as *ex post* measures are delayed in implementation. Second, there is a cost associated with providing subsidized financial support to countries under stress through programs. Third, there are contingent costs associated with the large Target2 liabilities that have been have incurred, and would not have increased as much in the presence of *ex ante* fiscal risk sharing. In order to give a sense of the magnitude of the implicit transfer, we compare actual interest expenses for crisis financing with the hypothetical costs if (i) similar amounts had been raised by crisis countries at current long-term yields, or alternatively, at rates reflecting fundamentals (derived from a model, as market rates might have overshot in the current context); or (ii) creditor countries had hedged their exposures at prevailing CDS rates to insure against the risks taken on their balance sheet. The implicit transfer is estimated at between €45 and €76 billion per year for Greece, Ireland, Italy, Portugal, and Spain. Netting out the contributions by these countries to crisis financing, the implicit transfer by euro area net creditors ranges between 0.75 and 1.25 percent of their GDP (Table 7.1). Taken together, these likely more than offset indirect benefits accruing to creditor countries from record low funding costs associated with safe haven flows.

In addition, the concept of fiscal union is not a zero sum proposition. It is often assumed that greater risk sharing would invariably morph into a system of permanent transfers, with financial costs systematically falling on those countries with a stronger tradition of fiscal prudence. So would risk-sharing mean redistribution? With appropriate safeguards, the answer is no.

Table 7.1 Implicit transfer to selected euro area countries (billions of euro, as of February 2013)

	Cost Paid	Cost Derived from Market Rates			Implicit Transfer per Annum		
		Bonds	CDS[4]	Model[5]	Bonds	CDS	Model
	(a)	(b)	(c)	(d)	(b)-(a)	(c)-(a)	(d)-(a)
EU arrangements[1]	5.8	20.5	20.1	31.0	14.7	14.3	25.2
ECB[2]	20.8	51.5	49.7	72.0	30.6	28.8	51.2
Gross Total	**26.6**	**72.0**	**69.7**	**103.0**	**45.4**	**43.1**	**76.4**
(percent of euro area GDP)	0.3	0.8	0.7	1.1	0.5	0.5	0.8
Net Total[3]	**25.2**	**69.3**	**67.6**	**100.2**	**44.1**	**42.4**	**75.0**
(percent of net contributors' GDP)	0.4	1.1	1.1	1.6	0.7	0.7	1.2

Source: IMF staff estimates.

[1]Includes EFSF, ESM, EFSM, and Greek Loan Facility.
[2]Includes increase in Target2 and currency issuance above allocation since December 2007.
[3]Totals net of the contributions by Greece, Ireland, Italy, Portugal and Spain.
[4]Germany bond yield plus CDS spread. Ten-year bond yield for Greece.
[5]Estimates for Ten-year yields, see Fiscal Monitor, October 2012, p. 40.

Deeper integration would provide insurance from fellow euro area members against bad events, thereby also preventing worse outcomes for the membership at large. But while support could span over several years if shocks are persistent – as they appear to be in the current crisis – no system should provide permanent transfers to compensate for a permanent lack of competitiveness or enduringly low income levels. Put differently, risk-sharing means that *at any given point in time* countries facing relatively better economic circumstances would support countries facing less favorable outcomes. But this does not mean that the same countries would *always* be on the receiving end. In fact, our analysis shows that the net beneficiaries would have varied greatly year-to-year, had a risk-sharing mechanism been in place over the last thirty years. Using the example of a rainy day fund described earlier, we find that since the late 1970s, all countries would have benefited from transfers at some point in time (Figure 7.9).

That said, the support afforded by centralized stabilization mechanisms may vary between small and large countries. On the one hand, activity in smaller countries might be more volatile than in larger ones. Their economies might also be more prone to idiosyncratic shocks if their business cycles are less synchronized with the euro area – for example if they trade relatively more with non-euro area countries. In that case, there could be instances where they resort more frequently to fiscal risk sharing mechanisms than do larger euro area members. On the other hand, when larger countries are affected by country-specific shocks, to the extent that inflation evolution in these countries weighs relatively more on euro area-wide price indices, some stabilization is also provided through monetary policy support. Fiscal risk sharing mechanisms at the euro area level would

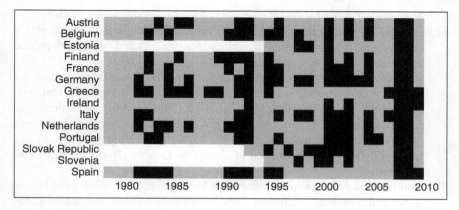

Figure 7.9 Transfers over a longer horizon

Source: Furceri and Zdzienicka (2013).

Note: Grey = zero gross transfer; Black = positive gross transfer.

thus naturally complement other policy instruments in fostering macroeconomic stability.

The proposals laid out in this chapter are to prevent future crisis. Yet, what are the immediate priorities? Crisis management measures taken since 2010 must remain in place to accompany the ongoing adjustment at the country-level. Banking union is in progress. The current proposals to strengthen fiscal governance are a major step in the right direction, and any element of fiscal risk sharing will have to be preceded by further strengthening in that framework and a stronger role for the center. However, deeper fiscal integration needs not and will not occur overnight, but defining a clear roadmap for the elements described above and beginning the journey will help anchor confidence in EMU viability and as such contribute to instilling confidence. Governance reforms in progress should proceed. Once the roadmap is agreed, legal requirements to support stronger center oversight, fiscal risk sharing, and eventually borrowing at the center should be assessed in a comprehensive manner.

However, one element is time sensitive: a euro area common fiscal backstop for the region's systemic banks should be put in place to sever negative sovereign-bank feedback loops and anchor confidence in the banking system. Hence, the single supervisory mechanism, which will be operational in November 2014, and the single resolution mechanism should be complemented by an adequate common fiscal backstop.

Finally, it is worth noting that the proposals here will not tackle the existing debt overhang. Dealing with it will remain a delicate issue, pertaining to burden sharing rather than risk sharing. On that issue, we offer the following concluding remarks:

- **Striking the appropriate balance:** On the one hand, relying entirely on national adjustment could trigger debt-deflation dynamics in the periphery, dragging the entire region into a period of prolonged stagnation, with heightened risk of financial instability. On the other hand, debt mutualization at this stage would be akin to selling insurance after the fact and could even reduce the incentives to restore competitiveness.

- **Conditioning support:** One compromise could be to transform part of the sovereign debt where it is excessive to common debt – in the sense that euro area entities would hold the debt – against a commitment from participating countries to repay that debt over time, and conditional on fiscal medium-term plans and structural reforms. The Debt Redemption Fund proposal, as put forward by the German Council of Economic Experts (2011), could be one such option.
- **Linking legacy issues to the roadmap:** More generally, resolving the legacy issues and providing a common fiscal backstop to banking union could provide for an embryonic framework for stronger fiscal risk sharing. It could also be a window of opportunity to generate momentum for some of the more ambitious reforms to strengthen fiscal governance and central oversight.

Appendix 7.1

Estimating the effectiveness of alternative risk sharing channels – A technical note on the Asdrubali, Sorensen, and Yosha approach

In their 1996 paper, Asdrubali, Sorensen, and Yosha use the national income and product accounts to measure the degree of risk sharing between subnational or regional entities; and in 1998, they extend the approach to national entities. They do so by breaking up the variability in output into various sub-components, and then relating that variability in output to the variability in consumption. They start with the following identity:

$$GDP_{i,t} = \left(\frac{GDP_{i,t}}{GNP_{i,t}}\right)\left(\frac{GNP_{i,t}}{NI_{i,t}}\right)\left(\frac{NI_{i,t}}{DNI_{i,t}}\right)\left(\frac{DNI_{i,t}}{\left[C_{i,t}+G_{i,t}\right]}\right)\left[C_{i,t}+G_{i,t}\right]$$

where i indexes countries, t indexes time (years), GDP is gross domestic product (output), GNP is gross national product (income), NI is net national income, DNI is net national disposable income, C is private consumption, and G is public consumption (government consumption expenditures).

This identity highlights a number of risk sharing channels, through which national consumption $(C + G)$ can be insulated from shocks to output (GDP):

- $GDP - GNP$ = *international income flows (factor income flows)*
- $GNP - NI$ = *capital depreciation*
- $NI - DNI$ = *net international tax and transfer flows (fiscal risk sharing)*
- $DNI - [C + G]$ = *saving*

Output shocks affect consumption to the extent that these risk sharing channels do not move counter-cyclically – they are unable to offset output shocks. For ease of discussion the international income flows and capital depreciation channels are aggregated into a capital markets channel, as the bulk of factor income flows are capital income. Since saving works through the credit market (fixed income securities and deposits), the saving channel is also referred to as the credit market channel.

By evaluating how much the various components in the identity move with output, Asdrubali, Sorensen, and Yosha derive a measure of the degree of income shock smoothing that each channel provides. Specifically, they assess these channels by estimating the following system of equations:

$$\Delta \log GDP_{i,t} - \Delta \log GNP_{i,t} = \alpha_t^m + \beta^m \Delta \log GDP_{i,t} + \varepsilon_{i,t}^m$$

$$\Delta \log GNP_{i,t} - \Delta \log NI_{i,t} = \alpha_t^d + \beta^d \Delta \log GDP_{i,t} + \varepsilon_{i,t}^d$$

$$\Delta \log NI_{i,t} - \Delta \log DNI_{i,t} = \alpha_t^g + \beta^g \Delta \log GDP_{i,t} + \varepsilon_{i,t}^g$$

$$\Delta \log DNI_{i,t} - \Delta \log \left[C_{i,t} + G_{i,t} \right] = \alpha_t^s + \beta^s \Delta \log GDP_{i,t} + \varepsilon_{i,t}^s$$

$$\Delta \log \left[C_{i,t} + G_{i,t} \right] = \alpha_t^u + \beta^u \Delta \log GDP_{i,t} + \varepsilon_{i,t}^u$$

where α coefficients are common time effects, absorbing any common shocks, and β coefficients indicate the average amount of income shock smoothing contributed by a given channel (measured as the percent of an income shock smoothed), with $\sum \beta = 1$. The β coefficients can be negative, when the channels in question exacerbate, rather than smooth the effect of income shocks. For example, β^m indicates the share of income shocks that are smoothed by international income flows. The last coefficient, β^u, indicates how consumption (private and public) moves with output – the larger it is, the less income shock smoothing is occurring. Full insulation of consumption from output is achieved if $\beta^u = 0$. See Furceri and Zdzienicka (2013), for further details and discussion on the estimation for the euro area.

Notes

We would like to thank Jochen Andritzky, Atilla Arda, Katharine Christopherson, Helge Berger, Xavier Debrun, Luc Eyraud, Florence Jaumotte, Petya Koeva Brooks, Geerten Michielse, Franziska Ohnsorge, Esther Perez Ruiz, Tigran Poghosyan, and Aleksandra Zdienicka, who have been working with us on this topic for the last two years.

1   The focus is therefore deliberately narrower than in the previous chapters. In particular, redistributive aspects, which are less relevant for crisis prevention and mitigation, are not looked at in this chapter.
2   The mobility of workers' and firms' across states can also increase competitive pressures at subnational levels to maintain fiscal discipline, while ensuring low taxation and high quality public services. Workers and firms effectively "vote" by moving.
3   Many comparative studies follow the Asdrubali, Sorensen, and Yosha (1996) approach, originally applied to the United States. This approach involves using the standard income accounting identity to highlight the role of saving, intergovernmental fiscal transfers (between the center and states/regions), capital depreciation, private factor income and insurance flows as the wedge between income (GDP) and consumption and is also used to estimate more specifically risk sharing in the euro area. See Appendix 7.1 and Furceri and Zdzienicka (2013) for further details.
4   While the euro area is not a federal state itself and legal arrangements differ significantly from existing federations, the degree of economic and financial integration between member states is of the same order of magnitude as that of the different regions of many federal states. This suggests that, on economic grounds, federal states offer the closest benchmark for the euro area.

5   Downturns are alternatively identified using financial (banking, currency, and debt) crises starting dates, taken from Laeven and Valencia (2012), and by applying the business cycle dating approach proposed by Harding and Pagan (2002) to quarterly GDP data.
6   As mentioned in Chapter 5, Canada and Mexico have centrally-financed stabilization funds that perform similar functions, with resources available to protect states from volatility in their revenues.
7   Even in Germany where the presumption that support to banks would come from the Länder, bailouts were provided on an ad hoc basis by the federal government.

References

Afonso, A., and D. Furceri, 2008, "EMU Enlargement Stabilization Costs and Insurance Mechanism," *Journal of International Money and Finance*, 27, 169–187.

Asdrubali, P., B. Sorensen, and O. Yosha, 1996, "Channels of Interstate Risk Sharing: United States 1963-90," *Quarterly Journal of Economics*, 111, 1081-1110.

Balli, F., S. Basher, and J. Rosmy, 2011, "Channels of Risk Sharing Among Canadian Provinces: 1961–2006," *MPRA Paper* No. 30876.

Carvalho Filho, I., 2014, *Trade Shocks in Europe*, IMF Working Paper, forthcoming.

European Commission, 1977, *Report of the Study Group on the Role of Public Finances in European Integration (MacDougall Report)*, available at http://ec.europa.eu/economy_finance/emu_history/documentation/chapter8/19770401en73macdougallrepvol1.pdf and http://ec.europa.eu/economy_finance/emu_history/documentation/chapter8/19770401en517macdougallrepv2_a.pdf.

———, 2012, *A Blueprint for a Deep and Genuine Economic and Monetary Union – Launching the Debate*, November 30, 2012.

European Council, 2012, *Towards a Genuine Economic and Monetary Union, Report by the President of the European Council, in collaboration with the Presidents of the Commission, the Eurogroup and the ECB*, December 5 2012.

Farhi, E., and I. Werning, 2012, *Fiscal Unions*, NBER Working Paper No. 18280 http://www.nber.org/papers/w18280

Frankel, J., and A. Rose, 1998, "The Endogeneity of the Optimal Currency Area Criterion," *The Economic Journal*, Vol. 108, No 449 (July), pp. 1009–25.

Furceri, D., and A. Zdzienicka, 2013, *The Euro Area Crisis: Need for a Supranational Fiscal Risk Sharing Mechanism?* IMF Working Paper No. 13/198.

German Council of Economic Experts, 2011, "Euro Area in Crisis," Chapter 3 of the Annual Report 2011/2012, available at www.sachverstaendigenrat-wirtschaft.de/

Harding D., and A. Pagan, 2002, "Dissecting the Cycle: A Methodological Investigation," *Journal of Monetary Economics* 49(2), 365–381.

Hepp, R., and J. von Hagen, 2013, "Interstate Risk Sharing in Germany: 1970-2006," *Oxford Economic Papers*, 65(1), 1–24.

IMF, 2013a, *A Banking Union for the Euro Area*, IMF Staff Discussion Note 13/01, February 2013.

———, 2013b, *Toward a Fiscal Union for the Euro Area*, IMF Staff Discussion Note 13/09, September 2013.

Jaumotte, F., and H. Morsy, 2012, *Determinants of Inflation in the Euro Area: The Role of Product and Labor Market Institutions*, IMF Working Paper No. 12/37.

Laeven, L., and F. Valencia, 2012, "Systemic Banking Crises Database: An Update," IMF Working Paper 12/163.

Pisani-Ferry, J., 2012, "The Known Unknowns and Unknown Unknowns of EMU," *Bruegel Policy Contribution*, Issue 2012/18, October.

Sorensen, B., and O. Yosha, 1998, "International Risk Sharing and European Monetary Unification," *Journal of International Economics* 45, 211–238.

Tommaso Padoa-Schioppa Group, 2012, *Completing the Euro: a Roadmap Toward Fiscal Union in Europe*, June 26, 2012, available at http://www.eng.notre-europe.eu/011-3317-Completing-the-EuroA-road-map-towards-fiscal-union-in-Europe.html.

Index

between governments in 167*t*, 185; fiscal balances in 166*p*; fiscal indicators targeted by 98*t*; fiscal responsibility laws (FRLs) in 141*b*; information on 3*t*; infrastructure spending by 28–9*f*; institutional constraints on 95*t*, 119*t*; public financial management (PFM) systems in 135*t*; social protection centralization 51*t*; sovereign credit default swap (CDS) spreads, change in 229*f*; subnational financing framework overview 159*t*; tax revenue by government levels in 19*f*, 39–40*t*; tax revenue structure of 20*f*; transfers and vertical fiscal imbalance 31*f*
Austrian Stability Program 7
Autonomous Communities' Council of Fiscal and Financial Policy 145

Bayoumi, T. 62, 64*t*, 65, 66, 71, 74–5, 74*t*, 76, 84–5
Belgium 2; breach of constraint corrective actions 123–4*t*; central government spending by 23–4*f*; central/subnational government gross debt of 162*t*, 165*p*; corporate income tax in, features of 44*t*; credit rating in 175*f*; debt allocation/tax capacity of 160*f*; education spending by 26*f*, 49*t*; expenditure financing decomposition 32*f*; financial linkages between governments in 167*t*, 185–6; fiscal balances in 166*p*; fiscal indicators targeted by 98*t*; fiscal responsibility laws (FRLs) in 141*b*; health care decentralization/harmonization 47*t*; High Fiscal Council of Finance (HFCF) and 110–11, 111*f*; information on 3*t*; infrastructure spending by 28–9*f*, 52*t*; institutional constraints on 95*t*, 120*t*; PIT tax, features of 45*t*; public financial management (PFM) systems in 135*t*; social protection centralization 51*t*; sovereign credit default swap (CDS) spreads, change in 229*f*; subnational financing framework overview 159*t*; tax arrangements in 41*t*; tax revenue by government levels in 19*f*, 39–40*t*; tax revenue structure of 20*f*; transfers and vertical fiscal imbalance 31*f*; VAT/sales tax arrangements, features of 46*t*; vertical imbalances in 5
Blue-Red bond scheme 180*b*
Bohn, H. 106
borrowing constraints 214–15

Brazil 2; breach of constraint corrective actions 124*t*; central/subnational government gross debt of 162*t*, 165*p*; consolidation of accounts in 142*b*; corporate income tax in, features of 44*t*; education spending by 26*f*, 49*t*; expenditure financing decomposition 32*f*; federalizing of state debts in 209–10*b*; financial linkages between governments in 167*t*, 186; fiscal balances in 166*p*; fiscal indicators targeted by 98*t*; fiscal responsibility laws (FRLs) in 93*b*, 140*b*; indirect public loans to states 170*t*; information on 3*t*; infrastructure spending by 52*t*; institutional constraints on 95*t*, 107, 120*t*; PIT tax, features of 45*t*; public financial management (PFM) systems in 135*t*; social protection centralization 51*t*; state debt by holders in 171*p*; subnational financing framework overview 159*t*; subnational fiscal crises in 200*t*, 204*f*; subnational net debt in 108*f*, 215*f*; tax arrangements in 42*t*; tax revenue by government levels in 19*f*, 39–40*t*; tax revenue structure of 20*f*; transfers and vertical fiscal imbalance 31*f*; VAT/sales tax arrangements, features of 46*t*
Budget and Fiscal Responsibility Law 140*b*
budgetary functions, distribution of 13–56; described 13; European Union (EU) budget 33–6; expenditure policies 22–9, 37, 47–54*t*; introduction 13–14; revenue responsibilities 14–22, 36–7; tax arrangements, features of 41–6*t*; tax revenues by levels of government 39–40*t*; transfers 29–30, 32–3, 38; vertical fiscal imbalances (VFI) 30–2, 38
budget classifications, use of common 148–50
budget execution 140–1
budget formulation 136–9; macroeconomic/fiscal projections 138–9; medium-and long-term fiscal objectives 136–8
Budget Stability Law (Spain) 108

Cabasés, F. 107
Canada 2; balanced budget rules and 7; breach of constraint corrective actions 125*t*; central government spending by 23–4*f*; central/subnational government